Holocaust Memoir Digest

Holocaust Memoir Digest

A Digest of Published Survivor Memoirs
With Study Guide and Maps

Volume 2

Compiled and Edited by

Esther Goldberg

With an Introduction and
30 colour maps by

Sir Martin Gilbert

VALLENTINE MITCHELL
LONDON • PORTLAND, OR

First published in 2005 in Great Britain by
VALLENTINE MITCHELL
Suite 314, Premier House, 112–114 Station Road
Edgware, Middlesex HA8 7BJ

and in the United States of America by
VALLENTINE MITCHELL
c/o ISBS, 920 N. E. 58th Avenue, Suite 300
Portland, Oregon 97213-3786

Website: http://www.vmbooks.com

British Library Cataloguing in Publication Data
A catalogue record for this book is available.

ISBN 0 85303 622 5

Library of Congress Cataloging-in-Publication Data
A catalog record for this book is available.

Cover illustrations Front cover: At a railway station in the Balkans, a passenger train (left) is opposite a train (right)
carrying Jewish deportees from Macedonia to the Treblinka death camp. Back cover: T`he spur railway line
leading into the Theresienstadt Ghetto, photograph taken in 1996.

Typeset in 11/13pt Ehrhardt by FiSH Books, London
Printed in Great Britain by MPG Books Ltd, Bodmin, Cornwall

"What does it mean to remember?

It is to live in more than one world,

to prevent the past from fading,

and to call upon the future to illuminate it."

Elie Wiesel

"I have learned that when we bring comfort to others,

we reassure ourselves,

and when we dispel fear,

we assuage our own fears as well."

Gerda Weissmann Klein

CONTENTS

Study Guide Maps

INTRODUCTION BY SIR MARTIN GILBERT

The memoirs of those who survived the Holocaust are one of the main sources of our understanding of that savage era. Each survivor who publishes a memoir contributes to a widening of our knowledge of the Holocaust years. Each memoir is different: no person's experiences are the same as those of any other. It is not only experiences that vary, but also perspectives.

In addition to the differing experiences and perspectives that each memoir reveals, the geographic range of the Holocaust was vast. Taking the five and a half Holocaust years as a single entity, hardly any two memoir writers were in the same towns, ghettos, slave labour camps, transit camps, concentration camps, death marches, and places of liberation, as there were so many locations, aspects of ghetto and camp life, and patterns of experience. In every recorded instance, even members of the same family had different sets of experiences.

Students, teachers, scholars, and anyone interested in the Holocaust era can widen their knowledge and insights from survivor memoirs. The *Holocaust Memoir Digest* aims to present the contents of individual memoirs in such a way as to facilitate understanding. Volume 1 examined nine memoirs; Volume 2 examines a further eight.

As with Volume 1, the memoirs in Volume 2 are presented in order of first publication, and have been chosen by the editor for their range and variety. They were published between 1957 and 2001, and they span a wide geographic area, extending from France in the west and Greece in the south, to present-day Lithuania and Ukraine in the east.

The first memoir to be looked at is *All But My Life*, by Gerda Weissmann Klein. It was one of the earliest memoirs to be published, only twelve years after the end of the war. It is a powerful story that has been the subject of an Oscar-winning documentary film.

Among the many important aspects of the memoir are Gerda Klein's description of the first weeks and months of the imposition of German rule in her home town of Bielsko–Biala in Poland in September 1939, her account of her slave labour experiences, and her account of one of the longest of the death marches in the final months of the war, starting in January 1945 and lasting for more than two months: "Everywhere we left some dead. Some we buried, others we simply left. Of two thousand women who set off, only one hundred and twenty survived."

Gerda Klein's strength of character is a feature of her memoir. Her reason for writing it reflects what many memoir writers have expressed. "I have discharged a burden," she explains, "and paid a debt to many nameless heroes, resting in their unmarked graves. For I am haunted by the thought that I might be the only one left to tell their story."

This aspect of the memoir-writers' motivation makes one of the categories of the *Digest* particularly important and poignant, the "Stories of individuals, including family members". One of the most powerful descriptions in this category is that of a sick girl in a transit camp to whom Gerda Klein offers her bowl of soup: "Her body was pitifully emaciated, her neck overly long. We looked at each other. For a fleeting moment I thought that she must be my age. I did not know her name or where she came from. I only knew that she was going to meet her death. ... She looked at me, perhaps wondering about the past, and I looked at her, wondering about the future, the bowl of unsavory food between us. I closed my eyes. 'God bless you, may you never know what hunger is,' she said to me."

The story of a family is seen most poignantly in *When Memory Comes*, the memoir of Saul Friedländer, who was only seven years old when the Germans entered his home town, Prague, in March 1939. Before the outbreak of war, Saul Friedländer and his parents had managed to reach Paris, apparently safe from any danger.

The Friedländers were an assimilated family in which "... Judaism as a religion had completely disappeared." Yet for the Nazi machine, it was Jewish blood, Jewish ancestry, not any Jewish religious identity or communal participation, that was sufficient cause for persecution and death: "... my father was hunted down for what he had refused to remain: a Jew."

After they had been in France for two years, the round-ups began. Putting their son into the care of French nuns, they accepted that he be baptized and brought up as Catholic to save him: "... my father had promised not only to accept my conversion but to assure me a Catholic education if later life resumed its normal course. ... in the same circumstances, in the face of the same drama, would not I, too, have written the same lines, given the same authorization, made the same promises? ... happily for them, no religious allegiance stood in their way. ... But what, I wonder, would a religious Jew have done if confronted with such a terrible dilemma?"

Saul Friedländer's parents made their way to the Swiss border as they sought to cross into another haven, neutral Switzerland. They were turned back at a time when the Swiss government's policy, rigorously enforced, was to send Jewish refugees back into France. Denied a place of refuge, Saul Friedländer's parents were deported from France to Auschwitz. One letter, thrown out of their deportation train, reached the young boy. He was never to see his parents again.

After liberation, he found his Jewish identity during the celebration of Passover, "it is the holy words that open the doors of imagination and allow the humblest of participants to understand, in his own way, the story and the feeling of liberation, knowing that these traditional words are his anchor and foundation within the community."

The third memoir in this volume, *Maus: A Survivor's Tale* (in two parts), is an unusual one, presented in cartoon form. The survivor is a Polish Jew, Vladek Spiegelman, who tells his experiences to his son Art, who transmits them in words and drawings.

Before the war, Vladek Spiegelman worked in the textile business in the Polish city of Czestochowa, a place of Catholic pilgrimage, and at the same time a vibrant Jewish centre. He married in 1937 and moved to the city of Sosnowiec, where he had a factory. He also had a factory in Bielsko-Biala, Gerda Klein's home town. When war came, he was conscripted into the Polish Army. Taken prisoner by the Germans, he recalled the harsher treatment meted out to Jewish prisoners of war than to their fellow Polish comrades in arms. He was fortunate, helped by a friend, to escape an imminent massacre of Jewish prisoners of war, of whom many thousands were murdered in the early months of the German occupation of Poland.

Vladek Spiegelman and his wife Anja spent many months in hiding, and in avoiding those Poles who were all too willing to betray Jews. When some Polish children in the street scream out that he is a Jew, he replies: " 'Heil Hitler. Don't be afraid, little ones. I'm not a Jew. I won't hurt you' ", whereupon a Polish passer-by apologizes to him with the words: " 'Sorry, mister. You know how kids are ... Heil Hitler.' "

When Vladek and Anja Spiegelman tried to flee across the border and make their way southward to Hungary, they were betrayed, with the same result as that of Saul Friedländer's parents, who had sought the safety of Switzerland and had been refused entry. The Spiegelmans were imprisoned in Bielsko, and then deported to Auschwitz. There Vladek Spiegelman learned the need to obtain extra food by barter: "If you ate how they gave you, it was just enough to die more slowly." Like all survivors, he reflects on the nature of survival, as he encourages his wife: "'To die, it is easy … But you have to struggle for life!'"

Part Two of Vladek Spiegelman's memoirs begins with his arrival at Auschwitz. For speaking to his wife, he is beaten. He teaches English to his Block Supervisor, who tells him: "Now the Allies are bombing the Reich. If they win this war, it will be worth something to know English." (Gerda Klein had been warned not to take English lessons, or she might be arrested as a spy – a German officer told her, sympathetically, "'Now run home as fast as you can, and forget your English.'")

No single account of Auschwitz is identical to any other. Each memoir writer who was in Auschwitz adds a fragment – even several fragments – to our understanding of man's capacity to survive terrible persecution and would-be dehumanization. Vladek Spiegelman is no exception. A Polish priest in Auschwitz adds together the six figures that make up his tattoo number: the number tattooed on all inmates of Auschwitz who were not destined for the gas chambers on arrival in the camp. His tattoo number was 175113. The priest points out that the figures add up to eighteen, the numeric equivalent – in Hebrew – of the word "chai" – "life". Vladek Spiegelman comments: "I started to believe. I tell you, he put another life in me." That Polish priest appears in the *Digest* under the category "Righteous Gentiles".

Like hundreds of thousands of Jews, Vladek Spiegelman was on a death march in the early months of 1945 "He who got tired, who can't walk so fast, they shot." His final reflection on survival in Auschwitz and in the East: "The Jews always lived with hope. They hoped the Russians can come before the German bullet arrived from the gun into their head."

The fourth memoir in this volume of the *Digest* is Fanya Gottesfeld Heller's *Strange and Unexpected Love· A Teenage Girl's Holocaust Memoirs*. This is a sensitive story of a teenage girl who survives in her small town of Skala, in Eastern Galicia, then part of Poland, today part of Ukraine.

Fanya Heller's memoir starts with an account of the "rich cultural and social life" in the Skala Jewish community, which is in stark contrast to the local anti-Semitism, where the local peasants "… were superstitious and still believed in the blood libel, and the priests told them again and again in church that the Jews had killed Jesus." Jews numbered 1,500 in a town of 5,500. Fanya Heller describes the Jewish school, the Jewish community house, and the Jewish library with its 5,000 volumes.

That world came to an abrupt end as the events of European history impinged upon every Jewish community. In the case of Skala, this began with the Soviet occupation of her town from mid-September 1939 to early July 1941, then the brief but vicious Hungarian occupation (Hungary was then allied to Germany), and finally the arrival of the German troops at the end of July 1941. With the arrival of German troops came the first anti-Jewish decrees, the first killings, "the struggle to find food", and, in September 1942, the first mass murder "action" (*Aktsia*): "Dead and dying people were strewn all over the street … Houses stood empty as if a cosmic cyclone had sucked their occupants to another planet. There were dead bodies lying on the beds and floors."

After the *Aktsia*, Fanya Heller had been in hiding for two weeks in her rescuer's barn when he brought her hot water and soap so that she could wash. As a result, she went "… from a state of terror of imminent, violent death to a feeling of calm bordering on joy, and even hope that the nightmare would end." The *Digest* includes this aspect of her story in the category of "Specific Escapes", as an example of psychological escape. As for all survivors, it was a long nightmare. She and her parents and younger brother hid first in a chicken coop, and then briefly in the forest, where they witnessed and survived a massacre. With liberation, she writes: "The phrase 'it's over' was as empty as the prayer of gratitude to God my mother instructed us to say with her."

Their nightmare did not end with liberation. Her father was killed after liberation. Neither his body nor his killer was ever found. Jews were murdered in Skala, as in so many towns, for many weeks and months after liberation: "Almost all the Ukrainians and Poles", writes Fanya Heller, "wanted the Jews dead whether the Germans were gone or not."

Like almost all those who survived the Holocaust, Fanya Heller was saved, as was her family, by a Righteous Gentile. In her case it was Jan, a Ukrainian, a former altar boy, whose own life was blackened because of the life-saving help he had extended: "A host with time-bomb guests on his threshold, Jan had every right to slam the door in our faces. ... I understood that he had protected us for so long that our lives no longer belonged to us, they belonged to him, too. For the rest of his life he would hear the door as it slammed shut in his face."

The geographic range covered in the memoirs is indicative of the vast extent of German-dominated Europe and the anti-Jewish policies pursued with such zeal and venom. One of the cities whose Jewish community was all but destroyed was that of Salonika, the Greek port that had provided a haven for Jews since their expulsion from Spain in 1492.

One of these Sephardi Jews, Erika Myriam Kounio Amariglio, has written one of the first survivor memoirs published in English in the twenty-first century, originally published in Greek in 1995, called *From Thessaloniki to Auschwitz and Back, Memories of a Survivor from Thessaloniki*. She was among more than 50,000 Jews from Salonika deported by train to Auschwitz, an 800-mile journey across Yugoslavia, Austria, and Czechoslovakia. The passage of time has not dimmed her memory or her power to convey the wide range of her experiences.

Unusually, Erika Amariglio's Sephardi Greek father had married an Ashkenazi Jewish woman from the Czech town of Karlovy Vary (Karlsbad). In 1938, her Czech-Jewish grandparents fled to Salonika as refugees. No one could have forecast that within three years the German army and SS would be the rulers of Salonika: "The hardships of the occupation were enormous; there was less and less food; people were dying from cold and hunger."

The deportation from Salonika to Auschwitz lasted six days. In this, as in every memoir in which Auschwitz is the destination, the account of that place includes many new details. Erika Amariglio worked, as did many Jewish women, in the SS offices. She worked as a Greek translator and record organizer. There she witnessed the meticulous record keeping, and heard about the destruction of Crematorium IV at Birkenau, an extraordinary act of defiance in which Greek deportees took a prominent part.

Erika Amariglio also gives an eyewitness account of one of the "walking dead" (a *Mussulman*) who was trying to explain to the SS – she was translating – that he was not Jewish, but had been selling bread sticks at Salonika station whenever a deportation train departed. He had been caught up in the crowd and deported to Auschwitz. "I tried to explain that he definitely was not Jewish. 'I can tell from his accent', I told them. ... The Germans did not let him continue speaking, they grabbed him and threw him outside."

In 1965 Erika Amariglio returned to Auschwitz with her mother, as part of an international conference. "How quiet," she writes. "My God, how quiet. But in my ears I could hear the lamenting, the screams of pain, the prayers, the howls of the dogs, the 'barking' of the SS. It was the souls of the dead who were wandering, I told myself."

Solomon Gisser was twenty years old when the Germans invaded his home town of Lodz in Poland. After the war, he emigrated to Canada, where he became a cantor in a synagogue in Montreal. His memoirs were published 52 years after his liberation in Buchenwald. Entitled *The*

Cantor's Voice, they give a voice – as all memoirs do – to a large number of those whose voices were cruelly silenced.

Once again, a memoir writer's individual recollections of Auschwitz add to the wider canvas. On reaching Birkenau, writes Solomon Gisser: "... they beat us with sticks. We were stunned. We didn't know why. We didn't understand what was happening to us." Leaving Auschwitz as Soviet troops draw near, he sees: "... a big fire. ... the Nazis were burning documents, burning papers. Burning the evidence of our humiliation."

Throughout much of the war, Solomon Gisser had been a slave labourer, the fate of many hundreds of thousands of Jews. Like them, he was in many slave labour camps, each with its own cruel agenda of torment. For him that slave labour camp torment began when he volunteered for work in Germany, in return for money promised to his family in the Lodz Ghetto: "The German who was head of the camp gave us a speech, and by the time he was finished, we knew that we were prisoners, not just volunteers."

In one slave labour camp, Babitz, Solomon Gisser was ordered to sing while the slave labourers worked: "I was singing and the workers were being beaten because they were not fast enough ... ." Among the slave labourers in Babitz was a Greek Jew from Salonika, who did not understand the commands being shouted at him, and was tortured because he did not respond to the orders he could not understand. When another slave labourer protested at the injustice of this, the guard looked at the protester "... with total disdain ... And he started beating up the man who had dared to ask the question."

In the category of "Resistance", the *Digest* notes the religious aspect of Solomon Gisser's survival. In the Lodz Ghetto he conducted a choir that chanted the High Holy Day services. "Our performance was supreme. ... The whole ghetto talked about our services for weeks on end."

The final memoir in this volume is Samuel Bak's *Painted in Words – A Memoir*. Published in 2001, it is the story of a young boy in Vilna who was a gifted painter. Today, his paintings – one of which was used on the cover of Yitzhak Arad's history of the Vilna Ghetto (*Ghetto in Flames*) – are a remarkable testimony to the power of an artist to convey the almost unconceivable.

Before the war, at the age of five, while returning from kindergarten, Samuel Bak was spat upon in the street and cursed for being a Jew. "Because my face had been spat on, I had to understand the why of it, to realize what it meant to be a Jew. I had to acquire our language and culture." At that moment, he recalls, his parents – who, like many Jews before the Holocaust, were assimilated – transferred him to a Yiddish school.

Samuel Bak writes of the time of torment with sensitivity and a painter's eye. Sent from the Vilna Ghetto by truck to a slave labour camp in the city shortly after his tenth birthday, he describes the scene: "Crowded to the maximum, piled up against each other, we look like a compact accumulation of human spare parts."

On 27 March 1944 the SS rounded up the children who were then working or hiding in one of the two slave labour camps where the surviving Vilna Jews had been incarcerated after the liquidation of the ghetto in September 1943. Samuel Bak was fortunate to have avoided being seized that day and taken with the others to the death pits at Ponar. He had been hidden with two other children, and his father had been able to slip a gold-plated rouble into the hand of one of the two Germans who were searching for the hiding place: "He closed his fingers, let it drop into his pocket, and called out to his companion that everything was all right, and suddenly both were gone."

Samuel Bak was then ten years old. His memory of that moment of the deportation of the children is poignant: "The sobs of the children fade with the rattle of the departing trucks, and the sound of retreating army boots leaves behind a silence of death." His account continues: "A mounting sound of moaning grows in crescendo and turns to a fortissimo of wailing cries, a chorale of hundreds of bereaved parents." He later learned: "Several mothers who clung to their children were taken away on the first of the trucks. Others, who opposed the soldiers, were gunned down."

The vividness of Samuel Bak's memoir is testimony to how, although memory may fade in general, when it comes to the specific aspects of a fearful time, it can be sharp and detailed even sixty years later. It was immediately after the war, in a Displaced Persons camp at Landsberg, that Samuel Bak found himself among survivors who, like almost all survivors: "... were in need of telling over and over again their experiences of recent years." Thus he was a witness of, and a participant in, the first impulses that were to lead, to date, to the publication of several thousand memoirs, including his own: "Pain, loss and bewilderment were everywhere. Talking about people from our past, and in particular about those who had perished, gave us a sense of rescuing them from extinction. As if the dead were being summoned to cleanse us of the guilt of having survived."

Readers of the *Holocaust Memoir Digest*, and of its Study Guide, will gain access to the world of the Holocaust through the eyes of those who were closest to it: the survivors from many lands, speaking many tongues, coming from diverse backgrounds, but each driven by the desire – the imperative – encapsulated by the venerable Jewish historian Simon Dubnow as he was shot down in the streets of Riga: "Write, and record!"

Martin Gilbert
Honorary Fellow, Merton College
Oxford
April 2005

EDITOR'S ACKNOWLEDGEMENTS

Laureen Nussbaum, a survivor of the Holocaust who now lives in Portland, Oregon, wrote to me after I had sent her Volume 1 of the *Holocaust Memoir Digest*. She described the reaction when she took the book to a speakers' bureau meeting organized by the Oregon Holocaust Research Center. "At one point, one of the survivors present deplored that after our generation will be gone, distortion of information will go unchecked," she wrote. "That was my cue. I held up your book and told the group about it and within minutes, the woman in charge collected money for nine copies! I let the book go around the circle and urged everybody present to take their copy to every speaking engagement and recommend it to both librarians and teachers."

To those who have the courage to speak of their experiences, to those who have the strength to write their memoirs, the *Holocaust Memoir Digest* seeks to honour their memories, to make their eyewitness accounts available, and to pass on the wisdom of their experience. I am grateful to those who have allowed me to include the summaries I have done on their memoirs in this, the second volume. I am grateful to Frank Cass of Vallentine Mitchell for believing in the value of the *Digest* as a teaching tool.

The Vallentine Mitchell team has been enormously helpful at all stages of the *Digest*'s production and I am grateful for their patience, encouragement, and goodwill: notably Sian Mills, Lisa Hyde, Toby Harris and Gary Lister. Lenny Gerson at ISBS in Portland, Oregon, has been professional and cheerful in dealing with every challenge.

The *Holocaust Memoir Digest*, aimed at both new and established students of the Holocaust and related human issues, is a distillation of the experiences of individuals. The path to its publication, and its use, also created a collection of relationships with individuals. Therefore my acknowledgements recognize the *Digest*'s supporters who have encouraged me, and are using it in their classes as a useful and informative approach to teaching the Holocaust.

I am especially grateful to Professor Deborah Dwork, Clark University, Massachusetts; Professor Jack Fischel, Millersville University, Pennsylvania; Professor Marilyn Harran, Chapman University, California; Professor John-Paul Himka, University of Alberta, Canada; Dean Ruth Linn, Faculty of Education, Haifa University, Israel; Professor Steven Norwood, University of Oklahoma, Norman; Professor David Patterson, University of Memphis, Tennessee; Professor Eunice Pollack, University of North Texas, Denton; Professor Haim Shaked, University of Miami, Florida; and Professor Froma Zeitlin, Princeton University.

At the high school level, the *Digest* has been recognized as a tool for teachers. I am particularly grateful to those who organize teacher-training program: Ilana Abromovitch, Manager of Curriculum, Museum of Jewish Heritage, New York; Avril Alba, Director of Education, Sydney Jewish Museum, Australia; David J. Bobb, Director, Hoogland Center for Teacher Excellence, Hillsdale College, Michigan; The Reverend Father Lawrence Frizzell, Seton Hall University, New Jersey; Rich Hitchens, Programming Manager and Public Educator, Association for the Elimination of Hate, and Director of the General Romeo Dallaire Summer Institute on Teaching the Holocaust and Genocide, London, Canada; Miriam Klein Kassenoff, Director, Teacher Institute/Holocaust Studies, University of Miami; Jeffrey Morry, Senior Program Manager, Asper Holocaust and Human Rights Studies Program, Winnipeg, Canada; Karen Murphy, Director of the International Program, Facing History and Ourselves, who took the *Digest* to

Rwanda to help students come to terms with their own history; Dan Napolitano, Mandel Teachers Fellowship Program, United States Holocaust Memorial Museum, Washington, DC; Karen Pollock, Chief Executive, and Anita Parmar, Education Officer, Holocaust Education Trust, Britain; Leonid Saharovici, and Ruth K. Tanner, Executive Director, Tennessee Holocaust Commission; Eva Unterman, Chair, Council for Holocaust Education, Jewish Federation of Tulsa, Tulsa, Oklahoma; Helen Walzer, Assistant Director, Holocaust Resource Center, Kean University, New Jersey; and former teachers, Charlene Abrahamson, San Diego, and JoAnna Ernst of Washington, DC. Also I am grateful to Jane Ploetz, a teacher in San Diego, and Margo Singagliese, a teacher in New Jersey, whose quests for knowledge are a benefit and example to their students.

Many educators have been helpful in promoting the *Digest*. They include Rabbi Shalom Berger, Lookstein Center for Jewish Education in the Diaspora, Bar Ilan University, Israel; Donald Braum, Deputy Director, Holocaust Issues, Bureau of European and Eurasian Affairs, United States Department of State, Washington, DC; Josey Fisher, Holocaust Education Consultant at the Auerbach Central Agency for Jewish Education, Philadephia; Dr Bonnie Hausmann, Program Officer, Partnership for Excellence in Jewish Education, Boston; Dr Shulamit Imber, Pegagogical Director, International School for Holocaust Studies, Yad Vashem, Israel; Allan Levine, St. John's-Ravenscourt School, Winnipeg, Canada; Bernie Pucker, Pucker Gallery, Boston; Eric Saul, Curator, "Visas for Life"; Adrian Schrek, Associate Director and Director of Education, Holocaust Center of Northern California, San Francisco; Paul Shaviv, Director of Education, Community Hebrew Academy of Toronto, Canada; Marc Skvirsky, National Program Director, Facing History and Ourselves.

Librarians have been helpful: Aviva Astrinsky, YIVO Institute of Jewish Heritage, New York; Elliot Kanter, Social Sciences and Humanities Library, University of California, San Diego; Michael Terry, Dorot Judaica Library, New York Public Library; Snow Zhu, Rita and Leo Greenland Library and Research Center, Anti-Defamation League, New York; Mark Ziomek, Director of Library, United States Holocaust Memorial Museum, Washington, DC.

I am grateful to Martin Goldman, of the United States Holocaust Memorial Museum, for his warm reception of the book; and to Dina Lanceter Cohen and the Generations of the Shoah International for connecting those of us who carry the names of our grandparents, aunts and uncles. I am grateful to the Anti-Defamation League for their belief in the value of the *Digest*: to Darcy Lorin, Assistant Director, Development, for her encouragement, and to Ann Shore, President, and Rachelle Goldstein, Vice-President of the Hidden Child Foundation/ADL for their belief in the book and their warm reception of it.

Shi Sherebrin has helped with all technical challenges involved with the creation and continuance of the *Digest*. Geoff Cain and Earl Pinsky of Digital Internet Group created and maintain the website (www.holocaustmemoirdigest.org). Mark Poznansky's generous support has again allowed me to continue to devote my energies to producing the *Digest*. Sean McCoy has put his enthusiasm towards making the *Digest* available, and I am grateful.

Sir Martin Gilbert has been a pioneer in his belief in the validity of survivor testimony as historical documentation. Conflicts must be studied and understood by listening to those who experienced them. His research, based in part on survivor testimony, brings a human element into view. The individual eyewitness links us to the bigger picture. The *Holocaust Memoir Digest* seeks to open up the view of the eyewitnesses, and to open our understanding to that view.

As the survivors' words give us a picture, the maps that accompany their descriptions give us a place, a geographic context. I am grateful to Sir Martin for the memoir maps, and also for the thirty colour maps in the Study Guide, which he created for the *Digest*, and to Tim Aspden, the British cartographer, who prepared them for publication.

I am grateful to my family: my mother, Helen Goldberg, who carries the past with her, my daughters Shoshana and Mirit, who move to the future, knowing where they came from, and my brother Rick, who believes in bearing witness. My late father, Ben Goldberg, is always there.

The fear of many of my generation is that some families may not have had any survivors who would be able to "light a candle" for them, to remember them. For the descendants of those in this book, and for the descendants of the Byk, Flejsz, Goldberg, and Shapiro families of Sarny, Czartorysk, Klesow, and Kiev, the candles are lit.

Esther Goldberg
London, Ontario, Canada
15 April 2005

THE DIGEST

The aim of the *Holocaust Memoir Digest* is to make the contents of each survivor's memoir available to schools, libraries, and institutions that deal with the Holocaust. Using the *Digest*, teachers, students, and researchers will know what is in the memoirs, and will be able to use them easily and effectively.

The memoirs appear in the order of their first publication. The memoirs chosen for this second volume of the *Digest* cover a range of regions and experiences, and include the earliest to the most recently published memoirs. Subsequent volumes of the *Digest* will continue to present a range of regions and experiences.

Outline

Each entry in the *Digest* covers the following:
Personal Chronology
Author
Title
Publishing details
Focus of the memoir: age of the writer, time frame, geographic locations
Features of the memoir: foreword, photographs, documents, works cited, maps, afterword, appendices, footnotes, glossary, bibliography, index
Topics particular to each memoir, with the page numbers from the memoir (given for every reference), according to the following themes:

1. Pre-war Jewish home and community life
2. Pre-war anti-Semitism
3. The coming of war
4. Life under German occupation
5. Creation of the ghetto
6. Daily life in the ghetto
7. Deportation
8. Mass murder sites
9. Transit camps
10. Death camps
11. Slave labour camps and factories
12. Theresienstadt/Terezin
13. Auschwitz–Birkenau
14. Death marches
15. Concentration camps
16. Witness to mass murder
17. Resistance, ghetto revolts, individual acts of courage and defiance
18. Partisan activity
19. Specific escapes
20. In hiding, including Hidden Children

21. Righteous Gentiles (also known as Righteous Among the Nations)
22. Liberation
23. Displaced Persons camps (DP camps)
24. Stories of individuals, including family members
25. Post-war life and career
26. Personal reflections

Places mentioned within Europe, including variant names or spellings, are listed with the page number of first reference. These places are also shown on individual maps specially drawn for the *Digest* by Sir Martin Gilbert to illustrate each memoir.

Places mentioned outside Europe are listed with the page number of first reference.

Memoir Digest

Gerda Weissmann Klein, *All But My Life*

8 May 1924: born in Bielitz (Bielsko–Biala), Poland

August 1939: vacations with her mother in Krynica, a summer resort

3 September 1939: Germans enter Bielitz

21 April 1942: moved to the Bielitz Ghetto

June 1942: ghetto liquidated, separation from parents, taken to a transit camp in Sosnowitz

2 July to August 1943: in the slave labour factory in Bolkenhain

September 1943: in the slave labour factory in Märzdorf

September 1943 to 9 May 1944: in the slave labour factory in Landeshut

May 1944 to January 1945: in the slave labour factory in Grünberg

29 January to 5 May 1945: leaves Grünberg on death march that ends in Volary, Czechoslovakia

5 May 1945: liberated, Volary, Czechoslovakia

1946: emigrates to America

Author: Gerda Weissmann Klein

Title: *All But My Life*

Publishing details

Hill and Wang, New York, 1957, 246 pages.
ISBN 0-8090-1580-3.

Focus

Gerda, a young Polish girl (who is 15 in 1939) survives slave labour camps and death marches and is liberated by an American Jewish soldier; the events take place between 3 September 1939 and 13 September 1945.

Features

Author's acknowledgements.
Preface written by the author.
Family photographs: Gerda's parents and brother Arthur, Gerda and Kurt, and their grown children and spouses.
Epilogue written by the author, August 1994, pages 247–61.

Contents (by topic, with page numbers)

Pre-war Jewish home and community life

(23–4) Gerda and her mother spend part of the summer at a resort in Krynica, but are called home to Bielitz early due to her father's illness, August 1939.
(74–6) Before their deportation, she says goodbye to their garden and home, remembering her life there: "There by the brook, thinking and crying softly, I bade farewell to my childhood."
(124–6) Photographs found and sent by Abek remind her of her father's family and her grandfather's return from Siberia.
(177) While in Grünberg, 1944, Gerda pictures her homecoming with memories: "Papa would kiss the Bible even as his father had before him, when he returned from Siberia."

Pre-war anti-Semitism

(5) The possibility to escape not taken: Uncle Leo cables from Turkey, mid–August 1939: "'Poland's last hour has come. Dangerous for Jews to remain. Your visas waiting at Warsaw embassy. Urge you to come immediately.'" But her father is too ill to be disturbed.

The coming of war

(3–4) 3 September 1939, the Germans arrive in her town of Bielitz: "I did not know then that an invisible curtain had parted and that I walked on an unseen stage to play a part in a tragedy that was to last six years."
(6–7) The possibility of sending the children, Arthur and Gerda, east: "'Mr and Mrs Ebersohn have asked to take you with them to look for refuge in the interior of Poland.'" But the decision is to remain together. Papa continues: "'I hate to cast out my children to complete uncertainty. I believe that God will keep us together under the roof of our house.'"

(8–12) Their neighbours welcome the German soldiers: "'We thank thee for our liberation!' … I realized that we were outsiders, strangers in our own home, at the mercy of those who until then had been our friends."

(22) After Arthur leaves, Gerda accompanies her mother to the cemetery to pray at the grave of her grandmother, Julie Mückenbrunn: "Then Mama stood upright and addressed the stone in a different manner. 'You're lucky, mother. If only I could be certain that someday my children would be standing on my grave.'"

Life under German occupation

(25–7) Gerda goes with her father's partner Mr Pipersberg to see their factory: "From where we stood we saw huge trucks parked within the gates. Heaps of costly pelts were being loaded onto them. … The accumulation of years of work was being carried off." Mr Pipersberg goes into the factory and is beaten up: "'Some of the workers moved as if to interfere, but they were afraid and they finally turned away.'"

(32–3) The deportation order is postponed; they move into the basement of their house: "Going downstairs, I passed Trude. She was already taking her things upstairs."

(38–9) Her father helps her with her studies: "'But never underestimate the teachings of the Torah and the wisdom of the Ten Commandments. In them you can find a whole way of life, ethics, and the basis of human actions. They were written thousands of years ago, yet they are the foundation of every law in the world.'"

(42–4) They support themselves with knitting and sewing, trading their handiwork for food. With their garden closed off to them, Gerda and her friend Escia Bergmann find peace at the cemetery.

(46–7) Her father has a heart attack and Gerda helps him take his pills: "The only physician who was allowed to treat Jews, Dr Reach, himself a Jew, lived a twenty minutes' walk away. I could not go out because of the curfew; the streets were patrolled. There were no phones for Jews."

(51–3) Gerda goes with her friend Ilse Kleinzähler and Ilse's mother to visit a camp outside Bielitz: "The camp – a converted factory – was a big square four-story building with a yard in the center. … antique furniture, paintings, and other valuables from the homes of Jews who had been liquidated were stored in the factory. Here they were repaired and refinished, if necessary, and then sent to furnish the apartments of German officers."

Creation of the ghetto

(72–3) "On the morning of the nineteenth of April all Jews were ordered to prepare to move to the shabby, remote quarter of town near the railroad terminal. Here, where cattle and produce were unloaded, there were a few unoccupied, decrepit houses. In two short days they would become our ghetto." Bielitz (Bielsko–Biala) 1942.

(76–7) Niania comes to say goodbye as they leave their home: "Papa and Mama and I followed the wagon with bowed heads, as though walking behind a hearse." 21 April 1942.

Daily life in the ghetto

(78–9) The move: "The thing that we had feared most was done. The act of moving was over." The security of home: "Somewhere in the back of my mind I had always felt that the walls of our home would protect us. Now I fully understood why we had dreaded the move to the ghetto." The security of the ghetto to the 250 remaining Jews: "To me those porches were symbolic of the way our lives were linked and I felt safer in the knowledge that we were not alone."

(82) 8 May 1942, Gerda celebrates her eighteenth birthday in the ghetto with a gift from her parents, an orange: "I hadn't seen one in almost three years. ... Later I learned from the Kolländers that Mama had given a valuable ring to obtain the one orange. It was the last birthday gift I was ever to get from my parents."

Deportation

(30–2) Deportation orders and the confiscation of property: "... all Jews to report on Monday, December 2, 1939, at six o'clock in the morning, to an armory on Hermann Goering Strasse. Each person was allowed twenty pounds of clothing. All valuable objects, money, and keys to all closets, clearly tagged to indicate to which lock they belonged, should be put on a table in the front hall of each house. Violaters of this order would be punished by death."

(86–92) Her father is taken with the men by train: "There he stood, already beyond my reach, my father, the center of my life, just labeled JEW. ... We watched until the train was out of sight. I never saw my father again." The next day the remaining Jews are marched to a field, go through a selection, and are marched away: "I knew Mama was marching on – in the opposite direction. I did not turn around. I could not. I knew she was looking at me as Papa had looked at us from the platform of the train. I knew that if I turned around we would have run to each other – and that they would beat us or shoot us. We had to go on alone." June 1942.

(95–100) She is taken, with her friend Ilse, by truck to the headquarters of the Militz (Militia), the Jewish police force, in Sosnowitz, where she knows Abek's family lives. She finds the strength within herself to obtain a pass to visit them: "Walking along the corridor, I suddenly felt a new freedom born from the realization that no matter what action I might take, only I would have to bear the consequences. Nothing that I might do now could harm Papa and Mama."

(111–13) The journey by train from Sosnowitz to Bolkenhain in Germany: "The two old SS men who accompanied us looked into our compartment every so often, but as the hours passed they no longer bothered to come, perhaps because they had fallen asleep in another compartment."

(135) Abek returns home: "The Jews of Sosnowitz had met the same fate as those in Bielitz and elsewhere. He had managed to get to Sosnowitz but by the time he arrived no one was left. Even the young people had been sent to Auschwitz and not to work camps."

(151) While unloading coal trains in Märzdorf slave labour factory: "Other freight trains passed, from them we heard faint cries and pleas for water; in those trains were Jews making their last journey to Auschwitz. Those trains rolled by swiftly. Like snakes, they rolled into the night, taillights blinking sadly, and with them disappeared lives, thousands."

Transit camps

(104) Sosnowitz, June 1942: "We were in a so-called Dulag, an abbreviation for 'Durchgangslager', or transit camp, which in this case served as a labor pool. We were to be chosen for work in the German war industry and would be trained by the people who had requisitioned us from the SS."

Slave labour camps and factories

(83) Registering for work, with its potential for security: her father to work in Sucha, "... where the Germans were fortifying the river"; her mother and Gerda, "... to work in Wadowitz in a shop that sewed military garments. ... The wages of course would be ridiculously small, barely enough to cover the train fare. But we would be safe now, and might be able to stay in the Bielitz ghetto." May 1942.

(114–15, 117) 2 July 1942, transfer by train to the Bolkenhain factory: "I read the firm's name in large gold letters over the entrance: 'Kramsta-Methner-Frahne,' and under it, 'Weberie' – weaving mill."

(118–20) Running the looms at Bolkenhain: "At first each of us tended one loom, then we were assigned two, then three looms, and finally, we watched four. Experts who had spent their lives weaving never handled more than three looms."

(137–40) Life at Bolkenhain: "Actually, we were well off. The work, once we got used to it, was not as difficult as it had seemed in the beginning. Frau Kügler was good to us, and never resorted to physical violence. … We could, of course, have eaten much more, but we were not really hungry and we were not cold." She receives packages from her Uncle Leo in Istanbul.

(142–4) They leave Bolkenhain, the end of August 1943. Mrs Berger, Litzi the nurse, Suse, and Lotte are in the group that goes to Landeshut; Ilse and Gerda in the group going to Märzdorf; presumably to work in factories which were subsidiaries of Kramsta-Methner-Frahne.

(151–6) Ilse arranges for Gerda and herself to be among those transferred to Landeshut: "Although everything in Landeshut was much more strenuous than in Bolkenhain it was heaven compared with Märzdorf." Gerda spends ten months working the weaving looms on the night shift.

(157–60, 164) A dentist, Dr Goldstein, visits Landeshut: "When he came with his equipment, we learned from him that the men were housed about an hour's march from us in what had formerly been a tavern on a hill called Zum Burgberg. It was shortly to be known as one of the most horrible men's camp in Germany." Gerda discovers that Abek is there. She visits there before she leaves: "The place spelled horror to me, from the machine gun over the entrance to the tomblike, windowless walls that housed the men."

(166–70, 173–4) The girls are transferred by train to Grünberg: "The camp was modern, well scrubbed, clean, and filled with suffering. That day in 1944, when we arrived, there were approximately a thousand girls there. Some were bursting with health and color, others were half-starved and walked about with bent backs, decaying teeth, the pallor of death already on their faces."

(178–9) November 1944, the girls go through an examination by the SS. Gerda, fearing the reason for it, sells her mother's diamond and pearl pendant for two packets of poison for herself and Ilse: "With Ilse on the lookout for intruders I went to my bunk and carefully removed the pendant from my coat. I kissed it quickly, remembering how well it had looked on Mama's throat. Then I went in search of the girl with the poison."

Auschwitz-Birkenau

(83) Those living in the Bielitz Ghetto are told to register for work: "A notice followed proclaiming that those who failed to register would be sent to Auschwitz, described in the notice as a newly created concentration camp about twenty miles away." May 1942.

(170–1) At Grünberg: "About every two months the spinning-room girls were X-rayed. Each time a number were found to have contracted tuberculosis; they were immediately sent to Auschwitz." July 1944.

(175–6) At Grünberg: "Deliveries of old clothes arrived daily from Auschwitz to be shredded up and converted into yarn. A number of the girls who ran the shredding machines insisted that they had recognized their parents' clothes." Autumn 1944.

Death marches

(180–1) January 1945, the last night in Grünberg, a group of Jewish girls joins them: "They had come from another camp and had been walking for five days. Now we were to join them. They thought they were going to Oranienburg, a concentration camp like Auschwitz, to be gassed." The camp was Sachsenhausen, near Oranienburg. It had no gas chambers.

(182) The march from Grünberg: "We learned later there were about three thousand from other camps; with our contingent from Grünberg we totaled nearly four thousand. We were divided into two transports amid much whipping and screaming by the SS. ... We four were in the column which was doomed; out of two thousand only a hundred and twenty survived. The other column was liberated much sooner."

(183–9, 191–3) "I thought: I am marching to death or to liberation. It was the morning of January 29, 1945." The march begins to the west, taking more than a week to reach Camp Christianstadt, three days later, they continue to the west: "A week passed, two, perhaps three. We lost count of time. ... Everywhere we left some dead. Some we buried, others we simply left." They pass through Dresden as it was being bombed, and through Freiburg.

(189–91) Gerda comes up with a plan for her and Ilse to escape from the death march: "Only when Ilse showed her fear did my doubts come to the surface. ... But now I hesitated. The decision was not mine alone: Ilse's life was as dear to me as my own. ... I closed my eyes and held Ilse's hand tightly. We marched on."

(194–6) They march through Chemnitz, Zwickau, Reichenbach, Plauen: "We were ... more than five hundred kilometers from Grünberg. There were perhaps no more than four hundred girls left. It must have been around the twentieth of March; we had been marching for almost two months. Now we came to another camp, Helmbrechts. It wasn't a death camp; we saw with relief that there were people there, and no furnaces."

(209–10) Their death march ends in a factory barracks in Volary, Czechoslovakia; the SS try to set off a bomb, which fails, they return to shoot, and then flee: "Much later we heard shouting in Czech. A man and two women enter the factory calling: 'If someone is inside, come out. The war is over!'"

Witness to mass murder

(13–14) Near Kielce, early September 1939, Aunt Anna reports: "What they had mistaken for shooting stars had been German paratroopers. Now they had their first direct experience with the Nazi methods. First, the men were segregated from the women. ... The men were lined up, and every tenth one was shot. The rest were marched toward the forest."

(16–21) All men from ages sixteen to fifty are ordered to register: "One of the boys, a classmate of Arthur's, told us that after registering, many boys from other towns were taken to camp and killed. 'Nonsense,' Arthur said to the boy, 'what foolishness people try to invent.'" On 19th October 1939, Arthur leaves.

(30) Mid-November 1939, news of Arthur's October transport: "For eight days the boys had been locked in cattle cars, taken to the 'Gouvernement', and turned loose in the woods. Then the SS troops had beat and shot them at random. Those who were able to ran away. Thirty-six prisoners were said to have been killed."

(68–70) January 1942, friend Erica's letter arrives describing the massacre in her town, the death of her mother, her baby brother, and her boyfriend Henek. "I never heard from Erica again."

(105–6) At the Dulag, Sosnowitz: "Several living skeletons, clad in rags that crawled with vermin, stretched out begging hands. ... They knew they were now going to Auschwitz to be gassed and cremated. They were useful no longer to the glorious Third Reich. They had given their strength, their youth, their health, and now they had to give their lives."

(158) The dentist Dr Goldstein tells those in Landeshut of Zum Burgberg: "Dr. Goldstein kept us informed of the incredible excesses the SS guards indulged in: the slaughter, the wild orgies, the transports to Auschwitz."

(200–1) Two and a half months of the death march: "Since leaving Helmbrechts, we had had a horse-drawn wagon with us on which the sick and dead were transported until there were enough for a mass grave. Then the dead would be unloaded and the sick shot."

Resistance, ghetto revolts, individual acts of courage and defiance

(115–16) Malvine Berger is chosen as the "Judenälteste" at the Bolkenhain slave labour factory: "'Girls, I hope you know what our position is here. How we feel is beside the point; we have to please the people here.' ... She made it clear where we stood. She dared to say, 'How we feel is beside the point.' At that remark I saw how the director knit his brow. Thus she made our captors understand that we were no fools. Nor was there any humble begging in her manner."

(127) The girls decide to fast on Yom Kippur, 1942 in Bolkenhain: "Meister Zimmer somehow heard about it. He warned that severe punishment would be meted out to anyone who feigned illness or did not produce the prescribed amount of material. Nevertheless, we all fasted. We worked harder than ever but no one touched food until there were three stars in the evening sky. There was a proud serenity about every one of us, a sense of accomplishment."

(140–2) Gerda writes and arranges plays at Bolkenhain: "After the merrymaking and fun, that note of hope was the right one to strike. The hope for a normal life, for children and grandchildren who could live in a world where our experiences would seem too fantastic to be believable – that was our dearest wish. ... I thank God that I was able to make them forget. Even now, when I meet the few girls who survived and they remind me of those performances, I feel humble and grateful. I know that that was the greatest thing I have done in my life."

(145–50) In Märzdorf, she rebuffs the advances of the supervisor: "There was so much I wanted to say, but I knew that my life was in his hands. I was afraid even of silence. ... From that day on, Märzdorf became hell." The consequences: she unloads flax bundles by day, and coal at night: "Flax dust, coal dust, blood, sweat, all mixed together into a crust that covered my body. We were only a handful of girls who were chosen for both the flax and coal details, but I was always among them."

Specific escapes

(80–1) Her father escapes a raid by hiding in a closet: "We learned later that the Gestapo had combed the ghetto in search of someone and that the sound of the horn was a signal that the victim had been found."

In hiding, including Hidden Children

(45) Mr Pipersberg in hiding in the "Gouvernement": "We knew that there were people who obtained 'Aryan' papers and hid with farmers in villages. ... We did not know that this was to be the last message from Mr Pipersberg."

Righteous Gentiles

(34–5, 74) Family friend Niania Brenza: "Niania was the only person who had come to see us regularly and who didn't seem afraid of what the Germans would say or do. ... Although the Germans had summoned her to the police station and warned her not to enter our house,

Niania came and went as before. … a proud and simple woman; her spirit shone brightly in that world of betrayal."

(48–51) Gerda takes English lessons but is caught with her English grammar book, and is taken to the police station: "'It is almost espionage to learn English while we are at war with England.' … As soon as the policeman left, the bald officer turned to me. His voice softened to a more human tone. 'Now run home as fast as you can,' he said, 'and forget your English.' … I met many hundreds of Germans in the years that followed, but only two, and he was the first, who behaved as though they were human!"

(114–15, 132–3, 157, 165) Frau Kügler, "Lagenführerin", camp supervisor at Bolkenhain weaving factory; she saves Gerda from a selection by SS "Obersturmführer" Lindner: "The German woman who worked for the SS had saved my life." She reconnects the girls at Landeshut with the men they know at Zum Burgberg. On 9 May 1944 the girls are transferred from Landeshut: "Her face was wet with tears. 'Good-by, Gerda,' she murmured under her breath. 'Don't forget me.' … She stood there, a solitary figure, and waved a soundless farewell. … She was a good woman. … She displayed humanity, she gave us hope that perhaps not all Germans were cruel."

(223, 231–2) Herr Knebel: "… the owner of the factory in which we were hiding on Liberation Day … told me that he had known either my father or one of his business associates. The following day his two daughters … came to visit me. The day after that they came again, and brought me a dress. It is hard to describe the joy that I felt, and the eagerness with which I looked forward to being able to get up and wear it."

Liberation

(162) Mid-December 1943, Italian prisoners come to Landeshut: "We knew now that the war had taken a different turn. Apparently the Italians were no longer gallant Axis partners."

(179–80) December 1944, air raid sirens begin at Grünberg: "The German workers ran for shelter while we stayed in the factory. … We tried hard not to look too pleased. Then we were told that we must go to the shelter when the alarm sounded. Apparently nobody wanted to risk his skin watching us."

(214–16) Liberated in a factory building in Volary, Czechoslovakia, by the Fifth US Infantry Division: "Shaking my head, I stared at this man who was to me the embodiment of all heroism and liberty. He greeted me. I must tell him from the start, I resolved, so that he has no illusions about us. … 'We are Jews,' I said in a small voice. 'So am I,' he answered."

(215) Lilli, thanking their American liberators: "Her hands were shaking as she gently, unbelievingly touched the sleeve of his jacket. In the exchange that followed, I made out the word 'happy.' … Then she sighed, released his hand and, looking at him, shook her head and whispered, 'Too late.' … Shortly afterward, Lilli died."

(216–17) From the factory they are moved to a hospital: "The hospital we were taken to was a converted school. Wounded German soldiers had been moved to the third floor so that we could be installed in the first two floors. How strange – in a matter of one day, the world had changed: Germans were put out to make room for us."

(217–19) Her second day in the hospital, she hears that the war has ended, 8 May: "'It's my birthday, my twenty-first birthday, and Germany capitulated!'" Her recovery begins: "I was weighed – sixty-eight pounds. The nurses joked about being able to circle my thigh with their fingers."

(220–1) Kurt Klein, an American serviceman, speaking with Gerda, who was among the prisoners he liberated: "... he told me some of his experiences with the Germans' surprise when they heard about their concentration camps. 'It seems we fought a war against the Nazis, but I haven't met a Nazi yet,' he said wryly."

(224–33) While in hospital, she overcomes pneumonia, typhus, and the possibility of having her feet amputated; instead she tries other treatments: "At first there was not much sensation. Later the hot and the cold were equally excruciating, but I rejoiced in the pain, for it meant that I had life in my legs, that I would be able to walk."

(234–5) While still recuperating, she visits the Knebels: "I felt painfully alone and forlorn in that house which so closely resembled that of my childhood, in a country so much like my own, standing next to a man who was so much like my family. Yet nothing there belonged to me."

(236–42) Deciding not to return home, she moves with the American Army to Cham in Bavaria, then proceeds to Freising and Munich.

(245–6) Hearing from her Uncle Leo in Turkey, she realizes she is the only one of the family to survive: "Now at last I knew that I would never go home again." She decides to follow Kurt to America and marry him there.

Stories of individuals, including family members

(13–14) Father's sister Anna and her two children Miriam, aged 15, and then David, aged 19, come to the family seeking help; her husband had been killed when their train bound for Warsaw had been bombed, they had survived a massacre in the forest near Kielce: "Finding my father gave her new hope. They had no clothing, except the garments they wore during their flight. They had no food, no money. Everything was lost."

(15) Arthur, searching for Gisa Ebersohn, who had fled with her family to the East, finds only: "'The dog lies dead in front of her house.'"

(28–9) Aunt Anna and her daughter Miriam leave Bielitz for their former home in Czortkow, November 1939: "For a while we had letters from them, but in December, 1940, our letters came back. ... We never learned what happened to them, except that they never reached Czortkow."

(36–7, 40–1, 71, 131, 133–4) Rumours of Arthur's whereabouts precede a letter from him: "Both Arthur and David were safe in Russia. Even more miraculous, on their first night in Lwow, as they walked the streets looking for food and shelter, they had met Uncle Aaron, David's father, who was believed dead!" She receives letters from Arthur at Christmas 1942, and in January 1943: "It proved to be the last message I ever got from my brother. ... His quiet words gave me the strength and trust to go on and face what was to come."

(54–7) She meets the painter Abek Feigenblatt at a "boys' camp" near Bielitz: "Inasmuch as he worked outside the camp, restoring paintings and hanging them in German homes, he came and went unchallenged. He seemed to enjoy more privileges than anybody else in camp, perhaps because he painted portraits for the guards."

(58, 201–5) Ilse Kleinzähler plays her piano before it is confiscated: "Away from her piano Ilse was shy and withdrawn; only through her music was she able to express herself openly." She survives with Gerda for three and a half years. She dies in Czechoslovakia in April 1945 on the death march: "'If my parents survive, don't tell them I died like this.'" She was 18.

(59–68, 84, 136–7, 142–3, 163) Abek proposes to her: "'All I want is your promise to marry me after the war. It will give me all the courage I need to get through.'" Her answer: "'I would like to continue seeing you but I think it would be better if you didn't mention love until after the war.'"

(79–80) Their neighbours in the ghetto: "The Kolländers were very religious. The pious old mother alternately cried or prayed. ... Mrs. Freudenreich.... Her room was like a shrine for her young daughter, who had died in an accident in Vienna a few years before. ... Downstairs lived a young woman with charming twin girls. ... In another room near ours a middle-aged woman lived with her old mother. ... When I thought of our neighbors, I sometimes had the feeling that we were the only normal family there."

(85–6) Her parents, Julius, 55, and Helene, 45, spend their last night together before they are separated and sent to different labour camps: "And so they talked on through the night, animated and happy. They faced what the morning would bring with the only weapon they had – their love for each other. Love is great, love is the foundation of nobility, it conquers obstacles and is a deep well of truth and strength. After hearing my parents talk that night I began to understand the greatness of their love. Their courage ignited within me a spark that continued to glow through the years of misery and defeat."

(101–3, 106–10, 135, 244) Abek's mother and sisters Paula and Lola Feigenblatt try to help her remain in Sosnowitz with them: "They hoped that in exchange for one of their machines they would be able to obtain a working card for me. They would then take turns on the remaining machine and fill their quota by working day and night." They are able to offer her refuge but she decides to remain with her group: "But I couldn't accept his family's sacrifice and reject him. The certainty remained that if I accepted freedom now I would have to marry Abek." Abek's family is taken a short time later along with all the Jews of Sosnowitz. Their deaths are confirmed.

(105–6) Gerda offers her bowl of food to a sick girl at the *Dulag*: "Her body was pitifully emaciated, her neck overly long. We looked at each other. For a fleeting moment I thought, she must be my age. I did not know her name or where she came from. I only knew that she was going to meet her death. ... She looked at me, perhaps wondering about the past, and I looked at her wondering about the future, the bowl of unsavory food between us. I closed my eyes. 'God bless you, may you never know what hunger is,' she said to me."

(112–13, 213) Suse Kunz, born in Vienna, becomes Gerda's friend from the train journey from Sosnowitz until the end of the war. She dies on the day they are liberated.

(121–4) The realization of her parents' death when her letter to her father comes back marked: "'Return to sender, moved without forwarding address.'"

(128–30) Lotte's story: as a child she meets her father and has the possibility of her parents reuniting, but then her father is tragically killed; Lotte dies in February 1945, on the death march: "I cannot help but want to tell her story, for I might be the only one left in the world who knows it."

(161) Abek finds Gerda in Landeshut: "When the camp in Bielitz had been disbanded, all the men went to Blechhammer since the Dulag in Sosnowitz was no longer in existence. ... Later, when he heard that a men's camp had been opened in Landeshut, he begged to be sent there in a transport, much against the advice of his friend, who knew of the camp's reputation."

(168, 215, 222, 237) Liesel Stepper from Czechoslovakia, Suse's friend, reunited at Grünberg, together until liberation: "I continually asked for Liesel, and was finally told that she had died after an amputation. I was alone again! None of my close friends remained."

(172–3) Her friend in Grünberg, found to have tuberculosis, deported to Auschwitz, survives, is reunited with Gerda in Munich after the war.

(196–9) Tusia, from Bolkenhain, shares Gerda's birthday, inspires her in Helmbrechts: "'... you have given me belief in humanity. ... Your spark has not gone out, it never will. You will hurt people but you will make them happy. ... You are going through mud, but your feet are still clean.'" Tusia dies in Helmbrechts.

(201, 205–8) Hanka, her friend from Grünberg, keeps Gerda on her feet during the last days of the march: "Thus Hanka had become a guardian angel to me whose kindness I shall never forget."

(203) Rita Schanzer escapes the death march shortly before liberation: "Perhaps she had gotten safely away. I hoped so."

(221–2, 243) Kurt Klein, a refugee from Germany, a soldier in the US Army, reunited with his brother and sister in America, their parents deported to Gurs: "For a while letters reached them from America, then in July, 1942, a letter had been returned, stamped 'Moved – left no forwarding address.'"

(239–42) Mala Orbach leaves Volary with Gerda, for Munich.

(252–3) Aunt Pepi, her 17-year-old daughter Rose, and her 10-year-old son Josef taken to Auschwitz.

Post-war life and career

(Epilogue) Gerda and Kurt moved to Buffalo, raised three children, enjoyed eight grandchildren, and retired in Arizona. In the fall of 1946, Gerda began speaking publicly about her Holocaust experiences and has been involved with Holocaust-, Israel-, and Jewish-related issues since.

Personal reflections

(Preface) On writing her memoir: "I have discharged a burden, and paid a debt to many nameless heroes, resting in their unmarked graves. For I am haunted by the thought that I might be the only one left to tell their story."

(32, 150) December 1939, before deportation from home, Gerda contemplates suicide, but her father tells her: "'Whatever you are thinking now is wrong. It is cowardly.' ... 'Promise me that no matter what happens you will never do it.' ... in the years to come, when death seemed the only solution, I remembered that promise as my most sacred vow."

(247) "Survival is both an exalted privilege and a painful burden. ... The acuteness of those recollections often penetrates the calm of my daily life, forcing me to confront painful truths but clarifying much through the very act of evocation. I have learned, for the most part, to deal with those truths, knowing well that a painful memory brought into focus by a current incident still hurts, but also that the pain will recede – as it has – and ultimately fade away."

(248) On America: "I love this country as only one who has been homeless for so long can understand. I love it with a possessive fierceness that excuses its inadequacies, because I deeply want to belong. And I am still fearful of rejection, feeling I have no right to criticize, only an obligation to help correct."

(253) "I am awed by the marvel of creation, the mysterious spark in these new lives, which continue the chain of generations stretching back to time immemorial, imbuing it with the divine. To close the gap of what was left uncompleted, to create an existence that was meant to be denied represents a triumph over evil. I realize with wonder and gratitude that in my body reposed some part of shared ancestry with those deprived of life and that I was given the privilege of being a link between generations."

(260) "I have learned that when we bring comfort to others, we reassure ourselves, and when we dispel fear, we assuage our own fears as well."

Places mentioned in Europe (page first mentioned)

Amsterdam (255), Andrychow/Andrichau (85), Auschwitz Main Camp/Auschwitz I (79), Austrian Alps (233), Austro-Hungarian Empire (4), Bavaria/Bayern (224), Beskid Mountains (4), Bielsko–Biala/Bielitz (4), Blechhammer slave labour camp (Blachownia Slaska) (161), Bolkenhain slave labour camp (Bolkow) (113), Britain (9), Burgberg slave labour camp (157), Carpathian Mountains (23), Cham (239), Chemnitz (194), Christianstadt camp/Krzystkowice (188), Cracow/Krakow/Krakau (3), Czechoslovakia (4), Czestochowa (73), Czortkow (28), Denmark/Danmark (44), Dresden (193), Elbe river (193), France (9), Freiburg (193), Freising (239), Germany/Deutschland (9), Grünberg slave labour camp (Zielona Gora) (166), Gurs internment camp (222), Helmbrechts camp (194), Katowice/Kattowitz (96), Kielce (13), Kramsta-Methner-Frahne Factory (Bolkenhain) (114), Krynica (4), Lärchenfeld (Bielitz) (88), Landeshut slave labour camp (Kamienna Gora) (144), London (England) (247), Lvov/Lemberg/Lwow/Lviv (40), Märzdorf slave labour camp (Marciszow) (144), Munich/München (172), Norway/Norge (44), Oswiecim/Auschwitz town (28), Paris (44), Perlacher Forest (Munich) (242), Pfarrkirchen (224), Plauen (194), Poland/Polska (6), Reichenbach/Dzierzoniow (194), Sachsenhausen concentration camp (Oranienburg) (180), Silesia (189), Sosnowiec transit camp (104), Sosnowiec/Sosnowitz (59), Sucha Beskidzka slave labour camp (83), Switzerland/Schweiz/Suisse/Swizzeria (86), Teschen/Cieszyn/ CeskiTesin (4), Vienna/Wien (23), Volary (208), Wadowice/Wadowitz slave labour camp (83), Warsaw/Warszawa/Warschau (5), Wolfgang lake (256), Zwickau (194)

Places mentioned outside Europe (page first mentioned)

Arizona (255), Bosphorus (122), Buffalo (New York) (226), Israel/Yisrael (248), Istanbul/Constantinople (37), New York City (248), Russia/Rossija (11), Siberia/Sibir (125), Turkey/Turkiye (5), United States of America (11), Washington (DC) (256)

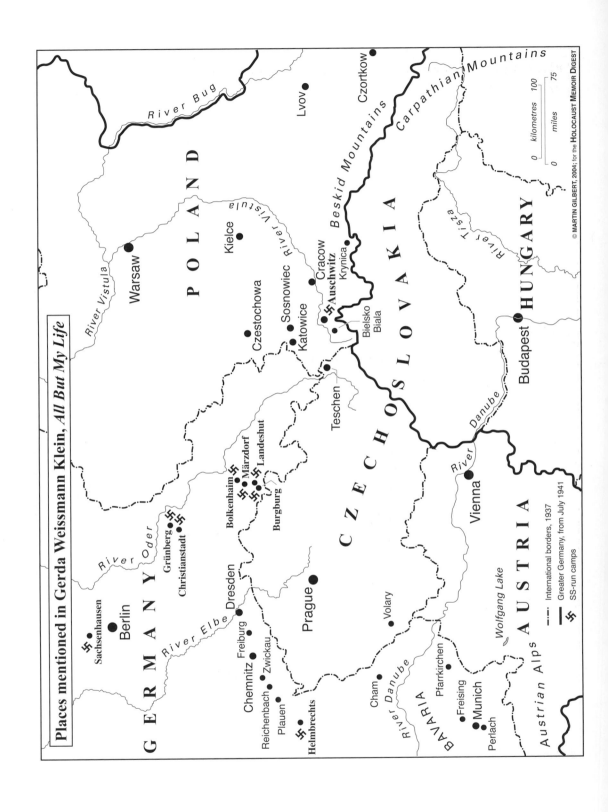

Places mentioned in Gerda Weissmann Klein, *All But My Life*

River Bug

Lvov •

Czortkow •

Carpathian Mountains

Beskid Mountains

P O L A N D

River Vistula

Kielce •

Warsaw •

River Vistula

Czestochowa •

Sosnowiec •

Katowice •

Cracow •

⚜ Auschwitz

Krynica •

Bielsko Biala

HUNGARY

Budapest •

River Tisza

C Z E C H O S L O V A K I A

Teschen •

Danube

River

Vienna •

Bolkenhain ⚜

Märzdorf ⚜

Landeshut

Burgburg

⚜ Grünberg ⚜

Christianstadt •

River Oder

Dresden •

Freiburg •

Chemnitz •

Reichenbach •

Zwickau •

Plauen •

Helmbrechts •

River Elbe

Prague •

Volary •

Wolfgang Lake

A U S T R I A

⚜ Sachsenhausen

Berlin ●

G E R M A N Y

River Danube

Cham •

B A V A R I A

Pfarrkirchen •

Freising •

Munich •

Perlach •

Austrian Alps

© **MARTIN GILBERT, 2004**; for the **HOLOCAUST MEMOIR DIGEST**

0 kilometres 100

0 miles 75

- - - International borders, 1937

── Greater Germany, from July 1941

⚜ SS-run camps

Places in the Auschwitz region mentioned in Gerda Weissmann Klein,
All But My Life
Czestochowa
International borders, 1937
SS-run camps
0 kilometres 20
0 miles 15
P O L A N D
Blechhammer
Sosnowiec
Katowice
Oswiecim
Cracow
Birkenau
Auschwitz
River Vistula
River Wieprzowka
Wadowice
Andrychow
River Biala
Bielsko-Biala
(Bielitz)
River Vistula
River Skawa
River Sola
Sucha Beskidzka
SLOVAKIA
© MARTIN GILBERT, 2004; for the
HOLOCAUST MEMOIR DIGEST

Saul Friedländer, *When Memory Comes*

Late 1932: born in Prague

September 1938: begins private school; Jews not allowed in public schools

12 March 1939: family attempts to flee to Hungary, returns to Prague

Summer 1939: family flees to Paris

Autumn 1939 to spring 1940: in a Jewish children's home, Montmorency, near Paris

Spring 1940 to August 1942: with parents in Néris-les-Bains

August 1942: two days in a children's home near La Souterraine

August 1942: a few days with parents in Néris, then taken to a Catholic boarding school in Montluçon

September 1942: escapes, returns to parents, they return him to school

October 1942: baptized, taken to Montneuf boarding school

September 1943 to 1946: at boarding school in Montluçon

August 1944: Montluçon liberated by the French Resistance

August 1945: realizes his parents are dead

February 1946: with the help of a priest, realizes he is Jewish

1946/47: transfers to a boarding school in Paris, reconnects with Judaism, becomes a Zionist

3 June 1948: leaves school, travels to Marseilles

11 June 1948: sails to Israel on the *Altalena*

Author: Saul Friedländer

Title: *When Memory Comes*

Publishing details

Avon Books, The Hearst Corporation, 1790 Broadway, New York, New York 10019, 1980, 186 pages.

ISBN 0-380-50807-9.

Originally published in French as *Quand vient le souvenir…* in 1978.

Translated from the French by Helen R. Lane.

The memoir also contains diary-like entries written from June through December 1977 in Israel, culminating in Anwar Sadat's visit and the "normalization" of relations with Egypt. For the purpose of the *Digest*, this summary focuses on his Holocaust experiences from his birth to his emigration to Israel.

Focus

Saul, a young boy (who is 7 in 1939), leaves Czechoslovakia with his parents to find refuge in France. He is sheltered in a Catholic boarding school, his parents are deported to Auschwitz. Saul emigrates to Israel on the *Altalena* in 1948, at the age of 15.

Contents (by topic, with page numbers)

Pre-war Jewish home and community life

(3–6) Saul, born in late 1932, in Prague, as was his father, Jan; his mother, Elli Glaser, came from Rochlitz, where his grandfather had established himself: "… his is fairly representative of a certain type of minor Jewish industrialist at the beginning of the century. … Jewish ingenuity did nothing to change the fact that everyone in our house felt German. … in our family . . .

Judaism as a religion had completely disappeared."

(13–15) Childhood fears of abandonment and death: his school director dies suddenly and is cremated: "For a long time the director's cremation haunted my nightmares. The mind of a child interprets the world in its own way, especially when that child is aware of a growing anxiety round about him which is still, however, difficult for him to identify." Saul is 6 years old.

(15–17) On his Czech governess Vlasta: "The influence of the Vlastas of all nationalities on the rapid assimilation of the Jewish bourgeoisie of Europe merits study. The Vlastas formed, quite naturally, the essential link between the Jewish child and the world around him."

(18–20) The Prague legend of the Golem, a mystical Jewish figure: "My father was less interested, I think, in its Jewish content than in its esoteric meaning, the one provided him by Gustav Meyrink's strange retelling of the legend, of which he possessed a magnificent copy, illustrated by the engraver Hugo Steiner."

(24) "In 1937 my mother and two of her brothers went on a cruise that took them to Palestine. … There was nothing at the level of religious tradition, certainly, but in the case of my mother and her brothers there was a more or less active interest in Zionism." The oldest, his Uncle Paul: "… was the mentor of this expedition. The youngest brother, my Uncle Hans, came back from this trip deeply disappointed. … Hence my Uncle Hans's break with Zionism and his turn to anthroposophy. … Her third brother, Willy, was interested only in chemistry."

Pre-war anti-Semitism

(25–9) September 1938, amid inflamatory speeches by Hitler, Saul begins to attend a private school: "… because Jewish children were no longer admitted to public schools. … during those first few days, on the eve of the final abandonment of Czechoslovakia, war seemed imminent. In Prague, alerts followed one after the other; I remember sirens, shelters, and above all the gas masks that everyone carried around like a talisman, in a cylindrical box slung across the shoulder."

(29–32) 12 March 1939, the family tries to flee to Hungary: "The real reason for our leaving the country was concealed from me. I was told that we were leaving Prague because the Germans had occupied Czechoslovakia and because we were Czech. I apparently did not notice that an essential link in this explanation was missing; it seemed altogether natural that my father should impress upon me my duty to remember Prague and our country. As for our status as Jews, we were taking it with us." However: "It was too late: the Germans were already there." They return to Prague.

(37–41) Spring, summer 1939, Saul and his parents flee Prague for Paris. Contemplating trying to get into Palestine, his father writes to a friend in England: "'… it will be a year at best before our turn for an immigration certificate comes up, and for people like us there is no way to decide things so far ahead.'" Saul is 6 years old.

(44–6) Saul stays in a children's home in Montmorency near Paris for more than six months: "Most Sundays … my mother did come. Till lunchtime every moment was happiness to me, but after lunch the fear of her leaving came over me."

The coming of war

(47–9) The Nazi–Soviet Non-Aggression Pact is signed on 22 August 1939; the next day his mother writes to a friend: "'All we can do now is wait as calmly as possible and let everything take its course.' … Eight days later, the German armies entered Poland and the war began."

(49–51, 65–7) Saul is reunited with his parents as they leave Paris. They spend the next two years in Néris-les-Bains: "The waters of Néris were well known before the war for their beneficial effects on nervous people, a fact that now became perfectly ironic. Hotels, family boarding-houses, and apartments for rent abounded … all of them filled up with a host of people taking a cure against their will. … Almost all of them, as I have noted, were Jewish."

Deportation

(70–1) "In July 1942, arrests of foreign Jews in France began simultaneously in the occupied and unoccupied zones. … On July 16, 1942, the great roundup began in Paris; nearly thirteen thousand foreign Jews, among them four thousand children, were herded into the Vélodrome d'Hiver. Adolf Eichmann let it be known that beginning on July 20 there would be sufficient space for children in the convoys destined to leave for the East before the end of August."

(72–4) His stay at the children's home of La Souterraine is cut short: gendarmes arrive in the middle of the night: "All the children over ten were being taken away. The next day, the gendarmes announced, they would be coming back for the others." The next night, the children hide in the forest. "Did the gendarmes come back? I couldn't say, for the next day Madame Fraenkel arrived and we returned to Néris." September 1942.

(88–90) From their deportation train from Rivesaltes, Saul's parents send three letters to Madame M. de L., the first from Saint-Gingolph at the border, a telegram from Rivesaltes, and a letter: "... thrown from the train of deportees to Quakers who waited in the stations as theconvoys passed through."

Transit camps

(88–90) 30 September 1942, Elli and Jan Friedländer are turned back at the Swiss border at the French village of Novel, arrested and taken to the French internment camp of Rivesaltes, then deported by train to "Germany" on 5 October.

Resistance, ghetto revolts, individual acts of courage and defiance

(69–70) Celebrating Hanukkah, December 1941, France: "When crises occur, one searches the depths of one's memory to discover some vestige of the past, not the past of the individual, faltering and ephemeral, but rather that of the community, which, though left behind, nonetheless represents that which is permanent and lasting. ... Perhaps the essence of a tradition, its ultimate justification, is to comfort, to bring a small measure of dreams, a brief instant of illusion, to a moment when every real avenue of escape is cut off, when there is no longer any other recourse."

(75–6) In Israel in 1967, the Warsaw Ghetto Uprising is commemorated, and the ghetto remembered, on its twenty-fifth anniversary: "That evening we listened to a radio program evoking memories of life in the ghetto."

(126–7) Two boys at Saint-Béranger, Jean-Marc, 13 years old, and Michel, 10 years old, voice their support for the French Resistance fighters even though the rest of the school supports Marshal Pétain: "Jean-Marc and Michel became heroes, in a modest way, by thus braving general opprobrium and giving proof of courage and independence at an age when children quite naturally follow the crowd."

Specific escapes

(89) In 1977, while tracing his parents' fate, Saul finds documentation at the French–Swiss border town of Novel: "'Novel – Memories, Reminiscences (1973).' And on the following page: 'A nightmare stay. From September 27 to October 6, 1942.' The story of a witness, Madame Francken, who lived in Novel at the time. ... In the course of her story, Madame Francken had written: '... Switzerland lets in the old, the sick, the families with children. The others are sent back across the border and into the hands of soldiers!'"

(185) A Jewish doctor from Sens escapes from the deportation train from Drancy. Saul's father gives him his Schaffhausen watch to send to Saul: "That was how the watch came to me. I never took it off."

In hiding, including Hidden Children

(76–80) "'... for today one can no longer have any confidence in a Jewish institution,'" writes Saul's mother to Madame M. de L. His parents agree that, in order to save him, Saul is to be baptized a Catholic: "... my father had promised not only to accept my conversion but to assure me a Catholic education if later life resumed its normal course. ... in the same circumstances, in the face of the same drama, would not I, too, have written the same lines, given the same authorization, made the same promises? ... happily for them, no religious allegiance stood in their way. ... But what, I wonder, would a religious Jew have done if confronted with such a terrible dilemma?"

(81) Saul's parents seek safety in Néris, but no hiding place can be found: "The vise was about to close. There was only one chance left: to cross the border and flee to Switzerland."

(82–4, 168–9) "Everything at Saint-Béranger stifled me: the austere discipline, the continual prayers, of which I didn't understand a word, the dreariness of our dark building, and, finally, the food, which seemed revolting to me. … I decided to run away." September 1942, Saul is 10 years old.

(85–8) Saul escapes from Saint-Béranger and succeeds in finding his parents at the hospital in Montluçon. He is told he must return to his school: "I was quite aware, however, that there was anxiety in these words: my parents were pleading with all the conviction of those who know that they are not going to be believed. … My mother put her arms around me, but it was my father who unwittingly revealed to me the real meaning of our separation: he hugged me to him and kissed me. It was the first time that that timid father of mine had ever kissed me."

(93, 95, 97–9) October, November, December 1942, the Montneuf boarding school: "… nothing seemed to be able to bring me out of the melancholic apathy into which I was sinking, little by little."

(94) "'Paul-Henri.' I couldn't get used to my new name. At home I had been called Pavel, or rather Pavlicek. … Then from Paris to Néris I had become Paul. … As Paul I didn't feel like Pavlicek anymore, but Paul-Henri was worse still. … Paul could have been Czech and Jewish; Paul-Henri could be nothing but French and resolutely Catholic, and I was not yet naturally so. … I subsequently became Shaul on disembarking in Israel, and then Saul, a compromise between the Saül that French requires and the Paul that I had been. In short, it is impossible to know which name I am, and that in the final analysis seems to me sufficient expression of a real and profound confusion."

(99–102) March 1943, Saul develops a nearly fatal case of croup, and the delirium of his illness brings back frightening memories of the train journey from Prague four years earlier, when he was temporarily separated from his parents: "But suddenly, by a miracle, I was saved: my mother, who had set out in search of me, appeared. I ran to her, threw myself in her arms sobbing, felt the coolness of her fingers on my face … I opened my eyes: it was Madame Chancel stroking my forehead to calm me."

(107–8) April 1943, Saul recuperates from his illness: "I felt fine; I had changed. The memory of my parents seemed further away somehow." In September, after nearly a year in Montneuf, he returns to Montluçon.

(109–16) Life in the boarding school in Montluçon: "I adapted and became a devoted Saint-Béranger student. I was placed in the fifth grade. Like many of my schoolmates, I soon felt a vocation: I wanted to become a priest."

(118–19) The distribution of mail at Saint-Béranger: "I waited, from one week to the next, for three years. … as the presence of my parents began to become blurred in my mind, their letter, the one that never arrived, became more and more important, more and more laden with nostalgia and vain expectations. … as time passed, the letter corresponded to a more immediate need than my parents' return; this symbol of love and attachment took the place of the persons themselves."

(120–2) At Saint-Béranger: "I had the feeling, never put into words but nonetheless obvious, of having passed over to the compact, invincible majority, of no longer belonging to the camp of the persecuted, but, potentially at least, to that of the persecutors. … Paul Friedländer had disappeared; Paul-Henri Ferland was someone else."

Righteous Gentiles

(65, 71–2) The director of his school in Néris accompanies Saul to his hiding place: "Pascal

Delaume, a quiet father of a family, probably close to fifty, a slightly ridiculous figure thanks to his plumpness, his toupee, and his clumsiness, has come to symbolize for me the good-hearted man in the full sense of the word.... Was there any reason for him to lift a finger when people were wary of giving us so much as a friendly glance?" August 1942.

(137–8) Father L., the Priest at Saint-Etienne tells Saul of his parents' fate at Auschwitz: "The attitude of Father L. himself profoundly influenced me: to hear him speak of the lot of the Jews with so much emotion and respect must have been an important encouragement for me. ... his sense of justice (or was it a profound charity) led him to recognize my right to judge for myself, by helping me to renew the contact with my past." February 1946.

Liberation

(125–8) August 1944, Resistance fighters liberate the city of Montluçon from the Germans: "Taking turns standing on the toilet seats at night, my classmates and I could see the lights of combat; we shivered with excitement at the mortar shots – and also because we were prolonging our stay in this suspect place longer than was strictly necessary."

(128–34) Writing to his godmother, Madame M. de L. on 25 May 1945, he requests her permission to remain at the school rather than joining his grandmother in Stockholm, he is 12 years old. He experiences panic attacks. His parents' friend Madame Fraenkel tries in August to persuade him to go to Sweden: "I asked for news of my parents once more. Then she stared straight at me and said, very slowly and very distinctly: 'My poor Paul, don't you understand that your parents are dead?' "

(135–8) A visit to Father L., a Jesuit and former teacher at Saint-Béranger, now in Saint-Etienne, who tells Saul about what had happened to Jews like his parents who had been deported to Auschwitz, February 1946: "I had the impression that the essential pieces of a puzzle that heretofore had made no sense were falling into place. For the first time, I felt myself to be Jewish – no longer despite myself or secretly, but through a sensation of absolute loyalty. ... A tie had been reestablished, an identity was emerging, a confusing one certainly, contradictory perhaps, but from that day forward linked to a central axis of which there could be no doubt: in some manner or other I was Jewish – whatever this term meant in my mind."

(147–50) Saul leaves Montluçon to attend a boarding school, spending weekends with a Russian Jewish family: "... instead of the almost total absence of a Jewish tradition, an atmosphere saturated with Jewish emotions, allusions, customs, mannerisms." Autumn 1946.

(151–2) With the help of his friends, he finds his Jewish identity, in the Passover Seder: "... it is the holy words repeated over the centuries, that give the general symbol its particular force, that mark the sinking of roots in a group, the sinking of roots in history and in time. Because they have never been entirely clear, and always open to exegesis and explanation, it is the holy words that open the doors of imagination and allow the humblest of participants to understand, in his own way, the story and the feeling of the liberation, knowing that these traditional words are his anchor and foundation within the community."

Stories of individuals, including family members

(27, 31) Aunt Martha in Prague, when Saul and his parents leave: "Two of my uncles were leaving for Palestine soon, and the third for Sweden, where he intended to send for my grandmother. My father's sister was going to stay behind: we never saw her again."

(51–7) Saul's parents Elli, 35, and Jan, 43, during the two years in Néris: "Quite naturally, my mother became our principal support. From this time on, she was to accept any and every task.... In the meantime, my father's health got worse and worse. The stomach ulcer that even in Prague had made him suffer now tortured him daily. … He finally contrived to give a few lessons – in German. Fate had chosen a fierce irony."

(54, 68) "Fraenkel, an obese, jovial Viennese Jew suffering from heart disease and asthma …." Friends with whom they celebrate Hanukkah in Néris, 1941: "Among those present were Fraenkel, his wife (an Austrian who was not Jewish), and their son Georges, whom I called Jojo, a boy of about eight …."

(64, 115) "Madame M. de L., who must have been already over sixty at the time, was one of my father's few pupils; it was she whom my parents were soon to turn to. … She ruled her library, her house, and everyone about her with an iron hand, but her authoritative manner could not entirely conceal a profound goodness that was all the more genuine for being hidden. … she was the only one of the persons in Néris who did their best to give us a helping hand." Later she throws the militiamen out: "A good deal more than one child's life had been at stake: Madame M. de L. was Jewish by birth herself."

(74) August 1942 following a raid at the Jewish children's home near La Souterraine: "The next evening they gathered us all together in the dining room: the big ones – I was one of them – held the little ones by the hand. My companion must have been five at most: I can't recall his name, but I remember that his nose was running, that he squinted terribly, and that despite his tender years he looked sad and resigned."

(97–8) "One day I saw a boy of about fifteen arrive at Montneuf: Davy, a boy I had known in Néris. If there is such a thing as a Jewish face, his was one, there was no doubt of that, but his name had become much more French than mine even with an aristocratic 'de' in it. … He passed through our midst like a hurricane and during the few weeks that he stayed at Montneuf he never gave a sign of recognizing me … ."

Post-war life and career

(32–4) In the spring of 1967, his book on Pope Pius XII is published in Czechoslovakia. He returns to visit Prague from Geneva, and visits his former governess Vlasta, with his former affection: "... for each of us who lived through the events of this period as children there is an impassable line of cleavage somewhere in our memories: what is on this side, close to our time, remains dark, and what is on the other side still has the intense brightness of a happy dawn - even if our powers of reason and our knowledge point to obvious links between the two periods."

(102–6) "It took me a long, long time to find the way back to my own past. I could not banish the memory of events themselves, but if I tried to speak of them or pick up a pen to describe them, I immediately found myself in the grip of a strange paralysis." In 1956 Saul visits his Uncle Hans in Sweden, and remains there for a year. His uncle is the director of a mental hospital and in trying to reach out to some of the children in the hospital, Saul understands the importance and the difficulty in communicating.

(116–18) A post-war discussion, recorded 20 September 1977, with Claude Lanzmann, about his film *Shoah*: "A mad wind turns the pages of the past."

(144–7) A 1962 meeting with ex-Grand Admiral Doenitz in Aumühle, Germany: "'I assure you that I knew nothing about the extermination of the Jews.' … Did one only have to deny the past, deny it steadfastly, in order for that past to disappear forever?"

(153–5, 157–91, 167) Autumn 1946, Saul enrols in Lycée Henri IV in Paris and revisits the neighbourhood where he had lived with his parents in pre–war 1939. At his guardian's house they follow the events in "Eretz Israel", and he attends a Zionist summer camp on Lake Chalain in the Jura Mountains.

(162, 165–6, 170, 175–9) Saul leaves Paris for Israel, 11 June 1948, on an Irgun ship, the *Altalena*. His letter to his godparents Madame de L. and her husband explains: "… recent events have awakened a feeling in my soul that had been dormant there for a long time, the feeling that I was Jewish. And I want to prove it by leaving to fight alongside all the Jews who are dying in Palestine … ." Saul is 15.

(180–1, 183–4, 186) Saul's voyage to Israel on the *Altalena*, one of the youngest of 940 passengers, among them Allied veterans, one of whom was among the 20 passengers who were killed when the ship was bombarded by the Haganah: "And then the wrecked vessel was sent to the bottom or sold for scrap, I don't know which, while along the shoulder of the road to Jerusalem, the charred remains of the trucks became monuments to memory."

Personal reflections

(20) "'When knowledge comes, memory comes too, little by little. Knowledge and memory are one and the same thing.' " from Gustav Meyrink's retelling of "The Golem of Prague".

(28–9) As a 6-year-old child in Prague, Saul hears Bible stories from the rabbi: "We took up the story of Abraham and the sacrifice of Issac: 'Take now thy son, thine only son Isaac, whom thou lovest, and get thee to the land of Moriah; and offer him there for a burnt offering upon one of the mountains which I will tell thee of …' … Why is this one of the first stories of our people? Why was it preserved in the Bible? … this text does not leave me in peace: 'Take now thy son, thine only son … and offer him for a burnt offering …' Abraham's obedience explains our entire history. Today most Jews no longer obey God's injunctions, yet they still obey the call of some mysterious destiny."

(52) On his parents: "I contemplate them from a distance, from very far off, and I ask myself: what blindness led them from mistake to mistake to the very end? What dark destiny? I endeavor to understand, to put myself in their place, to imagine what I would have done, but I am unable to … Even today, I look at them only through the eyes of a child."

(55) On his father, of their time in Néris: "… he could not have helped but bow to the evidence: his faith in complete assimilation was mistaken; his failure to recognize the Nazi danger total; his confidence in France ridiculous. We should have been in Palestine or Sweden, like my uncles or my grandmother, at least out of Hitler's reach. Doubtless the worst thing of all in those days was to go on waiting, reduced to complete passivity."

(56) "… my father was hunted down for what he had refused to remain: a Jew. What he wanted to become, a man like others, had been taken away from him, leaving him no possible recourse. He was being refused the right to live and no longer even knew what to die for. Much more than an impossibility of acting, his desperate straits had become an impossibility of being."

(114) On his earlier memories: "My image of the past is like a plot of land thirsting for water. The moment a drop falls, it disappears; the moment a torrent begins to flow, it is absorbed."

(134–5) "The letters are here, and two or three yellowed photographs. For the others, these traces will soon no longer mean anything. I must write, then. Writing retraces the contours of the past with a possibly less ephemeral stroke than the others, it does at least preserve a presence, and it enables one to tell about a child who saw one world founder and another reborn."

(155–6) "I wanted to write. … what was missing was not literary talent but rather a certain ability to identify. … I had lived on the edges of catastrophe; a distance – impassable perhaps – separated me from those who had been directly caught up in the tide of events, and despite all my efforts, I remained, in my own eyes, not so much a victim as – a spectator. I was destined, therefore to wander among several worlds, knowing them, understanding them – better, perhaps than many others – but nonetheless incapable of feeling an identification without any reticence, incapable of seeing, understanding, and belonging in a single, immediate, total movement."

Places mentioned in Europe (page first mentioned)

Adige river (4), Aix (114), Allier (49), Arnhem (181), Aumühle (144), Aurillac (44), Auschwitz Main Camp/Auschwitz I (117), Belzec death camp (155), Berry (98), Bialystok (117), Bonn (145), Bourbonnais (79), Braunau am Inn (116), Brittany (112), Brno/Brunn (29), Bubenec (Prague) (25), Bulgaria/Balgarija (11), Carpathian Mountains (4), Châteauroux (100), Commentry (50), Creuse (71), Czechoslovakia (5), Drancy transit camp (Paris) (185), Elsgård (Sweden) (105), Fourvières (Lyon) (164), Freiburg (145), Gablonz (3), Galicia (5), Gare d'Austerlitz (Paris) (151), Gare de l'Est (Paris) (37), Gare de Lyon (162), Geneva/Genève (32), Germany/Deutschland (24), Göteborg (107), Hanover/Hannover (7), Hradcany Park (Prague) (14), Indre (93), Jura Mountains (159), Kehl (37), Koblenz/Coblenz (145), La Souterraine (71), Lake Chalain (159), Le Blanc (100), Loire river (115), London (England) (39), Lorraine/Alsace-Lorraine/Elsass-Lottringen (83), Lvov/Lemberg/Lwow/ Lviv (5), Lyon (88), Majdanek concentration camp (155), Mannheim (144), Marseilles/Marseille (54), Midi (112), Montauban (94), Montluçon (49), Montmorency (44), Montneuf School (93), Moravia (29), Morge River (89), Mount Grammont (89), Munich/München (25), Néris-les-Bains (49), Normandy (126), Novel (88), Nuremberg (37), Orléans (49), Paris (37), Poland/Polska (48), Port-de-Bouc (178), Prague/Praha (3), Rhine river (37), Rhodes/Rodos (180), Rhône river (174), Rivesaltes internment camp (90), Roanne (135), Rochlitz (3), Romania (59), Rome/Roma (117), Saint-Béranger School (Montluçon) (79), Saint-Etienne (135), Saint-Gingolph (88), Sarre River (49), Stockholm (102), Strasbourg (37), Stuttgart (37), Sudetenland (3), Sweden/Sverige (31), Switzerland/ Schweiz/Suisse/Swizzeria (81), Theresienstadt/Terezin–ghetto/concentration camp (117), Toulon (114), Toussus-le-Noble (49), Treblinka death camp (116), Tulsa (Sweden) (102), Vélodrome d'Hiver (Paris) (70), Vichy France (49), Vienna/Wien (54), Vltava/Moldau river (18), Warsaw ghetto (35), Wilson Station (Prague) (31)

Places mentioned outside Europe: (page first mentioned)

Beit Itzhak, Israel (7), Beit Lid, Israel (22), Caesarea (60), Cairo (166), Cyprus/Kypros/Kibris (158), Egypt/Al Misr (151), Haifa/Hefa (24), Israel/Yisrael (7), Jaffa (62), Jerusalem/ Yerushalayim (9), Kfar Saba (Israel) (22), Kfar Vitkin (Israel) (180), Kibbutz Ein Shemer (57), Netanya (10), New York City (117), Nira (Israel) (7), Palestine (24), Plain of Sharon (7), Rabat (112), Ramallah (35), Ramat Gan (22), Ramleh/Ramla (Israel) (21), Sebastopol/Sevastopol (67), Shaar Hefer (Israel) (11), Siberia/Sibir (120), Sinai (43), Stalingrad/Volgograd/Tsarytsin (77), Tel Aviv (21), Tobruk (67), United States of America (21)

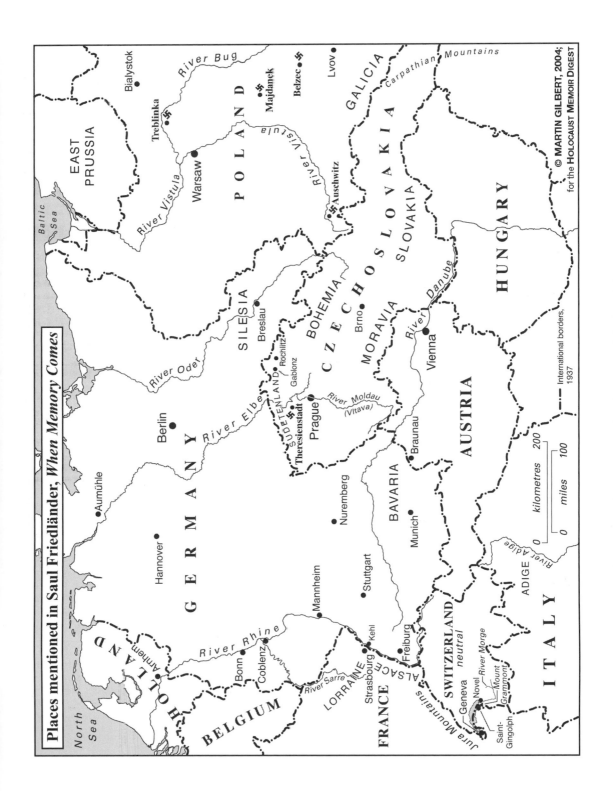

Places mentioned in Saul Friedländer, *When Memory Comes*

EAST PRUSSIA

Baltic Sea

North Sea

HOLLAND

Arnhem

BELGIUM

Bialystok

River Bug

Treblinka

River Vistula

Warsaw

P O L A N D

Majdanek

Belzec

Lvov

GALICIA

Carpathian Mountains

River Vistula

Auschwitz

C Z E C H O S L O V A K I A

SLOVAKIA

BOHEMIA

MORAVIA

Brno

Vienna

Danube

River

HUNGARY

SILESIA

Breslau

River Oder

Rochlitz

Gablonz

SUDETENLAND

Theresienstadt

Prague

River Moldau
(Vltava)

River Elbe

Berlin

G E R M A N Y

Aumühle

Hannover

Nuremberg

BAVARIA

Munich

Braunau

AUSTRIA

Stuttgart

Mannheim

River Rhine

Bonn

Coblenz

River Sarre

LORRAINE

Strasbourg

Kehl

ALSACE

Freiburg

SWITZERLAND
neutral

Geneva

Novel

River Morge

Mount
Grammont

Saint-
Gingolph

Jura Mountains

FRANCE

River Adige

ADIGE

I T A L Y

International borders,
1937

kilometres

0   100   200

miles

0

© MARTIN GILBERT, 2004;
for the HOLOCAUST MEMOIR DIGEST

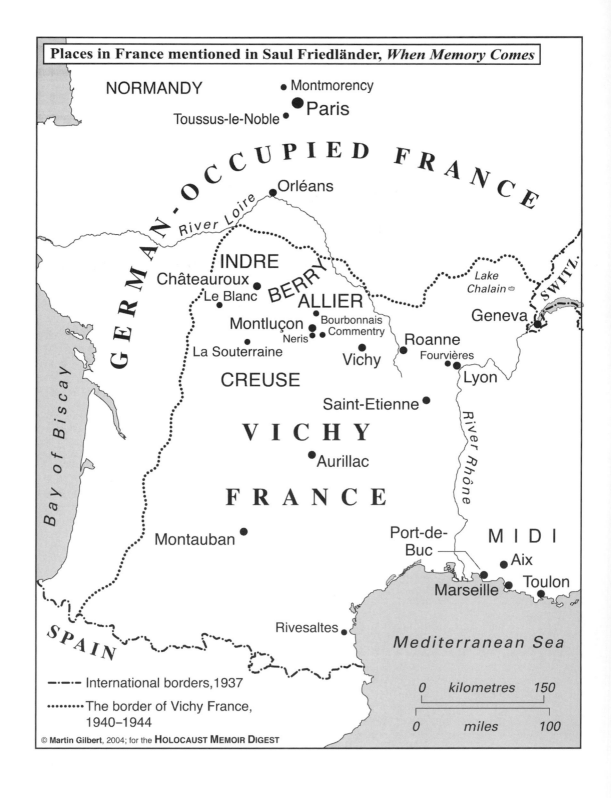

Places in France mentioned in Saul Friedländer, *When Memory Comes*

NORMANDY

Montmorency

Paris

Toussus-le-Noble

GERMAN-OCCUPIED FRANCE

River Loire

Orléans

INDRE

Châteauroux

BERRY

Le Blanc

ALLIER

Montluçon

Bourbonnais
Commentry

Neris

Roanne

Fourvières

La Souterraine

Vichy

Lake Chalain

Geneva

SWITZ.

CREUSE

Lyon

Saint-Etienne

Bay of Biscay

VICHY

Aurillac

FRANCE

River Rhône

Montauban

Port-de-Buc

MIDI

Aix

Toulon

Marseille

Rivesaltes

Mediterranean Sea

SPAIN

—·—·— International borders,1937

·········· The border of Vichy France,
1940–1944

© **Martin Gilbert**, 2004; for the HOLOCAUST MEMOIR DIGEST

0   kilometres   150

0   miles   100

"Writing retraces the contours of the past ...

it does at least preserve a presence,

and it enables one to tell about a child who saw one world founder

and another reborn."

Saul Friedländer

Art Spiegelman, *Maus: A Survivor's Tale, Part I*

1906: Vladek born in Czestochowa, Poland

14 February 1937: marries Anja Zylberberg, Sosnowiec

Early 1938: in a sanatorium in Czechoslovakia

24 August 1939: receives draft notice for Polish Army

September 1939: taken prisoner on first day of fighting

February 1940: transferred to a prisoner of war camp outside Lublin, escapes, returns to Sosnowiec

1 January 1942: ghetto established in Stara Sosnowiec quarter

12 August 1942: selection at the Sosnowiec stadium

1943: Jews moved to nearby village, Srodula

July 1943 to 1944: liquidation of Sosnowiec Ghetto, Vladek and Anja escape

16 March 1944: becomes number 175113 in Auschwitz

Author: Art Spiegelman

Title: *Maus: A Survivor's Tale, Part I: My Father Bleeds History*

Publishing details

Pantheon Books, New York, 1986, 159 pages.
ISBN 0-394-74723-2.
The book is done in cartoon form: the Jews are mice, the Poles are pigs, the Germans are cats, the Americans are dogs, the French are frogs, and the Gypsy, a moth.
The dynamics of the relationship between the survivor father narrator and his second-generation son, who records the events, are explored from the son's perspective. However, for the purpose of the *Digest*, this summary focuses on the survivor aspects.

Focus

A young married Polish couple, Vladek and Anja, survive in Poland, before being sent to Auschwitz. The husband (who is 33 in 1939) relates his experiences to their son born after the war; the events take place between 1931 and mid-March 1944.

Features

German Reich and Protectorate map, page 60; diagrams of hiding places, pages 110, 111; map of Poland's wartime divisions, with Rego Park neighbourhood map inset, back cover.

Contents (by topic, with page numbers)

Pre-war Jewish home and community life

(12–14, 20–2) 1935, Vladek in business in Czestochowa: "I was in textiles – buying and selling – I didn't make much, but always I could make a living."
(15–18) Vladek meets Anna Zylberberg, the daughter of a wealthy family in Sosnowiec: "Anja's parents were anxious she should be married. She was 24; I was then 30."
(19) Vladek meets Anja's family: "To see what a housekeeper she was, I peeked into Anja's closet. ... But what's this – Pills?! I wrote down every pill. If she was sick, then what did I need it for? Later, a friend, a druggist, told me the pills were only because she was so skinny and nervous."
(22) Vladek and Anja are married, 14 February 1937.
(26–9) Anja works for the Communists translating documents, Vladek objects: "When I found out this story, I was ready to break the marriage. I told her 'Anja, if you want me you have to go my way ... If you want your Communist friends, then I can't stay in this house!' And she was a good girl, and of course she stopped all such things."
(29–31, 34–5) Anja's father helps him build a factory in Bielsko-Biala; son Richieu is born in October 1937; Anja suffers from depression, Vladek takes her to a sanitorium in Czechoslovakia: "I understood much of such sicknesses, so I helped always to calm her down."

Pre-war anti-Semitism

(32–3) Traveling to the sanitorium in Czechoslovakia, they see swastikas and hear stories of: "'... a pogrom going on in Germany today!' ... each story worse than the other." Early 1938.
(36–7) They return from Czechoslovakia to find that their factory has been robbed and that there

have been riots in the town, Bielsko-Biala: "We thought then, that Hitler wanted only the parts from Poland, like Bielsko, what used to be parts from Germany before the First World War." (45–7) Vladek's army reserve examination: "... my father tried to keep all his children out from the army. ... Because when he was young, he had then to go into the Russian army. ... And there they took you for twenty-five years. ... To Siberia!"

The coming of war

(38) 24 August 1939, Vladek gets a letter: "A draft notice! I was in the Polish Reserves Army, and so I had to go right away!"

(44, 47–50) "We were given army trainings for a few days and then, by the start of September we were on the frontier. ... After two hours of fighting, the Nazis overcame our side of the river. ... They marched me to where there was more like me. War prisoners."

(51–9) They are taken to a prisoner of war camp, but the Jews are treated worse than the Poles: "'The Polish prisoners get heated cabins.' 'Yes, and we're just left to freeze in these tents.' ... 'The other prisoners get two meals a day. We Jews get only a crust of bread and a little soup.'"

Life under German occupation

(65, 75, 77–80) Sosnowiec: confiscations, beatings, food rationing, getting a work card, escaping a round-up: "I had to pass near – and they were grabbing Jews, if they had papers or no! What had I to do? Will I walk slowly, they will take me ... Will I run they can shoot me!"

(135–9) 1944, Vladek and Anja return to Sosnowiec from Srodula; they find a black market: "There even, I saw some Jewish boys I knew from before the war."

(140) While in hiding outside of Sosnowiec, 1944: "I traveled often with the streetcar to town. It was two cars. One was only Germans and officials. The second, it was only the Poles. Always I went straight in the official car. ... The Germans paid no attention of me ... In the Polish car they could smell if a Polish Jew came in."

(150–1, 154–6) Hoping to flee to Hungary, they are betrayed, imprisoned: "They marched us through the city of Bielsko. We passed by the factory what once I owned ... We passed the market where always we bought to eat, and passed even the street where we used to live, and we came 'til the prison, and there they put us."

Creation of the ghetto

(82) 1 January 1942, orders to move to Stara Sosnowiec: "It was no more the luxury life we had before."

(105) "Then in 1943 came an order: All Jews what are left in Sosnowiec must go to live in an old village nearby called Srodula. And the Poles of Srodula, we Jews had to pay to move them to our houses in Sosnowiec."

Daily life in the ghetto

(84–5) Black market business in order to survive: "When somebody is hungry he looks for business."

(106) Working as slave labour in Sosnowiec from the Srodula Ghetto "Every day the guards marched us about an hour and a half to work. ... And every night they marched us back, counted us, and locked us in."

Deportation

(86–7) Stara Sosnowiec, the first deportation order: "'All Jews over 70 years old will be transferred to Theresienstadt in Czechoslovakia on May 10, 1942 ... .' ... We thought it was to Theresienstadt they were going. But they went right away to Auschwitz, to the gas."

(88–91) 12 August 1942, selection at the stadium: "So it came to the stadium almost all the Jews of Sosnowiec, and from the other villages near, maybe 25 or 30,000 people. ... One from three they kept at the stadium ... maybe 10,000 people – and with them, my father."

(157–8) Deported by truck from the Bielsko-Biala prison to Auschwitz: "... we knew that from here we will not come out anymore ... ." 16 March 1944.

Mass murder sites

(60–1) Polish POWs shot in the forest outside of Lublin: "'Just before you arrived, there was another group of released war prisoners ... two days ago the Nazis marched them into a forest ... and they shot all of them – they killed 600 people!' We were the next party!"

Slave labour camps and factories

(116–17) Cousin Haskel arranges for Vladek to work in the Braun shoe shop, Srodula.

Witness to mass murder

(124) Pesach comes to the shoe shop bunker, persuades many of the group to leave: "They gave over the money and went past the guard. I stood, secret, behind a corner. I heard loud shooting ... ."

Specific escapes

(62–4) Friend Orbach helps him escape imminent POW massacre, he gets back to Sosnowiec hidden in the train.

(113–15) Betrayed from their hiding place in Srodula, they await the weekly van to Auschwitz; his cousin Haskel arranges to get his nephew Lolek out, then: "The day after, Anja and I carried past the guards the empty pails."

(149) Children in Sosnowiec scream that he is a Jew. He responds: "'Heil Hitler. Don't be afraid, little ones. I'm not a Jew. I won't hurt you.'" A Pole apologizes: "'Sorry, mister. You know how kids are ... Heil Hitler.'"

In hiding, including Hidden Children

(81) Possibility of hiding son, Richieu, in 1941, friend Ilzecki: "'I have a good friend, a Pole, who's willing to hide my son until the situation gets better. I think he'd take your boy too.'"

(107–8) Friend Persis offers to take Anja's sister Tosha and all the children to Zawierce to hide: "When things came worse in our ghetto we said always: 'Thank God the kids are with Persis, safe.'"

(110–12) He makes a hidden bunker in a coal storage cellar, then in an attic, Srodula: "We survived there a few Actions. But others, what didn't have such a good place like what I made, they kept being taken away."

(121, 123) Miloch Spiegelman makes a bunker in the shoe shop: "Everything was ready here so 15 or 16 people could hide."

(139–40, 144–5) At Mrs Kawka's farm: "'But, remember – if you're found there, I don't know you! ... You must say that the barn door was open and you just sneaked in.' 'Don't worry ... we won't betray you!'"

(141–3, 146–8) At Mrs Motonowa's home in Szopienice: "I walked with Motonowa as if she was my wife. And Anja, like a governess, went with the little boy behind. And nobody even looked on us."

(152–4) Cousin Miloch, his wife, and 3-year-old son hiding in a five-by-six-foot space in a garbage hole: "'… the decomposing garbage gives some heat.'" Vladek moves them to his hiding place with Mrs Motonowa: "… they all survived themselves the whole war … sitting there … with Motonowa … ."

Liberation

(126) He returns home to retrieve hidden valuables: "After I came out from the camps in 1945 I sneaked back to Srodula and – at night, while the people inside slept – I digged these things out from the bottom of the chimney."

Stories of individuals, including family members

(83) Nahum Cohn and his son Pfefer hanged: "… for dealing goods without coupons. … Cohn had a dry goods store. He was known all over Sosnowiec. … I traded also with Pfefer, a fine young man – a Zionist. He was just married. His wife ran screaming in the street."

(89, 91) Vladek's father chooses to remain with his daughter Fela and her four children at the stadium selection in Sosnowiec, 12 August 1942: "And what do you think? He sneaked on to the bad side! And those on the bad side never came anymore home."

(92–3) Mala's mother survives stadium deportation but: "'Eventually she and my father both ended up in Auschwitz. They died there.'"

(109) The Zawiercie Ghetto is liquidated. Tosha decides not to leave with the three children: her daughter Bibi, her niece Lonia, her nephew (their son) Richieu: "Always Tosha carried around her neck some poison … She killed not only herself, but also the three children."

(110) Tosha's husband Wolfe killed: "… on the train to Auschwitz he tried to escape and they shot him."

(115) Anja's parents taken to Auschwitz: "He was a millionaire, but even this didn't save him his life."

(118) Cousin Haskel Spiegelman survives: "… still in Poland, with a Polish woman, a judge, what kept him hidden … ."

(119, 124) Haskel's brother Pesach "organizes" a cake: "But, the whole ghetto, we were so sick later, you can't imagine … ." He is betrayed leaving the shoe shop bunker.

(120) Haskel's brother Miloch also survives, in hiding, but dies later in Australia.

(122) Nephew Lolek, 15, refuses to join them in the shoe shop bunker in Srodula: "'I'm a skilled worker. Wherever they take me, I'll be okay.'" He is deported to Auschwitz.

(124–5) Friend Avram leaves the shoe shop bunker: "That guy, Avram, his woman had friends to keep them. And the friends kept them … until Avram's money finished. Then they were reported."

Personal reflections

(6) Vladek to 10-year-old Artie, 1958: "'Friends? Your friends? … If you lock them together in a room with no food for a week. … Then you could see what it is, friends!'"

(110) Vladek describes the hiding place he'd built in the Srodula Ghetto to Art who is taking notes: "'Show to me your pencil and I can explain you … such things it's good to know exactly how was it – just in case … .'"

(122) Vladek's words of encouragement to Anja: "'To die, it's easy … But you have to struggle

for life! Until the last moment we must struggle together! I need you! And you'll see that together we'll survive.' This always I told to her."

Places mentioned in Europe (page first mentioned)

Amstow/Mstow (35), Auschwitz Main Camp/Auschwitz I (78), Bielsko-Biala/Bielitz (29), Brandenberg (33), Cracow/Krakow/Krakau (60), Czechoslovakia (32), Czestochowa (12), Dabrowa (89), Dekerta (Sosnowiec) (140), Hungary/Magyarország (145), Katowice/Kattowitz (77), Lodz/Litzmanstadt (76), Lublin (45), Nuremberg (51), Opole Lubelskie (109), Oswiecim/Auschwitz town (157), Radomsko (35), Sosnowiec/Sosnowitz (13), Srodula Ghetto (Sosnowiec) (105), Stara Sosnowiec (Sosnowiec) (82), Szopienice (141), Theresienstadt/Terezin Ghetto/concentration camp (86), Warsaw/Warszawa/Warschau (26), Zakopane (120), Zawierce/Zavshitz (106)

Places mentioned outside Europe (page first mentioned)

Rego Park (New York) (11), Siberia/Sibir (45), United States of America (16)

Art Spiegelman, *Maus: A Survivor's Tale, Part II*

1906: Vladek born in Czestochowa, Poland

16 March 1944: becomes number 175113 in Auschwitz

October 1944: arranges to move Anja from Birkenau to Auschwitz Main Camp

January 1945: begins death march from Auschwitz to Gross Rosen, then by train to Dachau

Early spring 1945: taken to the Swiss border to be exchanged as a prisoner of war

Spring 1945: liberated, moved to a Displaced Persons camp in Austria, is reunited with Anja in Sosnowiec

1946: post-war life in Sweden, both eventually emigrate to America

Author: Art Spiegelman

Title: *Maus: A Survivor's Tale, Part II: And Here My Troubles Began*

Publishing details

Pantheon Books, New York, 1991, 136 pages.
ISBN 0-679-72977-1.
The book is done in cartoon form: the Jews are mice, the Poles are pigs, the Germans are cats, the Americans are dogs, the French are frogs, and the Gypsy a moth.
The dynamics of the relationship between the survivor father narrator and his second-generation son, who records the events, are explored from the son's perspective. However, for the purpose of the *Digest*, this summary focuses on the survivor aspects.

Focus

A young married Polish couple, Vladek and Anja, survive Auschwitz and death marches. The husband (who is 33 in 1939) relates his experiences to their son born after the war; the events take place between mid-March 1944 and the summer of 1945.

Features

Immediate post-war photograph of Vladek, page 134.
Diagram of crematorium, page 70; map of death march, page 84; diagram of Auschwitz and Birkenau with Catskill region map inset, back cover.

Contents (by topic, with page numbers)

Auschwitz-Birkenau

(24–6) Arrival at Auschwitz Main Camp (Auschwitz I): "They registered us in … They took from us our names. And here they put me my number." #175113, 16 March 1944.
(30, 57) Brutality of "life" in Auschwitz, Vladek speaks to Anja, a crime: "So he beat me, what can I tell you? Only, Thank God, Anja didn't get also such a beating. She wouldn't live."
(31–3) Vladek teaches English to the block supervisor: "'Now the Allies are bombing the Reich. If they win this war, it will be worth something to know English.'"
(36, 47) He goes to work as a tinsmith under Yidl the Communist: "'They send drek like you here while they send real tinmen up the chimney.'"
(48–9) He "organizes" food and barter: "If you ate how they gave you, it was just enough to die more slowly."
(51–3) He finds Anja at Birkenau (Auschwitz II) and communicates with her through a Hungarian Jew, Mancie: "'If a couple is loving each other so much, I must help however I can.'"
(55–6) Vladek the tinsmith volunteers to repair roofs in Birkenau in order to see Anja, summer 1944: "'Just seeing you again gives me strength.'"
(60–1) He becomes a shoemaker: "I had here a warm and private room where to sit … ."
(62–4) By "arranging" a "fortune" in bribes, he is able to include Anja with the other women moved from Birkenau to Auschwitz Main Camp, October 1944: "It was the only time I was happy in Auschwitz."
(67–8) Doing "black work" in Auschwitz: "Carrying back and forth big stones, digging out holes, each day different, but always the same. Very hard … ."

(80–1) Plans to hide during the evacuation of Auschwitz are abandoned due to rumours that the camp would be set on fire: "It was already night. They gave to each of us a blanket and a little bit food to carry, and we went out from Auschwitz, maybe the last one."

Death marches

(82–3) On the march from Auschwitz: "All night I heard shooting. He who got tired, who can't walk so fast, they shot."

(84–5) One night in Gross Rosen, then they are herded onto a train; 25 survived in his car of 200. Vladek hooks his blanket into the ceiling to create a hammock: "In this way I can rest and breathe a little."

(103–4) Anja marched through Gross Rosen and Ravensbrück after the evacuation of Auschwitz.

(105) Marching from Dachau train towards Switzerland: "And I saw, it's not everywhere, my hell. It's still life things going on."

Concentration camps

(84) Death march from Auschwitz to Gross Rosen for one night: "Here was a small camp, with no gas. It was thousands of prisoners from all around being pulled back into Germany."

(88) Train ends in Dachau: "It was early February in 1945. It was no food and so crowded …."

(91–2) In Dachau he gets into the infirmary: "… a paradise … Here I had three times a day something to eat, and it was only two patients for each bed."

(95–6) He survives a bout of typhus in Dachau, keeps his bread ration: "I couldn't eat, but I cut pieces to pay for help to go down to the toilet."

(97) He leaves Dachau by train to be exchanged for a prisoner of war: "I was very weak, but, for my bread I had two friends what helped me."

Witness to mass murder

(55, 72) Summer 1944, working in Birkenau: "Thousands – hundreds of thousands of Hungarians were arriving there at this time."

(54) A German soldier returns from a few days working in Birkenau: "And he was afraid any more to speak."

(58) Surviving a selection: "The ones that had not so lucky the SS wrote down their number and sent to the other side."

(69–71) As a tinsmith, he is sent to dismantle the machinery of the crematorium in Birkenau: "You heard about the gas, but I'm telling not rumors, but only what really I saw. For this I was an eyewitness."

(86–8) Weeks on stopped train without food or water: "Near to the door we piled new dead ones. Each day the Germans opened: 'How many dead?' And we threw out, and soon we had room even to sit."

Resistance, ghetto revolts, individual acts of courage and defiance

(73) Why resistance in Auschwitz was hopeless: "It wasn't so easy like you think – everyone was so starving and frightened and tired they couldn't believe even what's in front of their eyes. … In some spots people did fight … But you can kill maybe one German before they kill fast a hundred from you. Then it's everyone dead."

(79) Four girls had blown up a crematorium, Birkenau: "They were good friends of Anja, from Sosnowiec. They hanged a long, long time." (Their names were Ella Gartner, Roza Robota,

Regina Safir, and Estera Wajsblum. The revolt occurred on 7 October 1944; the girls were hanged on 6 January 1945.)

Specific escapes

(65–6) Anja is caught with a food package from Vladek and escapes into the "evening appel" crowd, who are then tortured to give her up, Auschwitz Main Camp: "For a few appels it went so, but nobody of Anja's friends gave her out. You can imagine what she went through."

(67) Vladek escapes a selection by hiding in the toilets, Auschwitz: "Nobody looked, so I sat lucky the whole selektion."

In hiding, including Hidden Children

(109–11) Hiding first in a pit, then in a barn, Vladek and Shivek await liberation by the Americans.

Righteous Gentiles

(28) A Polish priest in Auschwitz Main Camp adds Vladek's number, 175113, together and gets "chai", the numeric equivalent of the Hebrew word for "life", which gives him hope: "I started to believe. I tell you, he put another life in me."

(31–6) His Polish block supervisor protects him in Auschwitz for two months in exchange for English lessons: "'I've kept you here in the "Quarantine Block" as long as I can. You'll have to be assigned out to a work crew ... Skilled workers get better treatment.'"

(93–4, 98) A Frenchman in Dachau shares his Red Cross food packages with Vladek: "He insisted to share with me, and it saved me my life."

Liberation

(104) Anja liberated separately: "I know only that Anja came out free by the Russian side and she came back to Sosnowiec before me. My liberation, it took longer ... ."

(106–8) Their German guards flee but then a Wehrmacht patrol captures them: "I didn't understand what is going on, but I was again here in German hands." Disaster is averted as these Germans also flee.

(112–13) Vladek and Shivek share their house with American troops: "So we worked for the Americans and they liked me that I can speak English."

(130–1) He travels to Hanover with friend Shivek, hopes to get news of Anja at Belsen, instead: "'Whatever you do, don't go back to Sosnowiec. The Poles are still killing Jews there.'"

(132–6) Anja returns to Sosnowiec; Vladek comes to find her: "... when I heard Anja is alive I stopped everything to go only back to Sosnowiec."

Displaced Persons camps

(129) Moved to DP camp in Garmisch-Partenkirchen: "Here we got identity papers and a place where to stay ... ." He develops typhus again, and diabetes.

Stories of individuals, including family members

(27) Abraham Mandelbaum and the Hungarian "escape" ends up in Auschwitz Main Camp: "'Well, so here's our Hungary.'"

(29, 33–5) Mandelbaum has difficulties in Auschwitz, Vladek gets him a spoon, a belt, and wooden shoes that fit: "'My God ... It's a miracle, Vladek. God sent shoes through you.'"

(43, 46) Pavel helps Art visualize the terror of Auschwitz: "'... From the moment you got to the gate until the very end.'"

(50) A First World War-decorated veteran in Auschwitz Main Camp appeals for mercy: "It was German prisoners also … But for the Germans this guy was Jewish."

(52, 104) A Hungarian girl, Mancie, protects Anja: "She had a lover, I heard later an SS man. He got for her a good position over 10 or 12 other girls from Birkenau."

(59) Felix the Belgian faces his terror, Vladek tries to calm him: "'Look, they're going to kill all of us here eventually … you this week, me the next … none of us can escape it. You must be brave … and, who knows, maybe it's not even your turn yet … .'"

(107, 135) Pre-war friend Shivek from Bedzin reunited with Vladek at the end of the war; they are liberated together.

(113–16) A box of family photos retrieved from Richieu's Polish governess reminds Vladek of family members and their fates.

(132) Baker's son Gelber returns to Sosnowiec after the war, is murdered by Poles: "'His brothers came from the camps a day later, and only stayed long enough to bury him … .'"

Post-war life and career

(123–5) 1946, they go by airplane to Sweden: "We wanted here to come, to Uncle Herman, but here was quotas, so Herman helped us to have a visa over to Stockholm to wait." Eventually they come to America.

(125) "I made in the States a living dealing diamonds, but never I had it again so good" (after Sweden).

Personal reflections

(44) Art's second-generation lament: "No matter what I accomplish, it doesn't seem like much compared to surviving Auschwitz."

(58) At a selection, Auschwitz: "They looked to see if eating no food made you too skinny."

(73) "The Jews lived always with hope. They hoped the Russians can come before the German bullet arrived from the gun into their head … ."

Places mentioned in Europe (page first mentioned)

Auschwitz Main Camp/Auschwitz I (16), Bedzin (107), Belsen/Bergen–Belsen concentration camp (131), Birkenau/Brzezinka/Auschwitz II (51), Blechhammer slave labour camp (Blachownia Slaska) (116), Breslau/Wroclaw (84), Cracow/Krakow/Krakau (84), Czestochowa (31), Dachau concentration camp (88), Garmisch-Partenkirchen Displaced Persons camp (129), Gross Rosen/Rogoznica concentration camp (84), Hanover/Hannover (129), Hungary/Magyarország (27), Innsbruck (109), Lodz/Litzmanstadt (56), Lvov/Lemberg/Lwow/Lviv (116), Oswiecim/Auschwitz town (25), Ravensbrück concentration camp (104), Sosnowiec/Sosnowitz (36), Stockholm (114), Switzerland/Schweiz/Suisse/Swizzeria (98), Theresienstadt/Terezin Ghetto/concentration camp (43), Würzburg (130)

Places mentioned outside Europe (page first mentioned)

Catskills (New York) (13), Florida (20), Queens (New York) (17), Rego Park (New York) (19)

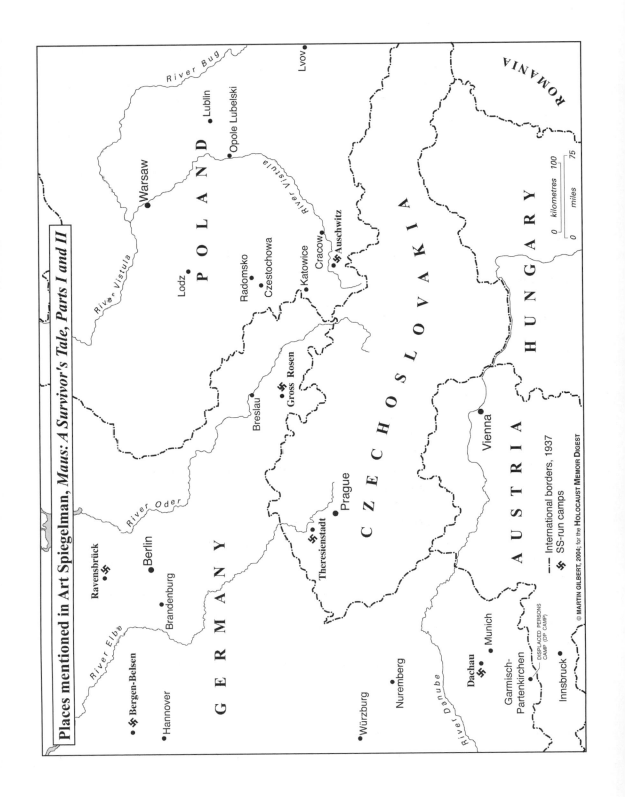

Places mentioned in Art Spiegelman, *Maus: A Survivor's Tale, Parts I and II*

ROMANIA

Lvov

POLAND

Lublin

Opole Lubelski

Warsaw

River Bug

River Vistula

Lodz

Radomsko

Czestochowa

River Vistula

Katowice

Cracow

Auschwitz

CZECHOSLOVAKIA

0 kilometres 100

0 miles 75

HUNGARY

Gross Rosen

Breslau

Vienna

Prague

Theresienstadt

AUSTRIA

River Oder

Berlin

Brandenburg

GERMANY

Ravensbrück

River Elbe

Bergen-Belsen

Hannover

Munich

Dachau

Nuremberg

Garmisch-Partenkirchen

DISPLACED PERSONS CAMP (DP CAMP)

Innsbruck

Würzburg

River Danube

International borders, 1937

SS-run camps

© MARTIN GILBERT, 2004; for the HOLOCAUST MEMOIR DIGEST

Places in the Auschwitz region mentioned in Art Spiegelman, *Maus: A Survivor's Tale, Parts I and II*

"To die, it's easy ...

But you have to struggle for life!

Until the last moment we must struggle together!

I need you!

And you'll see that together we'll survive."

Vladek Spiegelman

Fanya Gottesfeld Heller, *Strange and Unexpected Love*

14 October 1924: born in Skala, Poland

Mid–September 1939: Soviet occupation of Skala

Autumn 1939 to spring 1941: attends high school in nearby Borszczow, boards with a Jewish family

June 1941: Soviets leave Skala

8 July 1941: Hungarian occupation of Skala

End July 1941: German occupation of Skala

Autumn 1941: meets Ukrainian Jan at peasant market

Spring 1942: Jan tells her he loves her, will protect her

Summer 1942: hiding place constructed on grandfather's property

26–27 September 1942: Skala *Atksia*, family survives in hiding place

28 September to November 1942: hidden in Jan's barn attic hideout

November 1942 to summer 1943: returns to Skala

August 1943: hiding in Trujca with Sidor in attic, builds hiding place in chicken coop in the barn

September 1943: survives in hiding in three separate places

October 1943: returns to Sidor to hide in chicken coop

24 December 1943: comes into Sidor's house to bathe

December 1943 to March 1944: hiding in chicken coop

March 1944: Germans leave, family moves into Sidor's attic, then returns to Skala

September 1944: attends school in nearby Czortkow, then in Lvov

Spring 1945: returns to Skala

August to December 1945: leaves Skala for Bytom Displaced Persons camp

January 1946: marries, then eventually emigrates to America

Author: Fanya Gottesfeld Heller

Title: *Strange and Unexpected Love, A Teenage Girl's Holocaust Memoirs*

Publishing details

KTAV Publishing House, 900 Jefferson Street, Hoboken, New Jersey 07030, 1993, 282 pages. ISBN 0-88125-467-3.

Focus

Fanya, a young teenage girl in the Ukraine (who is 15 in 1939) survives with her parents and younger brother in hiding in their home town; her father is killed after liberation. The memoir takes place between her birth in 1924 and her engagement to another survivor in July 1945.

Features

Acknowledgements written by the author, pages ix–x.
Foreword written by Rabbi Irving Greenberg, pages xi–xvi.
Preface written by the author, page xvii.
Postcript written by the author in 1995, pages 281–2.

Contents (by topic, with page numbers)

Pre-war Jewish home and community life

(4–5, 7, 11, 22–7) Fanya's family in Skala, in September, 1942: Fanya, then 18, her brother Arthur, 8, her father Benjamin Gottesfeld, and her mother Szencia (Charlotte) (Wasserman) Gottesfeld. On her father's side, his parents Azriel and Hinda Gottesfeld, who had 13 children, nine of whom survived to adulthood: Benjamin and his siblings Mendel, Esther who married Mendel Gottfried, Usher, Krenia, Brana, Tuvia (all of whom lived in Paris), Leo (Leibish) married to Laura, and Sophia, who married Zygmunt (Zisha) Zimmerman. On her mother's side: her parents Jakob and Miriam (Horowitz) Wasserman, her mother's siblings Wolf and his wife Malcia, Lolla and her husband Mottel, and Suza and her husband Munio. Jakob and Miriam, with five children, had lost a 21–year-old son, Bubcio, to tuberculosis in 1928.
(19–21) Jewish life in Skala: "We had a very rich social and cultural life centered around our two–story Bet Am (community house). It had a large auditorium where lectures and concerts were held, an amateur theater troupe performed, and where we celebrated Purim and Chanukah and other holidays; a library with 5,000 books; a reading room; and a very high level Tarbut (Hebrew cultural movement) school which ran from kindergarten to the eighth grade." The Jewish population was 1,500, out of the town's total population of 5,500.
(28–9) The marriage of her parents: "... Jakob was opposed to my mother's marrying my father because he came from a poor family. My father threatened suicide, and the Wassermans finally gave in, but Grandfather Jakob refused to give my mother a dowry because she had married my father against his wishes."
(30–4) Fanya's family and her education: "My father wanted me to be educated, but my mother didn't care. ... She wanted me to get married, and worried that I wouldn't because there was no money for a dowry. ... When Lachmann gave me A's, Grandpa Azriel took me to the Cukiernia, a coffee house, for currant drinks and ice cream with waffle-wafers." Grandmother Miriam's view: "'Reading is bad for the eyes, and who's going to marry a girl who wears

glasses?' She reminded me that I wouldn't have much of a dowry. I'd tell her I wasn't interested in marriage, and she'd reply that this was all the more reason to leave school and apprentice myself to a seamstress."

(32, 103) Jewish self-help: "For an hour in the late afternoon after Hebrew school we went to the home of Sluwa Kassierer to do homework under her supervision. Sluwa and her two sisters, all of them seamstresses, supported their old parents and lived in two small rooms. They were close to 30, and their unmarried state was considered a 'shanda', an embarrassment. Every family who could afford a few pennies considered it proper to send their children to the Kassierers to do their homework. Actually, we didn't do much there – we usually ate apples and socialized."

(114) Reminiscences, while staying at the Sternberg's house, autumn 1942: "... my mother began to tell of the Friday nights when she was a girl, the only night the entire family sat down for a meal together. ... 'During the week we sat alone or stood about like a bird on one leg,' she said. 'But on Friday nights … .'"

Pre-war anti-Semitism

(19–20) Skala's pre-war population consisted of 3,000 Greek Orthodox Ukrainians, 1,000 Catholic Poles, and 1,500 Jews: "Our relationship with the Poles and Ukrainians was always strained. The peasants were superstitious and still believed in the blood libel, and the priests told them again and again in church that the Jews had killed Jesus. Sometimes when they drank too much after returning from church, they threw stones at Jews or beat them, and we always closed our windows when we saw them coming up the street."

The coming of war

(38–9) The Soviet take-over, mid-September 1939: "... The Jewish Communists in Skala embraced the Soviets the same way the Ukrainians later welcomed the Nazis – with a great feeling of exhilaration. ... The Russians closed all the stores and warehouses, and the peasants robbed and looted them. The Jewish merchants and storekeepers lost everything and became impoverished overnight. Every man became an employee of the state, working in agriculture, the stone quarries, or on road and rail construction."

(39–40) A Soviet officer who had bartered with Fanya's father: "... after a few months he admitted he was a Jew and showed his passport to prove it. ... All of his family had been transported to Siberia. Crying and eating, the sugar and salt mingling, he looked up and said, 'You don't know how good you have it, such a good life.' " Skala, late 1939.

(41–4) Fanya continues her schooling at high school in nearby Borszczow, by boarding with a Jewish family – Mrs Bradler, her married daughter Rose, and son-in-law: "The Russians had gotten rid of the pictures of Jesus and the Madonna and Child that had once hung in the classrooms and replaced them with portraits of Stalin. They had also fired all the Polish teachers and brought in Russian replacements. History was dropped, and the geography of the Soviet Union and the history of the Revolution were taught instead. Latin was also excised from the curriculum. All subjects, and of course, Marx's and Lenin's writings, were taught in Russian, the official language. We were forbidden to speak Polish or Hebrew; and many works of world literature, and of course, Polish literature, were forbidden as well. We had a lot of physical activities and calisthenics … ."

(51–2) In June 1941, news of the German advance into the Soviet zone: "The Soviets abandoned Skala, and its warehouses and stores were looted by criminals and Ukrainian peasants. ... Two weeks later, on 8 July 1941, Skala was occupied by the Hungarians, then allies

of Nazi Germany. The Hungarians descended on us like locusts – raping, pillaging and stealing.
… In the last week of July, Hungary expelled the Jews from the Trans-Carpathian region of
Ruthenia. … Mercilessly, they drove them across the Zbrucz River toward the Soviet Union."
(52–4) The Germans enter Skala, the end of July 1941: "From the cellar window, we could
see the Ukrainians – who wanted an independent state and believed the Germans would give
it to them – welcoming the conquerors with blue-and-yellow Ukrainian flags and swastika
armbands. Father Derewienko, the Greek Orthodox priest, greeted the Germans with the
traditional gift of bread and salt."
(54) "Even before the Germans' arrival, some young Ukrainians had on whim tossed a grenade
into the home of David and Rosa Herscher. Rosa was killed." Skala, July 1941.

Life under German occupation

(54–6) "It was the Ukrainians who supplied the Germans with a list of 15 Jewish leaders who
were ordered to meet and choose a seven-man 'Judenrat' (Jewish Council), whose unenviable
job it was to announce and carry out the German decrees. The 'Judenrat' was located in the
home of Rabbi Yehuda Drimmer on the main avenue. … One of the Germans' first decrees
was that Jews had to wear a white arm band with a blue Jewish star. Within a few days, the
Germans ordered the Jews to turn in their radios. Then they demanded Jews deliver up all
their valuables – furniture, linens and china to furnish their headquarters – and jewelry."
(60–4) The struggle to find food: "Each day the scramble for a little food occupied me totally.
I ran all the errands because my father had to stay off the street lest he be dragged off to a
slave labor camp and my mother certainly couldn't trust seven-year-old Arthur to ferret out
food. She herself stayed home out of fear that Arthur would fall under Engel's boot if he made
another surprise descent on the house."
(61–2) Seven-year-old Arthur in Skala during the German occupation: " 'Oh, go read a book,'
I hissed at Arthur when one of his incessant mock battles tangled him around my ankles as I
crossed the floor. 'I don't know how,' he said, and I stopped for a moment and tried to think
what that must mean for him. … But Arthur had only completed first and second grade in
the Russian school before the German invasion and he could barely read."
(73–5) Working for the Germans: "… my father had arranged a compromise with the
'Judenrat': I would work for an officer in a capacity that would permit me to live at home.
Since I had a knack for knitting, I became the personal sweater manufacturer for the Nazi
chief manager of the count's estate … ." While at the estate for fittings of his sweaters, Fanya
manages to rebuff his advances.
(80–2) "Gottschalk, a noncom in the Wehrmacht in his late twenties with a fleshy face, had a
thing for me." Although Fanya tries to stay out of his way, one night he comes looking for her.
When she is not to be found at home, her mother is beaten. Fanya and her friend Lotka
Sternberg spend the next two nights hiding in a crawl space the Sternbergs had constructed.
(85–6, 232) "We had two rings left; except for my mother's heart pendant, all the rest of our
jewelry had been bartered for provisions." Fanya goes with her father to give one of the rings
to Father Derewienko for safekeeping. It had been her grandmother Hinda's engagement ring:
" 'Someday,' he said, 'it will be yours.' "
(87–8) The synagogue is burned, ten old men are taken to the marketplace where they are
brutalized and then released: "They and other Jews put on their prayer-shawls, fasted and
prayed, and then took the burnt Torah scrolls they had pulled out of the flames down the hill
to the Jewish cemetery, where they buried them." Early September 1942.

(113–17) After the family is reunited in the home of the Sternbergs, Fanya's father procures a "W" badge: "... an insignia based on a certificate testifying that he was a 'Wirschaftswichtige Jude', a Jew essential to the economy. ... The 'W' badge served mainly to intimidate Ukrainian militiamen so that they wouldn't drag him off to the Gestapo, but for the Germans it had no meaning at all, and if they caught him, he would have been killed." Autumn 1942.

(118–19) Shimek's father arranges for Fanya to work as a laundress, but: "A short while later, the manager looked at my hands and said, 'You're not a washerwoman,' and put me to work mending socks and sewing on buttons, which suited my talents better."

(129–32) Summer 1943, a conversation with Jan, their Ukrainian friend and protector. Fanya tries to understand the anti-Semitism of the local Ukrainians, as Jan describes his friend Stanislaus whom Jan had witnessed murdering a newborn Jewish child: "'Should I say Stanislaus is crazy or that he holds a grudge because a Jew once cheated him? No. He wanted to do it. I went to school with him. He has a good head on his shoulders, he doesn't beat his wife. He goes to church. He wanted to do it, and there's no law against it. He's the law. The law is behind us. Kill. I'm supposed to kill you. And Stanislaus? He'll do it again, given half a chance.'" Fanya asks: "'Can't you talk to Stanislaus? Tell him what he does is ...' 'No, I do what I can. That's all I can do.' He looked at me. For the first time I saw a look of pity, not because I was a Jew or stupid, but because I talked like a child, an overgrown child who didn't know limits."

(201) February 1944: "By this time the Ukrainians no longer trusted the Germans or believed they were going to give them an independent state, as they'd once hoped and expected, but they hated the Russians more than the Germans, and they hated the Jews more than both put together."

Creation of the ghetto

(13) After the 29 September 1942 *Aktsia*: "... posters went up in Skala ordering the 700 Jews still remaining there to go to the ghetto in Borszczow 15 kilometers away. ... The drivers who returned reported that Jews from several towns were stuffed together in designated houses, ten or fifteen to a room."

Daily life in the ghetto

(98, 107) Fanya's father reports on conditions he and his wife had experienced in their short time in the Borszczow Ghetto, October 1942: "'Living there we were already dead,' he said. There was almost no food or fuel for the communal stove in the room he and my mother shared with eleven other Jews."

Mass murder sites

(68) Three Hungarian boys survive the slaughter of the Hungarians who had come through Skala on their forced march to the Ukraine: "The 3,000 Hungarian Jews, they told us, had been held by the Germans at Horynin. Then they were told they were being sent home but were led to a field and murdered by machine-gun fire. The Ukrainian militia had aided the Germans and were in the front ranks of the looters. The boys had wormed their way out from under layers of bodies. ... (Eventually, the 'Judenrat' got the boys false papers and arranged their escape to Hungary; they all survived the war.)"

Death camps

(14, 194) During the Skala *Aktsia*, September 1942: "... my father's widowed father, Azriel Gottesfeld, had been shoved into a boxcar of the train bound for Belzec. ... When someone betrayed to the Germans the hiding place he had built for his son Leo, and Leo's wife, Laura, and their daughter, and himself, Azriel had walked to the train in newly polished boots, as well-groomed and proud as when he had been a young soldier. He took with him only his 'tallis', his prayer-shawl."

(119–21) "During the *aktsia*, when our family hid in the egg warehouse, Zhenia had watched from behind the door of her house as the Germans took her widowed mother, grandmother, and uncle away. Hearing that they had been deported to Belzec, she bribed her way to an audience with the district commander. She asked to be sent to Belzec too." Instead she is sent to be a maid in the German officers' quarters.

Witness to mass murder

(11–12) Emerging from their hiding place after the *Aktsia*, 27 September 1942, Skala: "What we saw on the way was a scene out of Dante's 'Inferno'. Dead and dying people were strewn all over the street. Children were running around looking for their parents, and parents were looking for their children. Houses stood empty as if a cosmic cyclone had sucked their occupants to another planet. There were dead bodies lying on the beds and floors. The doors and windows were smashed open, and everything was gone – clothes, furniture, all the occupants had possessed had been taken either by the Germans or the Ukrainian militia or by Polish and Ukrainian looters."

(77) Among the brutalities at the Gestapo prison in Czortkow, April 1942: "A prisoner friend of my father's who was redeemed by an enormous bribe told us of 120 Russian POWs forced to walk in a circle for ten hours a day with their hands in the air. It only took a few weeks before they were all dead."

(85) "Barely credible stories began to float around, stories told by distraught escapees from different 'shtetls' and by malicious peasants about Jews forced to dig their own graves before they were shot." Summer 1942.

(182–3) While hiding in the forest enclave, the Germans and Ukrainians stage a pre-dawn-to-dusk raid on the 150 Jews hiding there: "Gunfire and explosions erupted ahead of and behind us, and bullets whizzed past our heads. … Smelling smoke from bunkers hit by grenades, hearing the screams of people trapped inside, I got to my knees before my father pulled my ankle and I fell flat again. The Ukrainians dropped piles of smoking and burning straw into the remaining bunkers to roast and asphyxiate anyone who did not crawl out. German and Ukrainian voices yelling orders mixed with the screams of people wounded or on fire, and the human sounds, mixing with the shooting and explosions, became louder, then ebbed, then became louder again. … By evening, when it was quiet at last, most of the Jews in the forest were dead." Late September 1943.

Resistance, ghetto revolts, individual acts of courage and defiance

(56, 68, 73–4, 88, 107, 147) "The 'Judenrat' was trapped between the community's distrust of their decisions and the orders of the Germans." Examples of their work for the welfare of the community: they help three Hungarian Jewish survivors of a mass murder, they supply to the SS regional commander Kelner: "'gifts' of leather and gold pieces in return for letting the Jews remain in town …" after the *Aktsia*, they help Fanya's parents escape from the Borszczow Ghetto.

(78–9) Spring 1942 in Skala. Fanya starts a school: "The children, who were seven and eight years old, came to my house, and Shimek and I shared with them as much knowledge as we could – a little reading, a little writing, some arithmetic. Sometimes Shimek brought an old book to read to them. We adjourned for the day when the children got too hungry to concentrate or when their mothers heard of rumors of a roundup and fearfully came to pick them up."

(88, 270) Father's sister Esther writes from Paris asking whether it would be safer to come home, as opposed to hiding in France: "My father wrote Esther a postcard with one sentence: 'When you come home, you will probably first see your mother.' " As Grandmother Hinda had died, they understood and hid in France. The aunts, uncles, and cousins in France survived.

(120) Zhenia, working as a maid in the German officers' quarters: "Knowing her relatives were dead, that they had died before she could have gotten to Belzec, she decided to use her position in the enemy camp to help other Jews." She passes on information to the underground: "I asked and she assured me there was one." She also passes on food to the Jews of Skala.

Partisan activity

(121) Shimek discusses with Fanya the possibility of joining a partisan band in the nearby forest: "I had heard about partisan groups, but not of any near our region. Some of them hated Jews more than Germans. I didn't want to tell Shivek that I preferred a quick death by a bullet to starving in a cold dark hole in the ground. Besides, how could I abandon my parents and Arthur?" Early 1943.

(162–3) "When I mentioned to my father the possibility of finding a partisan group, I touched off an explosion. 'In the forest,' he said, 'the partisans themselves are the greatest menace.' Frustrated by lack of supplies and limited military success, the avowedly anti-Semitic partisans massacred fleeing Jews. When I asked Jan about fighters in the forest he said my father was right. 'How can they fight if they have no arms and nothing to eat?' "

(211, 213) The *Banderowtzi* partisan gangs who, after liberation: "... swooped down on village or town and took what they wanted. No sport short of obliterating a German division would give them more pleasure than to roister through this place and kill Jews."

Specific escapes

(58–9) Fanya survives a visit to their home by an SS officer: "Standing in the doorway was Engel, a German officer who liked to be recognized as the lord of the town, the owner of each person and object. ... 'Very clean,' he said. With extended finger he tested an upper shelf. 'Clean Jews,' he said as if he had discovered a blue rose. ... I stood there desperate for something to appease the thrashing dog when Engel dropped the leash and the dog's fangs penetrated my side. Engel called him back with words of praise and they left."

(76–7) Fanya's father escapes from the transport to the Borki-Wielki slave labour camp near Tarnopol in February 1942, but: "In April, on the first day of Passover, all men between the ages of twelve and sixty were ordered to go to Borszczow to be sent off to the Borki-Wielki labor camp. My father, Uncle Wolf, and Lolla's husband, Mottel, were among them." They manage to escape while in Borszczow and return home.

(105–6) After two weeks hiding in the barn, Jan brings a pail of hot water, soap, and a cloth for a towel and Fanya has a bath: "It seems odd to me now that such a simple procedure as a makeshift bath could switch my mood from low to high or, to put it more accurately, from a state of terror of imminent, violent death to a feeling of calm bordering on joy, and even hope that the nightmare would end."

(106–8) Fanya's parents escape from the Borszczow Ghetto: "They had run the 15 kilometers from Borszczow to Jan's barn, and miracle of miracles: they were here."

(139–41, 158–60) At Sidor and Marynka's house, Jan and Fanya discover love: "... sudden elation overtook me. I longed for dejection, the familiar dark mood that had enveloped me since the coming of the Germans. I had to summon dread consciously from where it had taken a back seat."

(168–73) Jan and Fanya's father had dug a small hiding place in the chicken coop on the outside of Sidor's barn to which they could escape during a raid, which came soon after: "The Germans ordered the Ukrainians to dig holes in every part of the barn ... . As they dug, pitchforkfuls of straw and dirt piled up in front of the uncovered hole in the barn wall. They were sealing us in and covering our hideout without realizing it. We had barely enough air to breathe." Late the next day Sidor comes to find them safe. Autumn 1943.

(247–9) While in Lvov, Fanya hears the story of her mother's escape from being murdered by *Banderowtzi* on the way to the marketplace in Czortkow. Arthur's fear had delayed her; she got a ride with another farmer: "The 'Banderowtzi' had waylaid the first wagon, the one my mother usually rode in, killing the two Jewish women passengers, plundering their goods, and letting the others go." Early 1945.

In hiding, including Hidden Children

(4–9, 88–9, 93–4) Fanya's father Benjamin Gottesfeld had built a hiding place in their warehouse which they use to escape the *Aktsia*, 26–27 September 1942, in Skala. Sixteen members of the family hide there, plus a neighbour and her daughter: "Efforts to breathe rasped all around me. We pulled the same fetid air into our lungs and pushed it out again."

(85) "My father, who had come to realize that the Germans in Skala were not the Germans of the poetry he knew by heart, began to prepare hiding places for the family, not only the four of us, but my grandparents, aunts, uncles, and cousins as well. Jan procured materials for building the hideouts, and my father showed him their location. All the hiding places were on Grandfather Jakob's property." Summer 1942.

(98–101) With her parents in the Borszczow Ghetto, Fanya and Arthur hide in Jan's barn: "Time, plentiful time, added an ineffable peril to the real fears. 'True time,' during which I sat and stared at a clump of hay and followed my thoughts as they slipped wherever they wished, clashed with 'false time,' chronological time, during which I gave my attention to Arthur or Jan. How to orient myself from one variety of time to the other without feeling violently unsettled became the task of waiting." October 1942.

(109–11, 228) While the four are hiding in Jan's barn: "My father dispatched Jan to bring Marysia, the peasant woman from a nearby village who had worked for us after Arthur was born." Marysia eventually comes: "'I came to see Arthur ...' I knew she had stopped herself from saying 'for the last time' ... ." She does not offer help to them and risk her own life: "Jan personally knew a Polish family the Germans had shot when Jews were found hiding in their chicken coop."

(122–3) Lotke returns to her parents, her hiding place in Lvov betrayed: "Only the Polish couple she was living with had known of her Jewish identity, and every safeguard had been taken to hide it, but she must have slipped up in some way. A blackmailer had challenged her, and she had barely managed to escape by giving him her last 'zloty'." Fanya considers going with Jan to Cracow: "But Jan knew as well as I did that I looked Jewish by feature as well as by my 'sad eyes,' an unmistakable Jewish trait." Early 1943.

(145–6, 149–51) Sidor and his wife Marynka and their daughter Hania, take Fanya, her brother Arthur, and her parents into their cottage to hide in their attic. Fanya's mother refuses to eat from Marynka's common soup bowl: "My father, who used to have to 'walk on his hands,' as he put it, in order not to muddy the immaculate carpet at home, shook his head. … 'if you are going to be alive it won't matter. And if you're going to be dead it won't matter.' After five days of refusing food, she gave in." Autumn 1943.

(152–4) Time passes slowly in Sidor's attic: "The discomforts of hunger – gnawing emptiness, headache, dizziness, disorientation, all familiar sensations since the Germans had come – would have been easy to disregard with a distracting activity, but I had nothing to do but clack my knitting needles together when wool was obtainable." Autumn 1943.

(165–8) Fearing that their neighbour will discover and betray them, the family moves into Sidor's barn: "… our beds were clumps of hay in the barn between the wheezing horse and the cow that had stopped giving milk. … Arthur grew listless now that Hania no longer came to sit near him."

(174–6) After the raid on his barn, Sidor takes them into the forest where they come upon: "… an enclave of earthen dugouts … . About 150 Jews from Skala and 'shtetls' in the area had fled to the forest one or two at a time after the 'aktsia' and after the liquidation of the Borszczow ghetto, and these bunkers were their last shelter."

(178–81) The conditions for those hiding in the forest near Skala, late 1943: "It took months, Lotka said, to become familiar with the forest and learn how to build bunkers and cover them with earth in which young trees were planted. I had probably walked over the heads of dozens of people without knowing it. … I walked a crisscross path back to my parents, passing people sitting at the entrances of bunkers. Some, too weak to manage more of a greeting than a fleeting nod of the head, sat immobile, hoarding air in their lungs before another suffocating night underground. Some turned over bits of clothing in the hunt for lice. Others lay on the ground in an agony of high fever. Typhus. 'Water,' a little girl moaned as I passed, 'a little water.'"

(191–3, 198–9) Hiding in the chicken coop in Sidor's barn: "No more spending time spread out in the barn, and no more leaving the brick cover for my father to pull shut from the inside. Sidor sealed us in. … Braided like a horse's tail, we had spent a maximum of two full days in there during the raid. Now, coming out for five minutes would be the longed-for exception. … There were so many lice that my hair was moving."

(195–7) Christmas Eve 1943, the family comes into Sidor's house and bathes: "I cried as I washed my face, hands, and chest for the first time in many months."

(212) Aunt Sophia recounts their life in hiding with Wasil: " 'Once a month he brought a pail of water so I could wash our clothes.' Once a month! Ours hadn't been washed in six months!"

Righteous Gentiles

(10–11, 76, 124–5) The Ukrainian Jan, their protector: " 'Our Jan,' who was called a 'Jewish uncle,' by his compatriots … ." As he continues to protect them: "The people in Father Derewienko's Orthodox church, where he had once been an altar boy and had taken his job very seriously, told him that what he was doing was sacrilegious and a defiance of the church. They made it clear that his absence would be welcomed." Autumn 1942.

(13–15, 83–5, 93–4, 183–90, 228) September 1942, Jan builds a hide-out for them in the attic of his barn: "His mother had forbidden him to bring us to her place, and his sister and brother-in-law had taken him aside and told him that they would turn us and him in if we were found on the premises." October 1943, Jan finds them hiding in the forest and brings them to hide in his barn while he searches for someone to take them in: "A host with time-bomb guests on his threshold, Jan had every right to slam the door in our faces. … I understood that he'd protected us for so long that our lives no longer belonged to us, they belonged to him, too. For the rest of his life he'd hear the door as it slammed shut in his face."

(29, 70, 230, 256) Moizesevich, the pharmacist in Skala: "He had on several occasions during the war supplied my father with medicine through Jan, and Aunt Sophia through Wasil. … Moizesevich had not had an easy time during the war. An Armenian who by name and looks could well have been a Jew, he had repeatedly been forced to prove otherwise by lowering his pants."

(29, 163, 211–12, 220–1, 256) Ulanowski, who had helped them, had hidden Dora: "Her parents and sister had been deported during the 'aktsia'. At some point, she had found shelter with Ulanowski. 'Some women threw stones at her when she stepped out onto the street, and one of them hit her in the eye.' Ulanowski blamed himself for not stopping Dora from leaving his house." After the liberation, March 1944.

(39, 128–9) The Polish peasant Sidor (Isidore) who works with Fanya's father on the labour brigade on the bridge over the Zbrucz river after the Soviet takeover: "… when he didn't fullfill his work quota, he was accused of sabotage. My father … intervened on Sidor's behalf and saved him from punishment. This was something Sidor never forgot."

(64–9) September 1941, Jan first sees Fanya in the marketplace and brings his fiancée to barter food for their silver cutlery. Her mother's fears: "He had seen what we had left and would come back with a gang of militia who would help themselves and take us away. No, my father counseled, this one was different: 'I have a hunch he's a decent guy.'"

(70–2) Jan fetches a doctor from Borszczow to treat Suza's husband Munio: "All of us were stunned that he had done something like this for us. And he refused to accept any payment, not even to cover the hay for his horse."

(83–4, 93–4, 102–4, 126–7, 200–6) Jan breaks off his engagement and reveals that he is in love with Fanya and will protect her: "Jan's declaration of love came as a surprise – totally unexpected. But it made me calm, gave me a sense of protection, acting as a kind of shield around me as I navigated in an increasingly hostile and stormy sea."

(113) "The Polish priest who had given religious instruction to the Catholic children in the Polish elementary school before the war, and who had since then sheltered several Jews, had taught Lotka Catholic prayers and liturgy every night for four weeks. He had gotten her 'good' Aryan papers – those of somebody who had died – and had made the arrangements for a middleman to take her to live with a Polish couple as their niece in return for money sent with him by Lotka's parents."

(135–8) Jan takes Fanya to Sidor, his wife Marynka, and their 9-year-old daughter Hania, to hide out for a short time, hoping to convince them to take in Fanya's whole family, August 1943: "'She's Ukrainian,' Jan explained to me after they left, 'and Sidor is a Pole, not a common combination.' I asked if he was as good-tempered as he appeared to be. 'In the morning,' Jan said, 'he gets out of bed on the right side and Marynka on the wrong side. What a couple!'"

(142–4, 155–7) Marynka overcomes her hesitations and agrees to hide the whole family: "In the neighboring village, a man who had sheltered Jews had seen his wife and children shot in front of his eyes. Then he was tied up within sight of their corpses, which everyone was forbidden to remove and bury."

(190–1) Sidor comes to Jan's barn to take them back: "Italy had capitulated, he explained, and he trusted my father's assertion, made months earlier, that the fall of Italy would be the sign that Germany would lose the war. My father nodded: the Germans were too smart to commit suicide, Napoleon-style, in Russia. The war would end before winter." September 1943.

(227) Fanya learns of the fate of a Polish friend of her father's at liberation: "... who had given sanctuary to Jews in Czortkow. He had been stopped while driving in his car on the outskirts of town. The car was set on fire with kerosene while he was inside, and he was burned so badly that he died."

Liberation

(208–12) Early March 1944, with Russian forces nearby, a group of Germans asks Sidor for help: "Germans begging for bread sparked our spirits more than the vision of a thousand tanks passing by our door." And then: "The phrase 'it's over' was as empty as the prayer of gratitude to God my mother instructed us to say with her."

(214–23) Uncle Zygmunt and Fanya's father go into Skala to find food; three days later Zygmunt returns to Sidor's alone. He had left Benjamin speaking to Soviet soldiers: "'I tried to tear Benjamin away,' Uncle Zygmunt said, looking at my mother, 'but I couldn't budge him. I told him I would meet him at the fountain around midnight, and left.'" Benjamin's fate is never known, nor his body ever found. Spring 1944.

(219, 221) Finio Finkel and Chaim Gottesfeld (no relation) are killed in Skala after liberation: "Almost all the Ukrainians and Poles wanted the Jews dead whether the Germans were gone or not."

(224–6) The six of them, Fanya, her mother and brother Arthur, her Uncle Zygmunt and wife Sophia, and their son Dolek leave Sidor for shelter in what is left of Grandfather Azriel's house in Skala. Fanya finds work in the office of the Soviet military command.

(228) "So far, fifty out of the fifteen hundred Jews who had lived in Skala before the German invasion had come back. For most of the townspeople it was too many." March 1944.

(231–3) In an attempt to find out the fate of her father, Fanya and her mother confront Dzsisiak, Jan's ex-fiancée's father, and Father Derewienko. Dzsisiak's response: "'Too many of you have come back,' he said." Father Derewienko, when asked to return the ring given him for safekeeping, claimed to have given it to Fanya's father: "That was impossible, my mother told him, because we had been in hiding at Sidor's at the time ... 'Wait here,' he said. He came back with a five-pound bag of white flour and told her it was to show that he forgave her for the accusation."

(234–5) "Now the storm was over and yet the wind blew harder than ever. I lived in a flux of daily needs and no prospects. Sleeping on the kitchen floor, hungry, in rags, lice-ridden, a turtle with carapace torn from its back, I felt exposed, half-blinded, deadened by sun and air, ignored by the world." Spring 1944, Fanya is not quite twenty.

(236–7) September 1944, Fanya moves to Czortkow: "... the nearest town with a functioning high school ... ." to finish her final year of high school: "The mental stimulation of schoolwork in the morning exhilarated me after three years of not having a book to read nor pen and paper for writing."

(237–40) "... I felt very conflicted about Jan – grateful to him for saving my life but tormented by the accusation that he had killed my father. I had feelings for him but was more aware than ever of the great disparity in age, religion, and background."

(241–6) Aunt Sophia had moved to Lvov, offers Fanya the opportunity to finish her studies there, and move away from Jan, but he decides his opportunities are also better there.

(250–5) At Easter 1945, Fanya returns from Lvov to Skala. She is invited to Jan's cousin Irena for Easter dinner: "I'm sure he wanted to make a statement to his family that it was I who was his girfriend, not the Ukrainian woman he was still officially courting. Still, I didn't like his showing people I didn't know that he owned me, and I felt uncomfortable."

(256–61) "The Polish government-in-exile and the Soviet government signed an agreement to permit non-Ukrainians – ethnic Poles and Jews – to leave for Poland. Skala's Jews decided to band together and go to the recently liberated section of western Poland called Upper Silesia. The Russians agreed to provide a train for us." Fanya says goodbye to her town, and to Jan. May 1945.

(262–5) The trip from Skala: "The Russians had sent cattle cars without roofs, not cars with seats. … We hadn't been told where in Silesia we were headed, only that the trip wouldn't take more than a day. It took four weeks. … After rolling along for fifteen minutes one day, we would sit derailed in an adjoining field for the next three." They arrive in the DP camp in Bytom. Summer 1945.

Displaced Persons camps

(269–70) "The DP camp consisted of wooden barracks with large halls which served as dormitories. Day after day, people lay on their cots without moving, small islands of despair and sorrow marooned by exhaustion, by malnutrition, and by illness. … Once a week I stood in line at the offices of the Joint Distribution Committee for our food package, setting aside the bare minimum we needed for ourselves and using the rest for barter." Bytom, Summer 1945.

(271–7) Moving out of the barracks, Fanya finds a place for her mother, Arthur, and herself with Miss Klampt: "Miss Klampt was an excellent seamstress but lacked clientele because fabric was unobtainable. She offered to sew a new outfit for me in order to attract a husband who would 'solve all your problems.'" In fact, Fanya is visited by a matchmaker who: "… sent three men in rapid succession … . All three proposed. I picked the one who took me to the movies. His name was Joseph." He and Fanya are engaged within the week. December 1945.

Stories of individuals, including family members

(32) Choneh Gottesfeld, a distant cousin, returns to Skala from America for a visit, around 1938: "When Choneh returned to America, he wrote a book in Yiddish about his visit to Poland."

(35–6, 112–13, 186–8) Fanya's childhood friend and second cousin Lotka, the daughter of Mottel and Szencia Sternberg: "Lotka was beautiful, with brown hair, green eyes, and heavy, dark eyebrows like her father's; and she played the violin. I always thought myself ugly in comparison to Lotka and was jealous because the boys I liked ran after her, not me." Lotka passes as a Christian in Lvov. She is betrayed. Her death with her parents, early spring 1944.

(36–7, 204) Growing up in Skala: "Zhenia was my closest friend and, secretly, my alter ego. Zhenia was radiantly beautiful; she looked like an angel. … I never saw her read a book in all our years together in Polish and Hebrew school. She didn't care about her studies and was a vivacious, happy-go-lucky type." Her death, February 1944.

(37, 259) Fanya's first boyfriend Izio: "He was ten years older than I, and this impressed me at the age of fourteen, as did his having served in the Polish Army, smoking cigarettes, and looking like a non-Jew. … He held my hand, he wrote me letters, and several times we kissed each other. In September 1939, Izio was called up to the army. War had broken out. I went with him to the train station to say good-bye."

(38–9, 51, 225–6) A cousin of Fanya's father, tortured in the Bereza-Kartuska Prison for being a Communist, freed during the Soviet take-over, fled with the Russians before the German advance. He survives and returns to Skala, learns of the murder of his family.

(41, 161) Rose Bradler: "... the daughter of the family I'd roomed with as a high school student in Borszczow. She was now hiding with her baby not far from us. Her milk had dried up and she needed sugar for the infant." Jan relays the message from Fanya's father: they have no sugar to send. Autumn 1943.

(45–6, 71–2, 118, 163–4) Shimek Bosek, Fanya's friend from Skala, in school with her in Borszczow, two years older than her: "How I admired his ease with languages! To dazzle me he'd switch from English to German to Latin to Hebrew in one sentence." Shimek's death, with his mother. Autumn 1943.

(46) Grandmother Hinda dies during the time Fanya is in school in Borszczow.

(70, 143) Dr Meir Steuerman: "... who had once relieved Sidor's agony during a gallbladder attack. The doctor had been hiding in a bunker under the Strusover Synagogue in Skala with his wife and daughter and a young woman who had run away from the Borszczow ghetto ... The Germans drove the four of them out of the hiding place and gunned them down on the sidewalk."

(112–13) The Sternbergs, who shared their house with Fanya and her family: "Mottel . . . Szencia, and Lotka had hidden during the 'aktsia' and the three days before Mottel got a 'hard' certificate – one that would stand up well under scrutiny ... What Mottel did in working directly for a Gestapo chief no one knew. ... Lotka was passing as a Christian in Lvov."

(147–8) Fanya's maternal grandparents Jakob and Miriam Wasserman are "murdered in the final liquidation of the Borszczow ghetto. ... They were taken out of town with the rest of the Jews, forced to dig a pit, ordered to undress, lined up, and shot row upon row into the pit."

(162, 180–1, 187) A letter comes from her father's sister Lolla asking for refuge with Sidor for her and her two sons: "... she had been stabbed in the head by the same Ukrainian peasants who had killed her husband in the fields where they were hiding after the 'aktsia'." They hide in the forest bunker, and are killed: "by a grenade thrown into their bunker."

(162, 202, 212, 224, 241, 250–1, 270) Father's sister Sophia, her husband Zygmunt Zimmerman, and son Dolek, in hiding with the peasant Wasil, appeal to Sidor for refuge: "... they expected to be turned out any minute because their funds were almost gone." They come to Sidor's with the German retreat. After liberation, they bring Fanya to Lvov, then leave for Cracow, and then Salzburg.

(176–7, 180–1, 187) Fanya's family find her mother's brother Uncle Wolf Wasserman and his wife Malcia and their two daughters hiding in the forest enclave, having: "... escaped to the forest from the Borszczow ghetto before its liquidation." They are killed in a German raid on their forest bunker.

(177–9, 181, 186–8) Lotke Sternberg's friend Rubcio in the forest, hoping to start a Jewish partisan unit. After the German raid on their forest bunker: "Rubcio, together with his mother and sister and other Jews, had been taken to another place in the forest and shot."

(213–20) Fanya's father's disappearance: he and Zygmunt leave Sidor's home to return to Skala to find food. After three days, Fanya sets off to look for them, finds Zygmunt on his return. Zygmunt recounts the story, that he had separated from Benjamin and had not been able to find him again: "'I don't know where he is.'" Sidor later reports: "... my father had been to see Jan, left to go to Ulanowski, never arrived there, and after that, no trace of him remained."

(228–9) The fate of Fanya's mother's sister Suza and her husband Munio, the dentist who: "... had been murdered a few weeks before the Liberation. ... We went from ditch to ditch, looking for traces of their bodies, but never found them."

(277–8) Joseph Heller, from a shtetl near Skala: "... he had lived like an animal for the two years he was in hiding underground, and had almost forgotten how to talk. … The youngest and only survivor of his siblings, he had nobody and was very lonely." He and Fanya marry.

Post-war life and career

(281–2) Fanya's family life with Joseph, children, grandchildren, her education, her mother's death in New York in 1982, her plans (1995) to visit Hania, Sidor's daughter. "We never found out who had murdered my father."

Personal reflections

(154) "My father's stance – to take what comes and go on from there, to avoid wasting time and energy by bemoaning our circumstances, not to curse God for turning away from us, above all to keep trying to stay alive – became my posture, too."

(199) "'Uberleben', the Yiddish word for 'survival', spelled doubt for me. Survive another day – and then what? All I could imagine was a ruined world populated by creatures out of a painting by Bosch who would torture me with hells I had not yet experienced. To live – if that word could be used for what we were doing in our coop – to live 'uber', 'over, beyond,' our current existence, what did it mean: 'over' in the sense of above it, disembodied, floating over everything as in a dream? Did it mean a challenge to prevail beyond physical existence?"

(206) Fanya and her parents and brother spend five months in hiding in a tiny chicken coop: "I frequently woke with the same inner vista: a bare tree standing alone in the tundra after a cataclysmic storm, one twisted branch on the icy ground still tossing in the wind."

Places mentioned in Europe (page first mentioned)

Austria/Osterreich (270), Belzec death camp (12), Bereza-Kartuska (38), Berlin (81), Borki-Wielki slave labour camp (76), Borszczow (13), Breslau/Wroclaw (272), Britain (38), Bucharest/Bucuresti (277), Budapest (277), Bytom Displaced Persons camp (265), Cracow/Krakow/Krakau (27), Czechoslovakia (51), Czernowitz/Cernauti/Chernovcy (28), Czortkow (27), Dnieper river (201), Dniester river (129), Galicia (256), Holland/Nederland (281), Horynin (68), Hungary/Magyarország (51), Italy/Italia (190), Jagelnica (84), Janowska slave labour camp (12), Kiev/Kyjiv (121), Lvov/Lemberg/Lwow/Lviv (12), Munich/München (281), Paris (22), Poland/Polska (19), Prague/Praha (35), Romania (38), Ruthenia/Sub-Carpathia (51), Salerno (168), Salzburg (270), Sarny (210), Sicily/Sicilia (168), Skala (3), Soviet Union/Union of Soviet Socialist Republics (19), Stanislawow (26), Tarnopol (76), Turilcze (128), Ukraine/Ukrajina (51), Upper Silesia/Oberschlesien (256), Vichy France (88), Vienna/Wien (26), Warsaw/Warszawa/Warschau (103), Zbrucz River (19), Zhitomir (121)

Places mentioned outside Europe (page first mentioned)

Israel/Yisrael (21), Leningrad/St Petersburg (46), New York City (281), Palestine (38), Siberia/Sibir (38), United States of America (32)

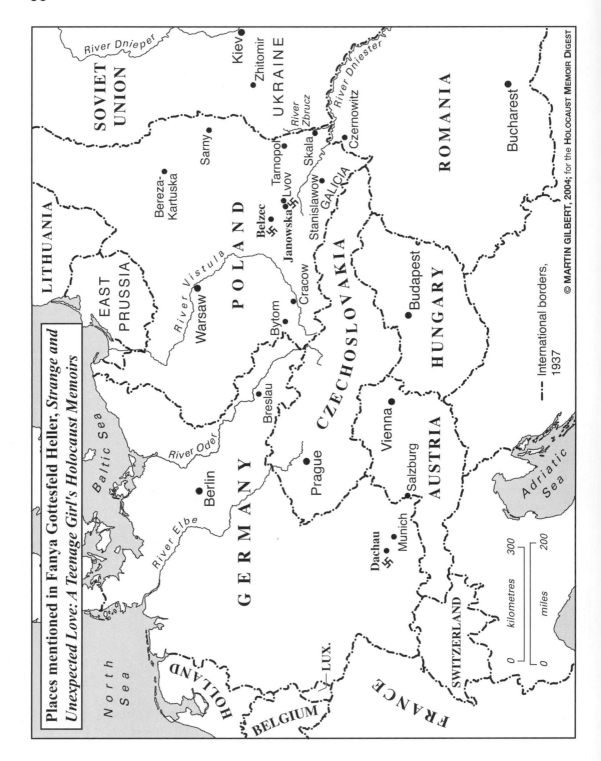

Places mentioned in Fanya Gottesfeld Heller, *Strange and Unexpected Love: A Teenage Girl's Holocaust Memoirs*

© MARTIN GILBERT, 2004; for the HOLOCAUST MEMOIR DIGEST

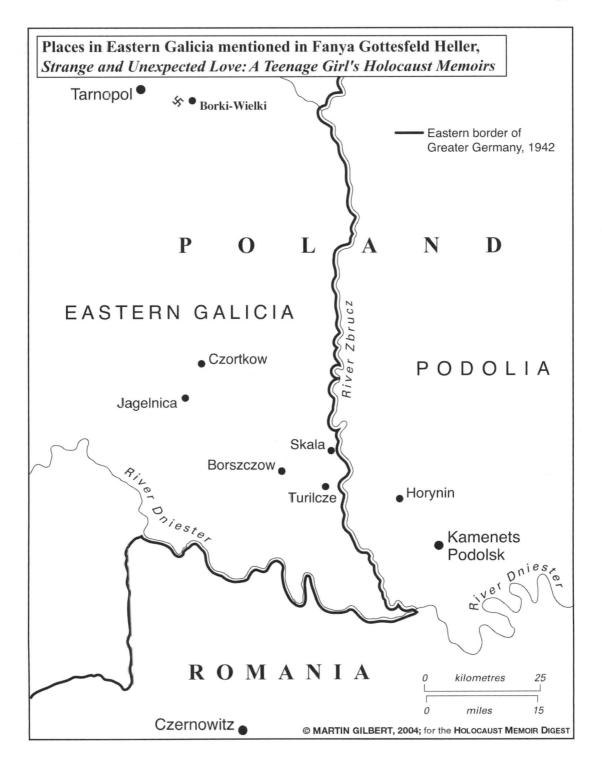

Places in Eastern Galicia mentioned in Fanya Gottesfeld Heller,
Strange and Unexpected Love: A Teenage Girl's Holocaust Memoirs

Tarnopol

Borki-Wielki

—— Eastern border of
Greater Germany, 1942

P O L A N D

EASTERN GALICIA

River Zbrucz

PODOLIA

Czortkow

Jagelnica

Skala

Borszczow

Turilcze

Horynin

Kamenets
Podolsk

River Dniester

River Dniester

R O M A N I A

0 kilometres 25

0 miles 15

Czernowitz

© MARTIN GILBERT, 2004; for the HOLOCAUST MEMOIR DIGEST

Erika Kounio Amariglio, *From Thessaloniki to Auschwitz and Back*

March 1926: born in Thessaloniki, Greece

Summer 1937: the last summer spent with grandparents in Karlsbad, Czechoslovakia

Autumn 1938: not allowed to join Greek youth group

October 1940: Italy invades Greece

April 1941: Germany invades Greece

9 April 1941: German troops enter Thessaloniki

November 1942: news reports reach Thessaloniki of mass murder in Lublin

8 February 1943: Nuremberg Laws imposed in Greece

22 February 1943: moves to ghetto

10 March 1943: moves to Baron Hirsch transit camp

14 March 1943: deported from Thessaloniki by train

20 March 1943: becomes number 38912 in Auschwitz

March to June 1943: works at the Gestapo office in Birkenau recording transports from Greece

8 June 1943: transferred to Auschwitz to work in the staff building

May, June, July 1944: records transports from Hungary

September 1944: during bombing raid, briefly reunited with father and brother

12 October 1944: learns that Greece has been liberated

December 1944: records transfers of prisoners evacuated to camps in Germany

18 January 1945: begins death march from Auschwitz

February 1945: on foot and by train, arrives in Ravensbrück

March to May 1945: taken to work in Malchov slave labour camp

1 May 1945: Malchov evacuated, escapes from death march

6 May 1945: liberated by Soviet forces

Summer 1945: returns to Thessaloniki via Belgrade

June 1947: marries, remains in Thessaloniki

Author: Erika Kounio Amariglio

Title: *From Thessaloniki to Auschwitz and Back, Memories of a Survivor from Thessaloniki*

Publishing details:

Vallentine Mitchell, Suite 314, Premier House, 112–114 Station Road, Edgware, Middlesex HA8 7BJ, 2000, 157 pages.
ISBN 0-85303-390-0.
Originally published in Greek in 1995. Editions also in German, French, Serbian, and Hebrew. Translated from the Greek by Theresa Amariglio Sundt, the author's daughter.

Focus

Erika, a teenage Greek girl (who is 13 in 1939) is deported with her parents and brother to Auschwitz, where she and her mother work in the Gestapo office as translators. The four survive and return home. The events take place between 1924, when her parents meet, and 1965, when she returns with her mother to Auschwitz as part of an International Conference of Auschwitz Survivors.

Features

Biographical Note, page viii.
The Library of Holocaust Testimonies, written by Martin Gilbert, page ix.
Acknowledgements, written by the author, page x.
Prologue, written by the author, page xi.
Preface, written by the English translator, Theresa Amariglio Sundt, page xiii.
Photographs of Erika and Heinz, grandparents, parents, childhood friends, husband, children
    and grandchildren, pages 3, 16, 17, 21, 33, 152–3, 157, and back cover.
Reproductions and translations of letters sent from Birkenau to friends in Greece, January
    1944, pages 98, 99.
Heinz Kounio's Auschwitz registration form, page 55.
Samuel Amariglio's exemption from restrictions certificate, page 49.
Epilogue, written by the author, page 159.
Glossary, page xv.
Works cited: Danuta Czech, *Auschwitz Chronicle 1939–1945*, New York, Henry Holt, 1990.
    Heinz Salvator Kounio, *I Experienced Death*, Thessaloniki, 1982 (in Greek).
    Lore Shelley, *Secretaries of Death*, New York, Shengold, 1986.

Contents (by topic, with page numbers)

Pre-war Jewish home and community life

(1–2, 5) Erika's father, Salvator Kounio, born in 1900 in Thessaloniki, the owner of a photography shop, travelled to a photographic exhibition in Leipzig in 1924, where he met the 18-year-old Hella Löwy from Karlsbad. She abandons her medical studies, they marry in 1925, and she returns with him to Thessaloniki: "In the 1920s Thessaloniki was really unlike the rest of Europe. She needed a lot of inner stength to overcome the barrier of being a 'foreigner', as everybody called her – even her friends and relatives – and to be accepted by Thessalonikian society." Erika is born in 1926, her brother Heinz in 1927.
(2–9) Erika's home and early childhood, their next-door neighbours the Vozios and the Polats,

and Gregorius, who keeps his boat nearby: "I loved listening to him and looking at his smiling blue eyes and big mustache, rising and falling as he talked. I often wondered how he could eat. Didn't his mustache get in the way?"

(9–10) Erika's brother Heinz is dared by their friends to lift a prize watermelon owned by the neighbour Vozios. The inevitable accident occurs: "When father came back at lunch-time, with lowered heads we went to tell him about our 'deed'. I don't remember him being angry with us, although I am sure he must have said something to us. He went straight to Vozios and paid for the watermelon. I remember that my brother didn't mention his being a 'muscle man' again for a long time afterward."

(10–14) Summers, and their evenings: "Our neighbor's eldest daughter, Gloria, was very much sought after, and our street was very popular among the troubadours, to my great delight. I very much loved to hear their songs, and I sang with them and dreamed of the time when I would come of age and they would come to sing for me as well! Sometimes I could also hear the odd splash of a bucket of water thrown at them to make them stop singing."

(14–15) Celebration of the Jewish holidays: "Yom Kippur, and in the springtime, Passover, was what made us sense the religious differences between us and our Christian friends. But this did not affect our relationships. We never felt different, we were all the same and we all believed in the same God."

(15–16) Her paternal grandparents, her "nono" Mosche and her "nona" Myriam Kounio: "... I could not communicate that well with my nona. My nona's Greek was very poor, because her language was Ladino … which we never spoke at home. We spoke our mother's native language, German, and my father's, Greek." Her "nono" spoke to them in Greek: "... and even today I feel the warmth of his hand holding mine."

(17–18) Her maternal grandparents, Ernst and Theresa Löwy of Karlsbad: "He was very fashionable and reserved. Only his eyes beamed. My grandmother, most beautiful – at least in my own eyes – with her hat on one side of her well-groomed hair, always wore smart dresses with her gloves and her little handbag. She opened her arms wide to embrace and hold me tight."

(17–19) Erika's family spend several weeks each summer in Karlsbad with her mother's parents: "The last time we went there was in 1937. I was already eleven, and I have the best memories from that particular summer. I watched with great fascination my grandmother's friends holding their parasols, some open, some closed. The gentlemen, with elegant gestures, took off their hats to greet any passing acquaintance and gracefully bowed quite low to the ground."

(19–20) June 1938, Erika and her father visit Athens: "Full of reverence I went up to the Acropolis, and full of awe I stood in front of the Kariatids. I was so happy to walk on the 'sacred mount', and I felt so small in front of the Parthenon. It was really one of the big days in my life."

(20–1) Autumn 1938, Erika has private French lessons, and piano added to her schedule: "My teacher, Mrs Mitza Abravanel, although my mother's close friend, never let me have any privileges, and she made me practice scales and exercises by Carl Czerny (1791–1857) for hours on end. I definitely felt very resentful at having to sit in front of the piano while my friends played outside."

Pre-war anti-Semitism

(19, 22) Spring 1938: "'We are not going to Karlsbad this summer,' my mother told us, 'but don't you worry, grandfather and grandmother will come to us, to stay with us forever and ever.'" Early 1939: "The Germans had overrun the Sudetenland and there was no place for Jews there anymore. Those who could flee did so. Grandfather and Grandmother, a suitcase in each hand, left their house and all their belongings and came to us as refugees to find shelter in their daughter's house."

(20–1) Autumn 1938, Erika is not allowed to join the Metaxas youth group; her friend Rose's sister is not allowed to join the tennis club: "It was the first time I realized that I was not on equal terms with my Christian friends."

The coming of war

(24–6) October 1940, Greece enters the war against Italian invasion: "The only thing for us girls to do was to knit for the war effort. We frantically knitted gloves, socks and hoods for the soldiers. We knitted and sang Sofia Vembo's latest hit, 'Fie on you Mousolini, none of you will be left.'"

Life under German occupation

(27–9) 9 April 1941, the Germans enter Thessaloniki, arrest Erika's father, and let him go after taking photographic equipment from his shop. A Gestapo officer requisitions two rooms of their house and moves in. He is polite: "'You see,' said our grandfather, who had recently arrived from Czechoslovakia, 'it is unnatural for Germans to behave badly. They are civilized, they are cultured. A nation that gave us Beethoven, Goethe and Heine could not be savage. It is only the SS who act brutally, and they are only a handful of people.'"

(29–31) Summer to winter 1941, food shortages that Erika's mother tried to overcome: "I remember one time when she cooked lentils and maggots floated to the top in the boiling broth. Patiently she spooned them out until there were none left. It didn't occur to her to throw the lentils away."

(34–8) Late summer 1942, Erika's parents and grandfather are arrested, taken to the Gestapo prison for a month, then are transferred to the Eptaphyrgion Prison, and eventually released. Erika's fluent German enables her to get food and medicine to them. They had been arrested as a result of their friendship with Helmut Held, a German soldier.

(40) Erika reports: "It could not be possible – but indeed, they were destroying the Jewish Cemetery."

(40) Late autumn 1942: "My friend May Benrubi came to school one day crying. They had turned her father's shop into an army center."

(40) Winter 1943: "The hardships of the occupation were enormous; there was less and less food; people were dying from cold and hunger. There were more cold and hungry people huddled on the sidewalks; many had already died."

Creation of the ghetto

(40–2) 8 February 1943, the newly arrived SS "committee" led by Alois Brunner and Dieter Wisliceny impose the Nuremburg Laws: "All the Jews were now required to put a yellow star on every piece of clothing they wore. Jews were not allowed to use public transportation. All the Jews had to move to special areas the SS had specified, i.e. ghettos. ... we moved to our new residence two weeks later, and grandfather went to live as the guest of a Christian Bulgarian family, very close to our house."

Deportation

(45–6) In the Baron Hirsch transit camp, Thessaloniki, plans for deportation: "... they would take us to Poland and we could even change Greek drachmas for Polish zlotys, so we wouldn't arrive there without money." Erika's father asks her mother whether they should leave on the first transport: "Mother, discouraged by the terrible living conditions, said to him, stressing every word: 'Salvator, whatever will be, let it happen as soon as possible. Let's leave at the first opportunity.'"

(50–1) Walking from the Baron Hirsch camp to the deportation train: "This picture remains vivid in my mind. The four of us proceeding like one person, and all around us disheveled women, some with babies in their arms, trying to calm them, all the while crying themselves, another dragging a bawling child in each hand, elderly people trying to walk faster, men with suitcases and bundles trying to push their way through the crowd to arrive even faster! Where to go? And the Germans' voices! Their wild yells … ." 14 March 1943.

(51–3) On the train: "My God how desperate! Some babies never stopped crying, sometimes quietly, sometimes screaming. Women were lamenting and some of the men took out their prayer books and were quietly singing hymns. It was dark in the railroad car, and they couldn't see to read, but they kept their eyes open, they turned the pages, they knew every line by heart."

(53) Her father, because of his fluency in German, had been chosen by the Germans to be an interpreter. On the third day, he lobbies for the train to stop and let people out for a bit of air, "for half-an-hour": "We must have been in Yugoslavia. The surroundings were deserted, not a soul to be seen. … The 'Schupos', guns ready, watched us, and whenever someone strayed too far they ordered him back. They did not allow us to get out of the cars again." The train journey lasts for six days, from Thessaloniki to Auschwitz.

Transit camps

(43–4) 10 March 1943, the SS arrest the family and send them to the Baron Hirsch camp, near the railway station, her father having been betrayed for having sold his business to protect his assets: "Fortunately, grandfather was not at home, and father sent somebody to warn him to stay where he was and hide."

(44–6) Three days, four nights in the Baron Hirsch camp: "Men, women, children, babies in perpetual aimless motion. … Our living conditions were terrible. We were cold and hungry, and because of our cold and our despair we couldn't sleep that night. … Another terrible night followed, with the rain dripping from the roof into little tin containers we had arranged to catch the drips. Emptying them as soon as they were full, shivering in the cold, we began another day."

Slave labour camps and factories

(32–4, 38, 40) "A German decree called for all Jews aged eighteen to forty-five to gather in Elevtherias Square at 8:00 am on 11 July 1942." They are taken to a slave labour camp run by the Todt organization. "… it must have been around mid-October, we heard that all the men compelled to do forced labor had returned. They were ill, thin, wretched. Many had died. I cannot remember many details, only my parents' relief."

(38) Rosa's uncle returns from the slave labour camp, autumn 1942: "He was a shadow of his former self, Rosa said, and he couldn't seem to pull himself together again. They had been forced to work under the burning sun, Rosa said. They had not given them enough to eat, and many had collapsed from exhaustion." Also taken are Rita Saltiel's and Dorin Kovo's cousins, and Sarika's father.

(126–32) After a few weeks in Ravensbrück, Erika, her mother, and the three Greek girls from the death march are taken with a group of women to Malchov, a slave labour camp affiliated with Ravensbrück. Erika's mother works in the "Garden Kommando"; Erika works for a short time in a box factory and then in the SS kitchen, from which Erika and her friends manage to smuggle out quite a few vegetables concealed under their clothing: "Our good fortune lasted only twenty days. We were losing vegetables more and more often – given our big loads – and leaving a trail behind us like Hansel and Gretel." The girls are caught and put to work in a *Wald-Kommando* (Forest Commando), sawing logs in the forest. March to May 1945.

(130–1) Hunger on the *Wald-Kommando*: "I would bend down to pull out grass stems that had started to grow from the frozen earth. I discovered an herb which was difficult to find but tasted vaguely like onions! Like goats we grazed, trying to satisfy our hunger."

Auschwitz-Birkenau

(54, 56–7) The train stops, 20 March 1943, at night: "Stunned by the long journey, stiff, hungry, frightened, desperate, everyone tried to jump out of the railroad cars, throwing their bundles and suitcases to the ground. There was confusion, screaming. The SS were running about everywhere. … It suddenly struck me that I could not tell who were more savage, the SS-men or their dogs."

(57–8) Erika's transport: arrival at Auschwitz, 20 March 1943, with about 2,800 Jews from Thessaloniki. 417 men and 192 women are admitted to the camp, including Erika's father Salvator (#109564), her brother Heinz (#109565), her mother Hella (#38911), and Erika (#38912): "What a coincidence it was that of the 2,800 people in the first transport, there was no one else who could speak German. And the Germans needed people to act as interpreters." The four of them are taken away in "… a car with a Red Cross emblem … ."

(59, 69–70) Separation from her father and brother: "… my brother and father had disappeared in the custody of an SS officer. I can still remember my father's look and feel his hand clasping mine before he climbed out. Where were they taking them? Would we see them again soon?" Some months later, Erika and her mother find out from their supervisor, "Unterscharführer" Klauss: " 'Your husband and son are fine! They are working in the camp tailor shop. I told them that you are fine too …' During the time I worked in Birkenau Klauss also brought us news on two other occasions."

(58–62) The first three days in the Auschwitz Main Camp, Erika and her mother are taken to their block directly from the train without the regular delousing, shaving, and tattooing: " 'But such a thing never happened before during the whole time the camp has been here! Are you Jews? One hundred per cent? – And you did not bring a safe-conduct letter from any important person? – Unbelievable, unheard of!' "

(61–2) Sarika tells Erika of the entrance into Auschwitz of the girls in their transport, the cold walk to the barracks, undressing and having their hair cut, the showers, the registration and tattooing: " 'We looked at each other in despair and didn't recognize each other. Leah broke into hysterical laughter. Allegrita couldn't bear it anymore, she started crying and called out for her mother. One crack of an SS whip and they all fell silent. Allegrita collapsed on the floor.' "

(62–5, 71, 77, 92) Erika and her mother are taken to Birkenau: "The living conditions in Birkenau were appalling." She describes their entrance, the uniforms, the "blocks" or barracks, the bunk beds: "They were wide enough for three or four people, but there were never less than eight or ten people in them. … We lay next to each other, all facing the same way, and when someone wanted to turn over, we all had to turn together." The morning roll call: "When the right number of prisoners were not present at roll call, the block would be searched until they found the inmate who had died or was too ill to get up. The 'Appell' lasted for hours. What a torture and how many of us could not hold out!" She describes their uniforms, and eating: "Around their waists was a cord from which their 'Menage' hung, a deep pot with two handles. It was their most precious possession. … Only those who had a 'Menage' were given the watery broth which was ladled out as a meal once a day."

(65) The work for some of the women in Birkenau: "Their job was to carry stones from one spot to another for no purpose at all. An SS woman with a dog oversaw the 'work' from nearby, and if she didn't like something – this happened continually – she would start yelling at them and let her dog loose on them. Others had to drag big iron rollers, the kind used to flatten the ground. A great iron bar was mounted like a shaft on each roller, and from eight to ten girls had to pull together, as they could be moved only with great effort."

(66–7) Erika's and Hella's area of work: "… the office of the Politische Abteilung (PA), the camp Gestapo, the SS. … That is where they kept detailed records of all the events that happened everyday everywhere in the Auschwitz and Birkenau camps. That is where they kept all the lists with the names of the people who had passed the selection and those who would be sent to the gas chambers. … The PA prisoners' 'Kommando' was divided into the following groups: the Document Section, the Interrogation Section, the Legal Section, and the 'Standesamt', the recorder's office, including the civil registry, and the 'administration' and 'management' of the crematoria."

(67–8, 71) In the *Politishe Abteilung* office: "My mother's job was to write the newcomers' personal facts on a specially printed form, i.e., the name and surname of each prisoner. Every time she wrote a name on the special forms, Sarah had to be written next to a woman's name, Israel next to a man's name. … I usually went to any of the secretaries who needed me to act as an interpreter. The transports from Greece arrived one after the other." March through June, 1943.

(70) "Prisoners who had reached the most miserable stage – the last stage of their lives – were known as 'Muselmänner' (the walking dead). … One day when I was in the toilet, a 'Muselweib' (one of these wretched women) dared to enter and sit down." When a political prisoner sees her, she pushes her off the bench and into the pit: "Together with two others who happened to be there, we pulled the unfortunate woman out in a sorry state. I wonder even now what she did after she got out, how she cleaned herself up, whether she survived?"

(71–4) Erika returns to work after a three-week stay in the *Revier*, the camp infirmary: "My strong constitution and 'will to live' were what kept me alive, as Dr. Ena told my mother." May 1943, Birkenau.

(76–7) "On 8 June 1943 the last transport arrived from Thessaloniki. Our presence was no longer needed in Birkenau." Erika and her mother are transferred to the Auschwitz Main Camp, to live and work in the "Stabsgebäude", the staff building: "The main thing was that it was clean, that we could wash and that we were fed regularly, though unappetizing, meals."

(79–80) Erika's work in the administrative offices at the Auschwitz Main Camp where she had the opportunity to read files of the political prisoners (non-Jewish): "Most of them were large, very thick volumes containing all the official documents of the prisons and the prisoners' previous records, which accompanied them to every prison and were updated after every interrogation. Why was someone arrested, what had he done, how had he been arrested, whether he had been tortured and what he had revealed. … A file could contain an entire life-story, starting long before a prisoner was arrested and ending on the day he was transferred to Auschwitz concentration camp."

(81–2) At the Auschwitz Main Camp, Erika is called in to translate the hysterical story of a Greek *Mussulman* who explains that he is not Jewish: "He had formerly sold 'koulouria', round bread sticks, at the station whenever a train had departed." He had been caught up with the crowd and deported to Auschwitz. "I tried to explain that he definitely was not Jewish. 'I can tell from his accent,' I told them. … The Germans did not let him contine speaking. They grabbed him and threw him outside. … I have never forgotten him to this day … ."

(83, 106, 114) "Throughout May, June and July of 1944 transports arrived daily from Hungary. The SS-people became extremely nervous and shouted constantly. Kirschner, the chief, was in a rage, and poor Edith Grünwald, his secretary, used to come out of his office white as a sheet to pass on his orders. Often their breath reeked strongly of Schnapps, and they worked in a semi-drunken state."

(84–6, 145) Erika's mother contracts typhoid fever and is taken to the infirmary, when she finds Erika's cousins Rosa and Emilia, and tries to have them transferred to better work: "With the help of 'Blockälteste' Maria and SS-woman Volkenrath, the names of Emilia and Rosa, as well as that of my dear friend May Benroubi, were added to the list. Unfortunately Rosa had died in the meantime, and May was in Block 25, where there was no chance of ever leaving alive. Only our Emilia came. She was the fifth member of our family who was saved. The rest, twenty-three people, did not survive." Emilia returns to Thessaloniki after the war, marries Albert Saul: "Her wedding took place in our house, because nobody from her family, her four brothers and her parents, had survived."

(88, 103) "The black wall that joined Blocks 10 and 11 was the wall where executions were held. Block 10 was the block where experiments were performed on prisoners by Dr. Mengele (PhD and MD) and Professor Dr. Clauberg. … they experimented in hopes of finding ways to sterilize men and women faster and more effectively. This was basically Dr. Mengele's speciality. Dr. Clauberg would bring as many twins from the transports as he wanted to the block. … They were known as 'Clauberg's twins'."

(89–90, 105) The work in "Canada"-Kommando: "The men did the heavy jobs; they carried the luggage belonging to Jewish deportees that had to be left on the station platform. … The workers had to sort clothes according to their style … . They had to check the hems, seams, soles of shoes and remove anything people had hidden there in their desperation. … Whatever was of good quality or useful the SS sent back to Germany, they kept the shabbier things for the prisoners."

(95) December 1943: "… 2,500 persons arrived from Theresienstadt. After the selection the people temporarily permitted to live were brought to the 'family camp', a new section at Birkenau."

(97, 100) Erika and her mother are rejected by a German researcher who makes plaster heads in order to find physical connections between nationalities: "It seemed that he likewise found me insufficiently representative of either the Jewish race or the Greek."

(102–3) "Unexpectedly, we started receiving inventories from the RSHA (German Security Department) with lists from Theresienstadt (Fall 1944). Nearly every day 2,500, 2,000 or 3,000 people arrived who, after the selection, were taken to a wing at Birkenau where they also kept the families together."

(105–6) 1944, "That summer, polka-dot dresses were in fashion – nearly every woman had such a dress. So many were collected in 'Canada' that one of the SS-officers decided to give them to us. … Suddenly we were no longer garbed in the striped prison outfits, but were all dressed in blue dresses with large or small white polka dots. … I wondered what unfortunate person had worn this dress, where could she be now?"

(108, 119) Autumn 1944, Auschwitz, with rumours of Allied advance: "Suddenly an order came from Oberscharführer (Staff-Sergeant) Kirschner: We were to collect all the files of those who had died up to now in the Auschwitz camp. They were loaded into a truck and, we learned later, were burned."

(109) 29 September 1944, a visit to their block by the camp commander and a visitor: "… the stranger was a Red Cross inspector . … Naturally the following day the carpet, curtains and flowers were all taken away."

(111) Transports arrive from Rhodes: "The numbers given to the men had the letter B in front, and those of the women had the letter A. These were the new numbers assigned, I believe, from 1943 or early 1944 on, I assume because the first series of numbers, which included our own, was getting too long."

(111–13) September 1944, a bomb falls on their building in Auschwitz. In the confusion, the men and women are not separated, and Erika finds her father and brother: "For days I could feel my father's embrace. My brother's image was constantly in my mind."

Death marches

(117) December 1944, Auschwitz: "Increasingly more branch camps were evacuated, and the still-healthy prisoners in the camp were transferred to camps in Germany. The girls of our 'Kommando' were constantly busy preparing the lists of transfers."

(120–2) 18 January 1945: "From Birkenau women prisoners were being brought to Auschwitz, and the SS gave each prisoner a loaf of bread, a piece of margarine and a blanket. They formed columns of five, and endless rows departed through the camp gates … ." Erika and her mother join the line, meeting three Greek girls, Esterina, Sarah, and Florika. They leave at noon and continue on to nightfall: "Every so often we heard gunfire and automatically accelerated our pace. The gunfire was meant for those who could not walk fast enough and fell behind, the last in the line."

(123–4) On the fourth day of their march: "The bread we had taken with us was gone; we were so hungry and thirsty!" They are taken to a railway station in Loslau, and into open boxcars: "We didn't have to walk anymore, but we were almost as stiff as pillars of ice. … eventually the train stopped. How many days were we on the train? Two or three, I do not remember. I only know that our only nourishment was snow." They had arrived at Ravensbrück.

Concentration camps

(124–6) Two or three weeks spent at the " 'Jugendlager' (concentration camp for youth), which they also called a 'Straflager' (punishment camp)" of Ravensbrück, where: "Very young women were kept in huts hidden behind large, beautiful trees. Various different experiments were performed on them … In the 'Youth Camp' at Ravensbrück they also had many pairs of twins the SS had obtained for the Experimentation Block."

Witness to mass murder

(39) November 1942, a BBC radio news broadcast on their radio at home: "At a certain point the news announcer said, in a very casual tone, that the same morning two Polish Jews had arrived at the radio station. They had escaped from a camp named Lublin. There – the announcer went on in the same indifferent voice – mass murders of Jews were going on. Without any additional comment he continued reporting the news." Her grandfather's reaction: "He stood up, red in the face, with big angry eyes and switched the radio off. He then turned to my parents and said: 'Rubbish, that is English propaganda.'" (This BBC broadcast

was a result of an eyewitness account that had just been brought to London by a Polish courier, Jan Karski, who had seen the transit camp of Izbica Lubelska, southwest of Lublin.)

(66) The morning and evening selections at the *Appel* in Birkenau: "On the left side of the gate the camp 'orchestra' stood and played military marches until all the prisoners had passed through. ... On the other side stood the camp's chief physician, Dr. Rohde. Next to him stood the two chief SS-women in charge, Drechsler and Mandel. Dr. Rohde, and in his absence Drechsler, made selections by pointing with a finger at the thinnest, palest and most terrified prisoners, who were then sent to Block 25 and from there to the gas chambers."

(74) Spring 1943, Birkenau: "About this time another big 'selection' was made, as happened whenever the camp got overcrowded. ... Lists of the 'candidates for death' had to be drawn up accurately and filed in an archive. This name registration took place after every selection, whether it was one of the mass selections, as in this case, or the daily ones held every morning when the prisoners went to work and every evening when they returned."

(77, 91) Late June 1943, Erika and her mother are transferred to the Auschwitz Main Camp: "We nicknamed our 'Kommando' the 'Himmelfahrts-kommando', which means the 'Ascension Detachment', because we were certain we would never leave the camp alive. ... We were important witnesses, just like those in the Sonderkommando (who worked in the gas chambers)." Their work involved preparing death certificates for prisoners transferred: "... from prisons or who had been captured in raids, and also for those who died in the camp from hunger, hardship, typhus, beatings, torture and so on."

(78) Erika's mother's job: "Every time a Christian died, a 'letter' was sent to the family expressing the administration's condolences ... Each letter ended with a postscript asking if the relatives would like to receive the ashes of the deceased, and if so, to send a certain amount of marks to cover the costs. We also had to separate the files of the people who died and bring them down from the top floor, the section of the living, to the basement, the 'Todesabteilung'."

(78–9) "The names of all the people selected in the Birkenau and Auschwitz camps were written on lists sent to the central office of the PA, where we worked, for registration. On each of those lists were the identifying letters SB which stood for 'Sonderbehandlung' (special treatment). The people on the SB lists had received 'special treatment', in other words they had been killed in the gas chambers. ... I was responsible for filing all the dead inmates' files in alphabetical order and for filing the SB lists which came in daily."

(87–8, 91–2, 115) Block 11, the punishment block, Auschwitz: "All the prisoners to be punished had to first go through an 'interrogation' by the PA Department. 'Interrogation' meant torture, and one of the worst torturers was SS Staff-Sergeant Friedrich Wilhelm Boger. Many times in the evening my workmates Maryla Rosenthal and Aranka Pollak would talk to us about the 'interrogations'."

(94–5) Yom Kippur 1943: "The biggest selection was held on the day of Yom Kippur. The sorting out – 'Sortierung', as the SS called it – started at the morning roll call. ... This happened in all three camps of men and women in Auschwitz and Birkenau. The typewriters in our office worked non-stop. We had to write the SB lists with all the names. There were over a thousand. ... Close to Christmas we heard of another big selection in the Birkenau women's camp. They 'selected' and burned more than 1,000 women one day."

(102) The Gypsy camp at Auschwitz: "Every time a child was born, he or she was also given a serial number, and the lists of the new-born babies were sent to our office for filing. The same applied to those who died. We had to separate their files from the 'section of the living' and transfer them to the basement, where the 'section of the dead' was located. ... one day

we learned that the gypsies' camp was being cleared out. They had all been sent to the gas chambers (2 August 1944)."

(104–5, 151) May to July 1944, transports arrive from Hungary: "A great line of prisoners was created, leading directly from the station platform to the gas chambers, instead of having the victims driven through the camp in trucks. The crematoria worked non-stop, yet still they could not keep up. They dug deep pits, threw wood and corpses into them and set them on fire. They burned the dead there, because the crematoria could not cope with such a massive influx."

(105) On the transports of Hungarians taken to the gas chambers, May through July 1944: "The smell of burnt flesh lingered in the air, and at night the heavens were glowing red – and this went on for weeks that seemed unending. … How could I ever forget all this horror, as much as I tried to erase it from my memory? The picture that I had in my mind has haunted me all these years."

(113) Autumn 1944: "In the women's camp at 'Auschwitz II'-Birkenau they held another big selection. More than 1,000 women were sent to die in the gas chambers. … After a few days we learned that another 2,000 people had been murdered during a cleansing of the men's camp. We received no inventory with the 'SB' stamp, however."

(115–16) "One big transport arrived in Birkenau from Ravensbrück, Germany. None of the prisoners were admitted to the camp; they were all 'Muselleute' (walking dead) and were sent straight to the gas chambers, the messenger from Birkenau told us. … One morning we learned that the gypsy camp had been totally liquidated (10 October 1944). They gassed and burned 800 people in all."

(117–19) Early January 1945, Erika and the girls in her office are taken to clean out Crematorium I, the one located in the Auschwitz Main Camp. It had not been in use for two years, and had been used for Christian prisoners who had died "… of hunger, hardship and torture – not in the gas chambers": "For three whole days we worked continuously without stopping. One small break to eat, nothing would stay down, and then back to work again."

(122–3) The second and third day of their march from Auschwitz: "And my mother repeating constantly: 'Go on … Don't stop … Don't look around …' I couldn't help looking at the fallen bodies, and I was sure that 'this one' was definitely my father."

Resistance, ghetto revolts, individual acts of courage and defiance

(27) April 1941, as Germany overran the Greek border en route to Thessaloniki: "Everywhere in town fires broke out. They were burning the warehouses so the Germans would not find anything. They set fire to the Alatinis warehouse, to the ammunition, to the gasoline, to the harbor. The depot's warehouses are opened; let the people help themselves so the enemy won't get anything! Full of awe, we watched the fires from our veranda. My parents were speechless."

(29, 37–8) Her father has a German friend whose son, Helmut Held, a soldier stationed in Thessaloniki, is befriended by the family. Helmut is transferred to Crete and begins a correspondance with Erika's father, for which Erika's parents and grandfather are imprisoned and then later released. In Crete: "It seems that he was in an anti-Nazi movement there and was being closely watched. … Helmut got drunk one night and cursed Hitler in the most explicit way. … we learned later that the National Socialists had imprisoned and condemned him to death."

(32, 36–7) Fall 1941, Erika and her friends conceive and organize an event for the following September: "… our president, Roula Tari, suggested arranging a lecture. It would be a cultural contribution to our city. … The attendance was big, many of the city's leading personalities came, including the mayor."

(40) January 1943, Against regulations, Erika's father transfers the title of his photographic shop to a friend: "… so that it wouldn't be expropriated by the German army. From then on his shop was not registered under his name."

(74–5) On the *Laüferinnen* messengers, Auschwitz: "Their job was to bring orders, lists and messages from one camp to the other. … Most of them were involved in the camp's Polish resistance, and in this way they were able to enter all the offices and talk to the men who worked there. Most of them were Polish Christians and were perceived as the camp's elite."

(85–6) The Polish prisoner Dr Vasilevsky, who operates on Erika's mother in the Auschwitz Main Camp: "He was also one of the people who formed the nucleus of the Polish resistance within the camp and had helped many prisoners, risking his own life in the process."

(87–8, 105) Aranka Pollak from Czechoslovakia, in Auschwitz since the spring of 1942: "She treated me as if I were her daughter … . 'You might survive. I certainly will not, and then you must speak out and tell what happened here.' Fortunately, both Aranka and Maryla Rosenthal survived … ."

(97) Erika's friends surprise her on her eighteenth birthday with gifts: "When we returned from work that evening, I found a small flower on my bed, around which several items had been arranged. I stood there, my mouth open wide with surprise, and a lump in my throat from emotion that left me speechless."

(98–9, 109–11) Reproductions of letters written on 26 and 27 January, 1944 by Erika and by her mother Hella in German to friends in Greece, with translation. Erika's letter asks: "'How are Elefteria and Pote?'" which she translates in the footnote as: "'Elefteria' means Freedom in Greek, 'Pote' means When." Hella's letter states: "'Here with us are aunt Friki and her daughter Tromara.'" Erika's footnote translates: "'Friki' means horror in Greek, 'tromara' means fright."

(100–2) Resistance in Auschwitz: "At first it was rather limited and insignificant, but starting in mid-1944 and continuing thereafter it became quite important. … To weaken the resistance, a large transport of Poles, mostly Christians, was assembled. All had low numbers, which meant that they had served the longest in camp. They were transported from Auschwitz to a camp in Germany."

(103–4) Erika's friend Vera from Belgrade, 21, a non-Jewish prisoner in Auschwitz: "For more than a year she had worked as a courier for the underground movement. In one of the German's 'razzias' she was caught together with some others. … she had seized the gun of the German who was leading her, walking in front, and shot him." Her singing at night is allowed to continue despite the ban on conversation and noise. "I never learned what became of her. I often wonder whether she survived or perhaps perished in the end."

(106–7) 24 June 1944, Mala Zimetbaum and Edward Galinski attempt to escape from Auschwitz; twelve days later they are captured, brought back, tortured and condemned: "During the time when one SS-man was reading her indictment she cut her veins. … She was transferred immediately to the hospital to stop her bleeding, but she died on the way. … Edward was hanged in the presence of all the prisoners. He himself kicked the stool from under his feet while singing the Polish national anthem."

(114–15) News of the destruction of Crematorium IV creates turmoil in their office; from Erwin they learn: "One team of the Sonderkommando, together with the 'resistance' group of prisoners, had been planning this explosion for some time. 'But where did they get the explosives?' we asked. 'From the Union! – The girls who worked there have been smuggling explosives to the men for weeks!' Turning to me he added, 'The Greeks were in the front line of this uprising!' ... Crematorium IV was not put back into operation again." October 1944. (117) On 6 January 1945 the four girls from the "Union-Werke-Kommando" are hanged: "They were Ella (Gärtner, Gartner), Roza (Roia, Robota), Regina (Safirstein, Saphierstein) and Esther (Estera, Wajsblum, Wajcblum)."

(131–2) End of April 1945, while on the "Wald-Kommando" at Malchov, working in the forest: "Instead of cutting the tree trunks into 80 cm lengths, as we were told by the forester, we cut 'plates', i.e. slabs of wood about 3 cm thick, which we took back to the camp to use as 'plates'. ... Every plate we cut took the same amount of work as cutting 80 cm lengths, as the forester wanted. This was our passive resistance."

Specific escapes

(42–3) February 1943. While living wth her family in the ghetto, Erika returns to her family's home: "One day I was so overcome by nostalgia that I took off my star and without saying anything went one last time to see our house in Koromila Street. I sat by the sea to bid farewell to the sun. It was to be the last time for many years."

(86) While at the Auschwitz Main Camp, 1943, near where Camp Commander Rudolf Höss and the SS lived, Erika hears music coming from one of the buildings near where she worked: "Unbelievable! There was still music in the world! A small butterfly lost its way and flittered through the barbed wire. ... A butterfly here! ... It was like a ray of light penetrating the camp's darkness."

(148–9) Erika's brother Heinz and their father escape execution with 18 others as a reprisal for 20 Russian prisoners of war who had escaped from their train en route to the Ebensee concentration camp: "After a while the junior officer reappeared bringing an order that they (the twenty) first had to be properly registered in the camp and after that executed, and he led them all into the camp." (Erika reprints this from the memoir *I Experienced Death* by Heinz Salvator Kounio, Thessaloniki 1982.)

In hiding, including Hidden Children

(47–8, 50) Why more Jews did not flee to the mountains in Greece: "The partisans encouraged them to join their cause; they would have helped them to escape." She mentions the issue of language: "Eighty per cent of the Jewish population spoke Spanish better than Greek. It was only in 1932 that a new law was passed that all Greek children should have compulsory education in the Greek school system for the first six grades. ... Jews could be recognized as non-Christians by their accents and risked being betrayed to the Germans." She mentions the money needed for someone to go into hiding: "Eighty per cent of the Jewish population were poor workers, porters, artisans or small merchants." She mentions the strengh of the family ties.

Righteous Gentiles

(32, 98, 109–11, 143) Some Christian families sought the safety of the Italian Zone of the occupation: "My dearest friend, Ritza Mamouna, left in 1940. They now lived in Athens, but we corresponded frequently and exchanged news." Their correspondance continues even from Auschwitz.

(33–4) July 1942, when the Jewish men are taken to work for the Todt organization: "And we, like all children, continued to play and swim. We were all together, Christian children, Jewish children, all wonderful friends."

(41) February 1943, Jews are required to wear the yellow stars: "The very next day we started wearing our yellow stars, but we went to school as usual. I still remember the love and

tenderness our teachers and our classmates showed us. Nothing had changed, I thought, and our lives would go on, wearing the yellow stars." The Kalamari school.

(42, 141) February 1943, with their move to the ghetto, items of furniture are given to a photographer friend of her father, Mr Melanidis, for safe-keeping: "Mr. Melanidis later returned everything we had entrusted to him in perfect condition."

(43) February 1943, in the ghetto: "How thrilled I felt when my Christian friends came to visit us in the ghetto. It was so kind, so moving, and all our friends came to see us. Some of them came everyday!"

(43) March 1943, with rumours of deportation: "That very day our old neighborhood postman came to see father in our house. I heard him saying to my parents, 'Give me the two children and I will take them to my mother, to the village, just outside Veria. They will be fine there – you must not worry.' And my father's answer, 'No, thank you. Thank you very much, but I don't want my family to be split up.'"

(48) Nineteen families in Thessaloniki were exempt from the restrictions as one spouse was Christian, a law organized by Georgios Papailiakis, and decreed by the head of the military administration, Dr Max Merten. Among these families was that of Samuel Amariglio, his Christian wife, and his three sons, one of whom married Erika after the war.

(59–60, 77, 80) Maria Maul: "... a German Christian imprisoned for political reasons", the *Blockälteste* in Auschwitz Main Camp: "Maria was a kind-hearted woman who always spoke to us in a considerate tone and often she spent the night comforting women who had awakened screaming, because of nightmares."

(73–4) Erika's bed-mate at the infirmary is a Polish political prisoner entitled to receive food parcels: "For a whole week while I was at the 'Revier' she shared her food with me and this helped me to recover even faster." May 1943, Birkenau.

Liberation

(116, 117–18) "One day (12 October 1944) my colleague Willy Pajak from the Auschwitz office came and whispered to me, 'Greece is free! The Germans have left!' This news struck me like a bolt of lightening." And in January 1945: "We constantly heard the thunder of cannons and rumors on the grapevine that the Russians were approaching and would soon free us."

(132) 1 May 1945, Malchov, a slave labour camp associated with Ravensbrück, is evacuated as the prisoners set off on foot: "The cannons sounded closer and closer, and the airplanes never stopped flying overhead, but the Germans, faithful to their duties, did not stop killing prisoners until the last minute. Here and there on the side of the road the SS would light a fire and burn files and folders of documents."

(133) Escape from the death march: "Finally we five Greek women decided to steal away and hide in the woods. The woods were teeming with people in hiding." French prisoners of war find them and take them to an abandoned barn: "They caught three chickens which they brought back triumphantly. Another found a sack of potatoes somewhere. ... for four days and four nights we did not budge from the spot, but ate constantly. After so many weeks of fasting we ate like kings!"

(133–4) On 5 May 1945 the Russians came: "... I heard my mother saying: 'Like Genghis Khan's hordes!' The Russian soldiers, as we heard later, had been given the order: 'Treat the Germans as they behaved in Russia. Burn, pillage and rape!' The prisoners of war who stayed with us in the barn would not let us go out. The Russians, full of hatred and desire to avenge themselves on the Germans, were destroying everything in their way. ... That lasted for twenty-four hours, and then the regular occupation army arrived. We could breathe more freely again … ."

(134–5) Esterina and Erika go out to forage for clothes in the abandoned homes of Germans who had fled the Russian advance for the protection of Allied occupation: "As we left I felt briefly ashamed because of the things we had taken, but our needs were so great that I did not allow myself to think about it."

(137–40) Erika and her mother travel to Belgrade en route home to Greece and stay with one of their Serb friends, Michael Ruszuklic and his family: "… Michael's mother welcomed us as if we were family, well-loved family, too! … They shared everything with us, although they had very little themselves. After a harsh occupation in which they had lost everything, money was scarce, but their hearts were big and their generosity even bigger."

(140–3) Their return to Thessaloniki, to father and brother, to their house, to the past: "I went in search of the houses where my classmates Dorin, May and Rita had lived, but it was as though they no longer existed. Strangers had moved in, and they did not even know who the previous owners were or how their houses had come to be deserted."

Displaced Persons camps

(135–6) "… the Russians settled us in a barrack where there were very many people, camp prisoners as well as prisoners of war." Erika and her mother meet four Serbian officers who invite the women to accompany them to the American Zone to be able to return to Greece.

Stories of individuals, including family members

(xii, 23) September 1939, Erika begins high school at S'china's Girls' School (run by Mrs S'china): "New teachers, new friends: Maria Stangou, Ilectra, Nina Saltiel, Dorin Kovo, May Benrubi, Rita Saltiel and Roula Tari were my best friends." Of her Jewish friends in this group, only Nina Saltiel survived; Dorin Kovo, May Benrubi, and Rita Saltiel were killed.

(24, 25, 26) After an illness of eight months: "On 26 December 1940, my darling, my most beloved grandmother, Theresa, passed away. It was my first experience of death. Why did people die? I could not cope with it. Today, 50 years later, I realize how lucky she was to die in her bed, surrounded by her children."

(40, 68) "Sarika bid us farewell, because they were leaving for Athens to stay with her grandmother." Late autumn, 1942. After finding Sarika in Auschwitz, March 1943: "A few days later I read her name on the list of Block 25, the death block. … I burst into sobs for the first time since our deportation, and the last time for many years."

(50) Erika sees an elderly couple "walking hand-in-hand" from the Baron Hirsch camp to the deportation train: "The grandmother had her shawl wrapped around her shoulders, and with her free hand she was clutching her walking stick. Her eyes, wide, dark eyes, stared right and left, frightened; and they were walking, walking! At a certain moment she turned her head and looked up at her husband. Her look changed, a faint smile appeared on her face and she looked up at him with such tenderness, telling him something. And then I lost sight of them as they disappeared in the crowd."

(52, 53) Little Moschiko on the deportation train: "Moschiko again climbed up on his father's shoulders to peep through the skylight to see where we were."

(52, 66) Esterina, a friend from the deportation train, describes her return to the Birkenau barracks at night: " 'As soon as I was close to the gate, I would raise my head, look straight ahead and try to walk confidently in my ungainly clogs, trying to deceive them so they wouldn't see the big boils on my feet!'" She is transferred to the "Schuh-Kommando" and works on shoes "'under a roof'".

(66) "For a while, Dr. Menashé's daughter played in the orchestra." Birkenau, spring 1943.

(68–9) The fate of Erika's grandfather Ernst Löwy who had been in hiding in Thessaloniki: "He felt so lonely away from his family that one Sunday morning he took all the decorations that he had earned as a Captain during the First World War, along with his diploma and went to the Gestapo." He asked: "'To be sent to where my daughter and her family went.'" He is deported to Auschwitz, as reported to Erika's mother by a woman on his transport: "Full of anguish, mother asked if he had been admitted to the camp. 'No, he was taken away in a truck, I don't know where they took him ... Do you know, Mrs. Kounio, where they took him?'" Mid-May 1943.

(70, 112) Erika tries to help her friend from their transport, Oriko, who is being attacked by an SS woman and her dog: "Suddenly I felt someone holding me back with great force. It was one of my co-workers, a Czechoslovakian girl named Edith Winter. She dragged me back to the offices. If Edith, who immediately grasped what I was about to do, had not been there, I might not be alive today." Birkenau, spring 1943. Edith's death when the camp is bombed, September 1944.

(80, 100) Three of the Polish political prisoners who had been brought to Auschwitz in 1940 and who also worked in the *Todesabteilung*: Wilibald Pajak, who corresponds with Erika after the war: "... according to his letter he became the block secretary in Block 16a in April, 1944." He tells her that Feliks Mylyk, No. 92, died in 1994, and that Marian Gemsky, No. 485, whose name is Jan Gemczyk, was: "... transferred to Buchenwald concentration camp (near Weimar) in 1944 and shot there in January or February 1945 for 'plundering'."

(83) "The camp was again overcrowded, and space had to be freed for the Jews who kept arriving in thousands everyday. ... After one such 'razzia' (police raid) in the women's camp at Birkenau, I found the names of my dear classmates Dorin Kovo and Rita Saltiel while reading the lists."

(83–4, 94) It is arranged for Erika to catch a glimpse of her father as he leaves his block in Auschwitz: "The sight of my father dressed in the striped camp uniform, a cap on his shaved head, looking so thin and haggard with his big eyes, still makes my heart ache, just as it did then. He could not see us."

(92) "One of our Politische Abteilung colleagues from Vienna, Berta, used to say, 'When I get out of here the first thing I will do is eat a schnitzel as big as a water closet cover!' Every time I cook a schnitzel I think of her."

(93) Friends in Auschwitz, Reni from Berlin, two years younger than Erika: "Her job was to wash the SS-personnel's clothes." And Jacqueline from France who worked in the tailor shop: "Jacqueline had five younger siblings, and when they arrived at Birkenau they were immediately sent to the gas chambers, together with her parents. She was often overwhelmed by despair and would cry in a heartrending way when she was depressed. She was a sweet, very intelligent girl with a great sense of humor. Unfortunately I lost touch with her, despite efforts to locate her. After the liberation I immediately got in touch with Reni, though. ... Today she lives in Israel."

(108) 30 June 1944, a transport arrives in Auschwitz with Jews from Corfu and Athens: "We read and examined the Athens file, looking for the name of my father's brother Vital. No, the name of Vital Kounio was not in the Athens file. Great relief. 'Unless he did not enter the camp, but was sent straight to the gas chamber,' said mother."

(120–3, 133–7) Erika and her mother join the evacuation of Auschwitz, and meet three Greek girls, Esterina, Sarah, and Florika, with whom they travel until reaching the American Zone after liberation. Erika and her mother plan to return to Greece: "Esterina, Sarah and Flora did not want to go back, they did not have anybody waiting for them, all their families had perished. They decided to seek a way to reach Palestine."

(131, 149–50) Mrs Cohen from Constantinople and her deck of cards in the camp of Malchov: "... everybody was after her to tell their fortune – they would give her a piece of bread or something else to thank her." April 1945. She tells Erika and her mother that Salvator and Heinz are still alive.

(138) While in Belgrade in the summer of 1945 Erika tries to readapt to life: "I was nineteen, but three years in a concentration camp had not taught me anything that would help me to be a 'charming' girl." She goes out with a group of friends: "One young man from the group sat down next to me and started to ask me about my life in Germany. ... After a while he disappeared and came back carrying a red carnation, which he presented me with! ... I never saw the young man with the carnation again. I do not recollect his name, but I shall never forget him!"

Post-war life and career

(144–6) In Thessaloniki: "My childhood friend and later husband, Rolli Amariglio, gave me much comfort and happiness. He was the first one to visit us after our return, and in the following months we became very good friends." They marry in June 1947. "Our dreams of owning a farm fell through. ... Together with one of his friends he decided to open a shop, the Rodam stationery store, which is still in business today ... ."

(146–8) 1947, Erika's husband is called up to serve in the army during Greece's civil war; Erika runs the shop: "I started doing business with the bank. ... I remember how anxious I was the first time I went there ... Will I manage? I wondered, and before I entered the bank I would pinch my cheeks to hide the pallor caused by my anxiety. At the concentration camp we used to pinch our cheeks before a selection. The camp was always lurking in my subconscious mind."

(150–1) "On 9 April 1951 our son Errikos–Riki, was born. Exactly ten years before, on 9 April 1941, the Germans had entered Thessaloniki. In my mind the past and the present coexist." Their daughter Theresa is born on 4 April 1953.

(151–6) "In 1965 the First International Conference of the Survivors of Auschwitz was held in Warsaw. Together, my mother and I represented the Jewish deportees from Thessaloniki."

Personal reflections

(46) "I remember saying, and hearing other people say: 'So, we shall have to wear a star; it's not so terrible.' And then: 'So, we will have to declare our assets, let this be the worse and nothing else.' 'So we have to move to a smaller house and live with all Jews together; it doesn't matter. It will be good to have all families together.' But the orders came one after another, without giving us time to figure out what was happening."

(47) "The orders fell like the blows of a whip, one after the other. Confused, overwhelmed, terrified the Jews succumbed to their fate. 'After all, they will be together again, wherever they are brought.' Hadn't the rabbi confirmed that they would all be reunited in Cracow? Hadn't they all changed their money to Polish zlotys? 'Let's not make things worse than they are. The main thing is to keep families together!' Optimism and hope always had the upper hand. 'We are going through a bad time, but it will end!'"

(80–1) On her work in the administrative offices in Auschwitz: "How can I understand anybody who believes that all our stories are figments of our imagination? Despite the attempts by the SS to destroy anything they put down in writing, not everything has been lost, and documents are available to everybody who wants to study them, in the Auschwitz museum, in Yad Vashem, and in other archives."

(89, 142) After the war: "The few times I tried to talk about my experiences, I realized that everything I had said was so horrifying that it seemed unbelievable that these terrible things could have happened. People wanted neither to listen to me nor to believe my story."

(134) On German refugees fleeing the Russians to zones controlled by the Allies, early May 1945: "Now it was their turn to carry their babies and drag their children behind them. The bewildered women, hair covered by turban-like kerchiefs, were pushing their carts. In many carts sat ill and elderly relatives wrapped in blankets. They had been sending our people straight to the gas chambers, I thought as I watched a woman bend lovingly over an old man to rearrange a blanket as she pushed the cart. Your turn has come, I thought with immense sorrow."

(155–6) Erika returns to Auschwitz with her mother in 1965, as part of the first International Conference of the Survivors of Auschwitz. She returns to Birkenau: "How quiet. My God, how quiet. But in my ears I could hear the lamenting, the screams of pain, the prayers, the howls of the dogs, the 'barking' of the SS. It was the souls of the dead who were wandering, I told myself … The sun was bright, but I could see shadows everywhere. Shadows of all the people who had perished. I walked along, and there was no mud or snow. My heart felt tighter and tighter. For the first time I could see the gas chambers and the crematoria close-up. It seemed that there were voices crying out of the smokestacks."

Places mentioned in Europe (page first mentioned)

Agia Triada (11), Agii Saranta (25), Ai-Jannis on Pilion (5), Argyrokastron/Gjirokastër (25), Athens/Athina (19), Auschwitz Main Camp/Auschwitz I (62), Austro–Hungarian Empire (2), Axios river (13), Baron Hirsch Transit Camp (Thessaloniki) (44), Baxe (11), Belgium/Belgique (24), Belgrade/Beograd (103), Belsen/Bergen-Belsen concentration camp (143), Berlin (93), Birkenau/Brzezinka/Auschwitz II (61), Buchenwald concentration camp (80), Canada/Kanada (Auschwitz II) (89), Cimarra/Himare (25), Corfu/Kerkira (108), Cracow/Krakow/Krakau (43), Crete/Kriti (37), Czech Republic/Ceska Republic (1), Czechoslovakia (1), Drama (147), Ebensee (148), Elevtherias Square (Thessaloniki) (33), Eptaphyrgion Prison (Thessaloniki) (36), Florina (140), France (24), Geneva/Genève (109), Germany/Deutschland (1), Greece/Ellas (1), Hungary/Magyarország (104), Kapoutsida (30), Karlsbad/Karlovy Vary (1), Katowice/Kattowitz (118), Kavala (147), Kifissia (Athens) (20), Korytsa/Korçë (25), Kozani (150), Leipzig (1), Lodz Ghetto (113), London (England) (39), Lublin (39), Malchow slave labour camp (126), Monastirioton Synagogue (Thessaloniki) (143), Netherlands/Nederland (Holland) (24), Niki (140), Oraiokastro (39), Panorama/ Arsakli (30), Paris (85), Pawiak Prison (Warsaw) (87), Peraia (11), Plasov (122), Poland/Polska (23), Politische Abteilung, "PA", (Birkenau) (61), Prague/Praha (17), Ravensbrück concentration camp (115), Rhodes/Rodos (111), Salonika/Thessaloniki (1), Serres (40), Slovenia/Slovenija (113), Sosnowiec/Sosnowitz (91), Spain/España (153), Switzerland/ Schweiz/Suisse/Swizzeria (109), Tepelene (25), Theresienstadt/Terezin-ghetto/ concentration camp (95), Verria (43), Vienna/Wien (2), Vodzislav/Loslau (122), Warsaw/ Warszawa/Warschau (151), Weimar (80), White Tower (Thessaloniki) (42), Yugoslavia (26)

Places mentioned outside Europe (page first mentioned)

Africa (32), Argentina (152), Australia (152), Brazil (152), Israel/Yisrael (93), Istanbul/Constantinople (131), Palestine (137), Russia/Rossija (32), United States of America (143), Yad Vashem (Israel) (81)

Places mentioned in Erika Kounio Amariglio,
From Thessaloniki to Auschwitz and Back

Malchow Ravensbrück

Warsaw

Bergen-Belsen

Berlin

Lodz

POLAND

Lublin

Leipzig

Buchenwald

Weimar

GERMANY

Katowice Sosnowiec

Loslau

Theresienstadt

Karlsbad Prague

Cracow

Auschwitz

CZECHOSLOVAKIA

Birkenau

Vienna

Ebensee

HUNGARY

SWITZ.

AUSTRIA

Geneva

ROMANIA

FRANCE

LUX.

BELGIUM

HOLLAND

ITALY

Adriatic Sea

YUGOSLAVIA

Belgrade

BULGARIA

ALBANIA

Salonika

GREECE

Athens

| 0 | kilometres | 300 |
| 0 | miles | 200 |

—·—·— International borders, 1937

© **Martin Gilbert**, 2004; for the **HOLOCAUST MEMOIR DIGEST**

Places in Greece mentioned in Erika Kounio Amariglio
From Thessaloniki to Auschwitz and Back

YUGOSLAVIA

BULGARIA

Adriatc Sea

MACEDONIA

River Axios

A L B A N I A

Lake Dojran

Lake Prespan

T H R A C E

• Drama

• Seres

Kavalla

Lake Ochrid

• Niki

Oraiokastro

Florina

Thessaloniki (Salonika)

Koritsa•

• Panorama

• Verria

• Peraia

Tepelene•

Kozani•

Argyrokastron•

Cimarra•

G R E E C E

Aegean Sea

—·— International borders, 1937

0   kilometres   100

CORFU

0   miles   60

© **Martin Gilbert**, 2004; for the **Holocaust Memoir Digest**

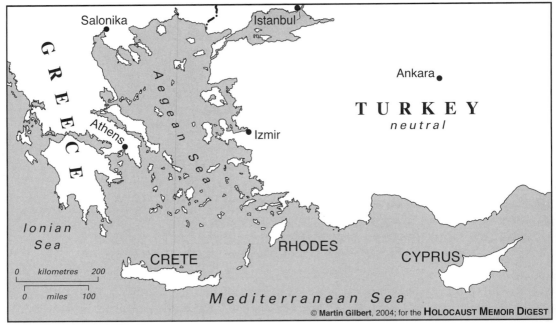

Salonika •

Istanbul •

G R E E C E

Aegean Sea

Ankara •

T U R K E Y
neutral

Athens •

Izmir •

Ionian Sea

RHODES

CYPRUS

0   kilometres   200

CRETE

0   miles   100

M e d i t e r r a n e a n   S e a

© **Martin Gilbert**, 2004; for the **Holocaust Memoir Digest**

"Women were lamenting

and some men took out their prayer books and were quietly singing hymns.

It was dark in the railroad car, and they couldn't see to read,

but they kept their eyes open, they turned the pages,

they knew every line by heart."

Erika Kounio Amariglio

Solomon Gisser, *The Cantor's Voice*

1918: born in Warsaw, moves to Lodz

1926: with older brother, joins a choir, begins singing career

Summer 1931: Bar Mitzvah in Lodz

September 1939: sick in bed during bombing; family remains at home

November 1939: witnesses destruction of Lodz Deutsche Synagogue, where he had sung

January 1940: Lodz Ghetto established

September 1940: organizes and conducts concert for High Holiday services in ghetto soup kitchen

Late 1941: volunteers for a work camp in Germany

Spring to autumn 1942: transferred to Camp Belitz

1942/43: in German work camps Kreutze and Dreetz

May 1943: deported to Auschwitz, sent to Babitz

18 January 1945: death march to Buchenwald, transferred to Ohrdruf, back to Buchenwald

11 April 1945: liberated at Buchenwald by American troops

Summer 1945: travels to Bergen-Belsen, and to Wetzlar in Germany

August 1946: marries, works as a cantor in Mannheim, in Amsterdam, and in Rotterdam

1952: emigrates to Canada

Author: Solomon Gisser

Title: *The Cantor's Voice*

Publishing details Serviceberry Press, Richmond, Virginia, 1997, 141 pages.
ISBN 1-882595-15-7.
Serviceberry Press is a division of New South Architectural Press, Richmond, Virginia and Memphis, Tennessee.
Edited by Dr David A. Patterson.

Focus

Solomon, a young man from a religious and musical family from Lodz (who is 21 in 1939), survives Auschwitz and several slave labour camps and becomes a cantor in Montreal. The events take place between 1918 and 1952.

Features

Author's Acknowledgements, pages 6–7.
Introductory Remarks by the editor, Dr David A. Patterson, pages 8–10.
Final Reflections written by the author, page 141.
About the Author, page 142.
About the Editor, page 143.

Contents (by topic, with page numbers)

Pre-war Jewish home and community life

(11–13) Solomon, born in 1918, to a poor, religious family in Warsaw, the seventh of ten children: "I have no memory of ever having enough food or clothing." The older children help to support the family: "My oldest sister was Rosa. After her came Isaac, Eva, Mordechai, David, Meyer, myself, Hyman … and Sam. Feivel, my youngest brother … ."

(15–16) Worries poor families faced in marrying their daughters: "In those days, if a girl didn't have a dowry, she could rarely expect to get married. Times were very bad, and if a poor boy wanted to marry, his station in life and his ability to rise economically depended upon his wife's dowry. No matter how beautiful the girl was, this was the economic reality, the way it was." Rosa saved her own money and got married; Eva: "… never got married, which was a tragedy for a Jewish girl in those days."

(17–19) Solomon and his brother Meyer develop their singing talent: "When I was eight and he was ten, we decided that we wanted to join a choir." They sing in the Old City Synagogue choir and a man, Zilberschatz, invites them to Nussn Farber's Restaurant for a weekly meal and to listen to cantorial records: "We didn't know whether to regard Zilberschatz as an angel or a human."

(20–1) His Bar Mitzvah, summer 1931, Lodz: "I turned thirteen and was supposed to get a 'maftir aliyah', the last call-up to the Torah. I expected to recite the Haftorah, too. … But these honours apparently were reserved for richer people than my father. … I am a Levi so they gave me the second aliyah, and I was deprived of getting the maftir. … Later that Saturday afternoon, ten boys came over for candy and cake. This was my modest bar mitzvah."

(21–2) He leaves school after his Bar Mitzvah to contribute to the family income, by beginning a "business" of collecting cloth scraps to sell to a tailor: "I didn't regard myself as a merchant selling used scraps of cloth; no, during this time I still had the love of my life, my singing." (24–6) The cantor controversy: "... Simcha Koussevitsky, younger brother of the great cantor Moshe Koussevitsky (no relation to Sergei Koussevitsky of Vilna). ..." auditions in a Lodz synagogue that needs a cantor: "His voice was so beautiful, so gorgeous that the people – even those who didn't want him to be present – listened with awe." But the leadership objects that he doesn't have a beard: "And how awful, how petty it seems in retrospect."

The coming of war

(27–9) 1939, Germany invades Poland: "... the night the Germans came in with their pounding artillery, I was sick with dysentery. Some of the people in our neighbourhood ran out and tried to escape, but my family decided to remain in our rooms because I couldn't get up from bed."

Life under German occupation

(28–9) Solomon and his brother witness the destruction of the Lodz Deutsche Synagogue in the fall of 1939: "It was still a little dark outside, and we watched, both wearing the Star of David on the front and back of our clothing. How sad and desperate we felt, afraid to look left or right. We saw the greatest synagogue, the most beautiful one in Lodz, and one of the most beautiful of synagogues everywhere, as it burned to the ground."

Creation of the ghetto

(30–3) January 1940, the Lodz Ghetto is established: "It was not hard to find a family who would take us in, even though we were three families in one room, a big room with no plumbing. The plumbing and toilets were downstairs in the courtyard. It was gruesome to live like this in the cold Polish winters." Overcrowded, with no food, no fuel for heat, no medical care.

Daily life in the ghetto

(32–3) With his father sick with gallstones and nothing in the house for the family to eat, Solomon appeals to a girl who works for Chaim Rumkowski, the head of the Lodz Jewish Council, for bread: "Right away she went over to her cupboard and cut off a quarter for herself and three quarters for me. ... To this day, I don't know how I ran home so quickly. And everyone in the family got a piece; it was like distributing a million, no, a billion dollars to a poor person." (36–7) Starvation in the ghetto: "More often, in the times that followed, we stood in the regular soup kitchen and waited a whole night to be able to be closer to the door when it opened in the morning. ... Sometimes the stronger ones pushed themselves in, grabbing all the food, leaving us with nothing when we finally reached the head of the distribution lines."

Deportation

(50–1) After a year in the ammunition camp at Dreetz, they are all to be transferred to a "work camp": "Wagons waited for us, and two hundred of us were crowded into the cars, as if we were mere cattle. We traveled all night, not knowing where we were going. We couldn't even ascertain the direction that the train was traveling."

Slave labour camps and factories

(38–40) In return for money promised to the family, Solomon and his brother Meyer volunteer for work in Germany; they are taken to a *Reichsautobahn Lager* in Neutomischel to do highway construction: "The German who was the head of the camp gave us a speech, and by the time he was finished, we knew that we were prisoners, not just volunteers."

(45–6) Camp Kreutze, located next to Camp Bielitz, where conditions are worse: "Because Kreutze was right next to the area where we worked, we sometimes could talk to the people who had been sentenced to live there. ... those unfortunate people worked many hours longer than we did. They were given less food to eat than we received. ... Those people were beaten every single day."

(42–5, 48–9) Camp Dreetz, near Neustadt-on-the-Dosse, where Russian prisoners work underground in an ammunition factory: "Being underground all the time, working with gunpowder, gave them a sickly appearance. Most of them did not last long."

(56–8, 61–8) At Babitz, he is ordered to sing while the labourers work in the fields: "I was singing and the workers were being beaten because they were not fast enough, and the guards were yelling and yelling. It was a symphony that one cannot imagine unless one was there." He is given the job of *Magaziner*, keeping an inventory of rakes and shovels in the storage shed.

(59–60) A Greek man from Salonika is tortured at Babitz because he didn't respond to a German command: "Someone asked the guard, 'How can you do this to a human being? After all, you are human too. And the man didn't understand what you were asking him to do. If he had understood you, he would have listened to you.' The guard looked at him with total disdain. ... And he started beating up the man who had dared to ask the question. ..."

Auschwitz-Birkenau

(51–3) Arrival at Birkenau (Auschwitz II): "Carrying big sticks and aiming them at whomever they wanted, they started beating us with the sticks. We were stunned. We didn't know why. We didn't understand what was happening to us." After one night there, they are marched to the Auschwitz Main Camp. May 1943.

Death marches

(73–4) 18 January 1945, they prepare to leave Auschwitz before the Russian advance: "As we marched out of the camp, we saw a big fire. ... the Nazis were burning documents, burning papers. Burning the evidence of our humiliation."

(74–5) Days of the march, then they are put in open wagons: "There was no water, and no food, so we drank snow."

(86–8) In the face of the British advance, they are marched from Ohrdruf back to Buchenwald: "One SS guard, weary of wearing a heavy knapsack, gave his possessions to an inmate to hold. How could we resist grabbing his rations? As soon as it grew dark, we all shared its contents. When the guard realized how he had been duped, he started yelling, 'Who did I give it to?' We weren't about to tell him."

Concentration camps

(75–7) They arrive in Buchenwald on the death march from Auschwitz: "There were 120,000 inmates squeezed into an unhealthy, filthy area. There were 2,000 men in a barracks that had been built for only 500." Miraculously, he finds his brother Meyer who, upon their arrival in Auschwitz, had been sent to Buna. After a short time together, they are separated again as his brother is sent from Buchenwald to another camp.

(78–81) With the potential of finding food, Solomon is taken with a group the few miles from Buchenwald to the bombed city of Weimar: "The Germans needed inmates to dig out the large holes in the ground where the dead were lying. We were the ones who were sent to perform this gruesome task."

(82–5) Solomon is transferred to Ohrdruf, where he is reunited with his brother, but: "In reality, this was actually the worst camp, the one to be dreaded the most. … Even though they lacked crematoriums, they planned to get rid of us so that we wouldn't be able to tell the Allies what had happened."

(89–91) The last days of confusion, humiliation, and starvation in Buchenwald: "Our hunger did not bring out sympathy in the SS guards. The high-ranking SS Führer stood mocking us."

Witness to mass murder

(46–8) Friend Feder from Lodz accepts the hope offered by the Germans at Dreetz: " 'If you wish to leave the camp to return to where you came from, you must register your names now.' " Those who register are taken in a van: "The Nazis closed the door of this green bus, packing in around ninety people, all of whom had registered. The unfortunate people were gassed five minutes later." Feder's brother, a rabbi in Montreal, inquired about the fate of his brother: "Sometimes it is better for people not to know the truth."

Resistance, ghetto revolts, individual acts of courage and defiance

(34–5) Abraham Brun chants the High Holiday Services in the ghetto in 1940, conducted by Solomon, with a choir chosen from all the previous synagogues. Brun survives the war, emigrates to America. "Our performance was supreme. … The whole ghetto talked about our service for weeks on end."

(40) Camp Bielitz near Frankfurt-on-Oder, at Purim he chants the Megilla by memory for the "two hundred Jews in the camp": "The Megilla reading was one of the rare happy events at that camp. The rest of the time was spent with us in agony, experiencing hardship after hardship."

(53–5) On their second day in Auschwitz, Solomon is separated from his brother Meyer when the men are divided into two columns. Meyer comes over to Solomon's side and is discovered. Solomon appeals to the SS officer: " 'He is my brother and if we are separated, I know I will never see him again. I don't want to be separated from him. I hope you understand.' " Solomon explains: "Too much of me had died already. I knew that we couldn't survive for long in that hell, so rather than be separated, I agreed to be shot." He is spared. His brother is sent to the I. G. Farben Industry camp at Buna-Monowitz, he is sent to work in the nearby agricultural camp of Babitz.

Specific escapes

(40–2) At Camp Belitz, he is saved from a beating by the camp foreman, Weiman: "For some reason, he had changed his mind and walked away from me like a tiger who had lost his hunger and decided not to attack. As he walked away from me without harming me, I was sure I saw the divine hand." Yom Kippur, 1942.

Righteous Gentiles

(63–7) The Oberscharführer of Babitz: "The director was a very intelligent man who knew exactly what he was doing. … He became very friendly with me in a way that was not usual for a high-ranking SS." He protects the men from the evil Kapo, Konrad.

(96) Meyer and Solomon leave Buchenwald for Bergen-Belsen after liberation. They spend their first night in a bed with sheets in a house owned by two sisters: "When we told them where we came from, they started to cry. And they really treated us wonderfully."

Liberation

(92–5) 1945, in Buchenwald: "And so it was at three o'clock in the afternoon, on the eleventh of April, when the first American tank came in. We were finally to be liberated." He spends the next month in hospital fighting typhoid, pneumonia, and severe malnutrition.

(95–8) The two brothers decide to travel west from Buchenwald before the Russian advance. They go to Bergen-Belsen, and then with a group of seven they travel to Wetzlar where they have an introduction to a Mr Neuberger, in the ultra-Orthodox community.

(99–100) While in Wetzlar, they are reunited with two of their brothers, Hyman and Sam, who had been in the Kaufering camp near Dachau, where they had lost another brother, David. They had been convalescing in Landsberg when they heard their two older brothers had survived.

Displaced Persons camps

(109–10, 114) He studies opera in Heidelberg with Richard Schubert. He gives concerts to raise money for Jewish institutions, and sings in DP camps: "I recall giving concerts in Landsberg, Feldafing, Munich, Frankfurt, Stuttgart, and many other places."

Stories of individuals, including family members

(11–12, 130–3) His father, Moshe, born in 1883 to a religious family: "He was shy and quiet, but when he talked, people listened with great interest. For he was a scholarly man." His mother, Sarah Golda Rothenberg, married at 17: "She came from a house of learning, and could speak and write Hebrew well." Her philosophy on the transience of life: "This world of ours is like a corridor. You go through it in order to come to the main dining room."

(12) Aunts and uncles: "My mother had three brothers and one sister. Her father made a livelihood by making cartons. ... My father ... couldn't maintain a family in Warsaw, so he ended up moving to Lodz, where his sister Esther lived. ... Esther was married to a wealthy man who sold dry goods and materials. She was the aunt who saved me from starvation by feeding me, they tell me, large portions of cream of wheat ... ."

(13, 99–100, 124–9, 134–7) The children in the family: Rosa, born 1906, married before the war; Isaac, married, died of typhoid three months after his wedding, his son Isaac, taken during a ghetto selection; Eva, who had no money for a dowry and thus didn't marry; Mordechai, "Motel", married with two children, one who died of starvation in the ghetto; David, born in 1912, died in Kaufering; Meyer, born in 1915, survived with Solomon, a painter, died in Montreal; Solomon, born 1918; Hyman and Sam, who remain in the Lodz Ghetto until its liquidation in 1944, sent to Birkenau and then Kaufering, liberated at Landsburg, reunited with Solomon and Meyer in Wetzlar, Hyman became a cantor in Montreal, Sam a businessman; the youngest sibling Feivel: "... came to Auschwitz and unfortunately was taken to the crematorium."

(14) No money available for food or books, yet Rosa, 12 years older than Solomon, helps to support the family: "My oldest sister was a brilliant student despite these hardships. But she had to leave school to go to work when she was about fifteen or sixteen. She learned bookkeeping. ... Eventually, she became a bookkeeper for the entire Lodz Ghetto."

(15–16) "My mother's brother, Chaim Yudel, was a kind of show-off who manufactured paper boxes for a living." He wins money in a lottery: "And because he was a very good-natured man, he helped us out."

(23) Solomon's music student Sturma, who returns to Bialystok from Lodz: "... I heard later that the Nazis had killed her."

(43–5) At Camp Dreetz, the starvation is so great that one boy eats mushrooms: "'The heck with it; I'll take a chance and eat them.' The boy died the same night ... ." Another boy takes an opportunity to steal rotten soup: "How sad it was that this poor boy thought he was lucky but was shot to death over a bowl of sour soup that had probably been sitting for a week in the sun."

(67, 87–8) Millstein, a friend at Babitz who shares his bread on the death march back to Buchenwald: "Was this not a gift from heaven? It was only a tiny piece … . But it was a piece of sustenance, just a little bit to keep us going. It gave us strength and a little optimism … ."

(69–72) At Babitz, a Russian prisoner of war, caught trying to escape, is beaten almost to death. After the guards leave, he manages to find a way to cut his own throat: "He had the courage to pick up the scythe, to pick himself up from the ropes, and to get up and cut his throat." Another Russian prisoner tries to escape by hiding in a barn hayloft; he is discovered by the SS: "They brutally led him to a little window very high up. They threw him out of the window and he was killed instantly, mercilessly."

(76) Yankel Gebrovitch from Radom, finds him in Buchenwald, reunites him with his brother Meyer.

(94) A Hungarian named Mermelstein convalesces in the hospital with him in Buchenwald: "We thought he was dead but the doctors knew better."

(104–5, 138–9) Anna, his wife, born in Cracow in July 1925, the only survivor of her immediate family of five. She had been hidden by a Polish family, was betrayed, tortured, and liberated at a camp, Braunschweig. They are married in August 1946.

(108) Friend at his wedding, Benzion Gold, helps him get established after Solomon's wedding. He later becomes the director of Hillel at Harvard.

(111–13) Their daughter Helen is born, prematurely, in 1947 in Giessen, Germany: "Helen is named after my grandmother, my mother's mother. … I was afraid to name her after one of my parents, because in truth I still wasn't sure that my parents were dead. With that little bit of doubt and hope still remaining, I didn't want to give her a name for someone who might still have been alive. In Hebrew she is Chaya Rasha. 'Chaya' usually is associated with life."

(116) His arrival in Amsterdam to become a cantor there: "Among the people who greeted me that day was Anne Frank's father, Otto Frank. He was to become my best friend in that city. He would come every Friday night to have dinner with us."

(124–5) His son David is born in Montreal, 1952: "We named the baby David after my own brother. I knew that he had died because he had entered the concentration camp with my two other brothers. They knew that he had passed away one night. His name had been Zvi David."

(140) Friend Morris Goldlust teaches Solomon and Meyer how to get extra soup at Babitz; he becomes a successful businessman in Toronto: "And whenever we meet, I remind him that I owe my life to him. … Having a little extra soup in those days could mean the difference between life and death."

Post-war life and career

(101–3) Solomon takes a position as a cantor in newly re-established synagogues in Mannheim and Heidelberg; he returns to Wetzlar to meet Anna: "To make the story short, I came home and I liked her very much."

(106–7) Their wedding with his congregation in Mannheim: "Unfortunately, during the whole wedding ceremony, under the canopy, both Anna and I were crying, and not a person could stop us. She cried because she didn't have anyone. No one in the world. I cried because I didn't have all of us. My parents and the rest of my family were gone."

(115–23) 1949. Solomon and Anna decide to leave Germany, and he takes a position in a synagogue in Amsterdam, for two years, and then in Rotterdam through the 1951 High Holidays. They decide to emigrate, with his three brothers, to Canada. They go to Montreal, where he is invited to become the cantor of the Shaare Zion Congregation, where he remains until his retirement in 1997.

Personal reflections

(141) "It is usual that you make the small decisions, but the big decisions somehow are made for you and are out of your control. These decisions seem to come from God. Everything works out in a different way than you had expected."

Places mentioned in Europe (page first mentioned)

Aachen (116), Amsterdam (115), Auschwitz Main Camp/Auschwitz I (13), Babice/Babitz slave labour camp (55), Bavaria/Bayern (100), Belitz slave labour camp (40), Belsen/Bergen-Belsen concentration camp (96), Berlin (42), Bialystok (23), Birkenau/Brzezinka/Auschwitz II (51), Braunschweig/Brunswick (105), Bremen (121), Buchenwald concentration camp (75), Budapest (62), Buna-Monowitz/Monowice/Auschwitz III (55), Cracow/Krakow/Krakau (104), Dachau concentration camp (99), Dillenburg (97), Dreetz slave labour camp (48), Feldafing Displaced Persons camp (114), France (39), Frankfurt-on-Main (97), Frankfurt-on-Oder (40), Germany/Deutschland (38), Giessen (111), Hanover/Hannover (105), Heidelberg (102), Holland/Nederland (117), I. G. Farben Industries (Buna-Monowitz) (55), Kaufering slave labour camp (99), Kreutze slave labour camp (45), Landsberg Displaced Persons camp (100), Lodz Ghetto (29), Lodz/Litzmanstadt (12), Mannheim (102), Munich/München (100), Neustadt-an-die-Dosse (42), Neutomischel/Nowy Tomysl (39), Ohrdruf concentration camp (83), Poland/Polska (11), Radom (11), Rotterdam (118), Salonika/Thessaloniki (59), Sighet/Maramarossziget/Sighetul Marmatiei (62), Stuttgart (114), Treblinka death camp (128), Umschlagplatz (Lodz) (39), Upper Silesia/Oberschlesien (39), Vilna/Wilno/Vilnius (25), Warsaw/Warszawa/Warschau (11), Weimar (78), Wetzlar (97), Wiesbaden (110)

Places mentioned outside Europe (page first mentioned)

Canada (93), Halifax (Nova Scotia) (121), Israel/Yisrael (138), Long Beach (New York) (34), Montreal (35), Outremont (Montreal) (122), Persia (40), Sinai (52), Toronto (140), United States of America (13)

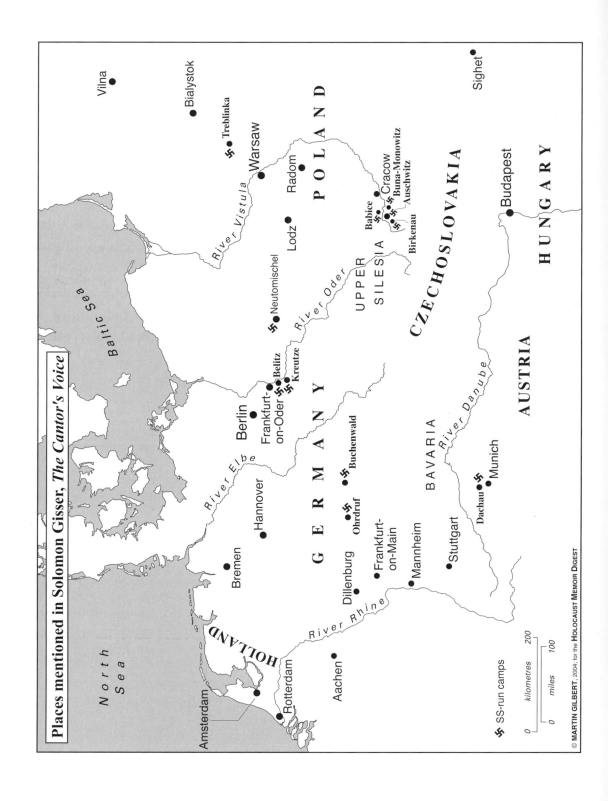

Places mentioned in Solomon Gisser, *The Cantor's Voice*

Vilna

Bialystok

Treblinka

Warsaw

Radom

Lodz

Sighet

POLAND

Cracow

Buna-Monowitz

Auschwitz

Babice

Birkenau

UPPER SILESIA

Budapest

HUNGARY

CZECHOSLOVAKIA

Neutomischel

River Vistula

River Oder

Berlin

Belitz

Kreutze

Frankfurt-on-Oder

River Elbe

Baltic Sea

Hannover

Bremen

G E R M A N Y

Buchenwald

Ohrdruf

AUSTRIA

River Danube

BAVARIA

Munich

Dachau

Stuttgart

Mannheim

Frankfurt-on-Main

Dillenburg

River Rhine

HOLLAND

Rotterdam

Amsterdam

Aachen

North Sea

卐 SS-run camps

0 kilometres 200

0 miles 100

© **MARTIN GILBERT**, 2004; for the HOLOCAUST MEMOIR DIGEST

Places in Germany mentioned in Solomon Gisser, *The Cantor's Voice*

Baltic Sea

North Sea

HOLLAND

Bremen

River Elbe

Neustadt-an-die-Dosse

River Dosse

River Oder

Bergen-Belsen

Dreetz

Hannover

Braunschweig

Berlin

Frankfurt-on-Oder

GERMANY

River Elbe

Aachen

Weimar

Buchenwald

Dillenburg

Wetzlar

Giessen

Ohrdruf

River Rhine

Frankfurt-on-Main

LUX.

Wiesbaden

River Main

CZECHOSLOVAKIA

Mannheim

Heidelberg

FRANCE

River Rhine

Stuttgart

River Danube

Kaufering

Landsberg

Dachau

Munich

Feldafing

Bodensee
Lake Constance

SWITZERLAND

AUSTRIA

0   kilometres   50

0   miles   30

© **MARTIN GILBERT**, 2004; for the **HOLOCAUST MEMOIR DIGEST**

Samuel Bak, *Painted in Words*

---

12 August 1933: born in Vilna

Autumn 1938: begins at a Yiddish school as a result of an anti-Semitic incident

Autumn 1939 to autumn 1940: refugees from Warsaw stay *en route* to east

June 1940 to June 1941: Soviet occupation

22 June 1941: Germany invades Soviet Union

6 –7 September 1941: moves to the Ghetto for one night

September 1941: hides at the Benedictine Convent at St Catherine's Church

Early 1942: escapes from the convent after it has been raided

1942 to September 1943: in the Vilna ghetto

8 March to 4 April 1943: contributes to an art exhibition in the Ghetto

23 September 1943 to March 1944: at the HKP slave labour camp, Vilna

27 March 1944: survives children's *Aktion* in hiding, HKP camp

April to July 1944: returns to Benedictine Convent and is hidden there

7 July 1944: liberated by Soviet Army in Vilna

Summer 1944 to summer 1945: under the Soviets in Vilna

October 1945: escapes from Soviet-ruled Lithuania, travels to Lodz in Poland

Late 1945 to 1948: in Landsberg Displaced Persons camp, Germany

Autumn 1948: moves to Israel, eventually settling in America

Author: Samuel Bak

Title: *Painted in Words – A Memoir*

Publishing details Indiana University Press, Bloomington and Indianapolis, 2001, 495 pages.
ISBN 0-253-34048-0.
Published in conjunction with Pucker Art Publications, Boston, Massachusetts.
Samuel Bak describes the lives of his family from the mid-1800s through his life to the present. He also writes of the development of and symbolism in his art. For the purpose of the *Digest*, this summary focuses on his Holocaust experiences.

Focus

Samuel, a child artist (who is 6 years old in 1939) survives in Vilna with his mother, escapes to the West and goes to Israel, eventually settling in the United States.

Features

Foreword, written by Amos Oz: "Painted in Words, Narrated in Colors and Light", pages vii–ix.
Author's Note, page xi.
Family photographs, and photographs of sites in present-day Vilnius.
Colour reproductions of some of Mr Bak's paintings.
Afterwords, written by the author, pages 497–8.
A Postscript, written by the author, pages 498–500.
Works cited: Janusz Korczak, *King Matt the First*, first published in Polish in 1923, in English in 1986, referred to on page 60.
Yitzhak Arad, *Ghetto in Flames* (1980), referred to on pages 311–12.
Ilya Ehrenberg and Vasili Grossman, *Black Book* (1946, banned by the Soviets and the proofs destroyed; one volume published in Bucharest in 1947; restored edition published in English, 1993) referred to on page 367. In 2002 a new edition, *The Complete Black Book of Russian Jewry*, translated and edited by David Patterson, Transaction Publishers, New Brunswick, NJ.

Contents (by topic, with page numbers)

Pre-war Jewish home and community life

(125–9, 247) Samuel's birth 12 August 1933, to Jonas and Mitzia: "'Bak' was the family name that Father received from his parents and 'Samuel' the name of Mother's grandfather who died a few days before I was born." His understanding of the meaning of the name Bak: "… from the times of the infamous Chmielnicki. Horrendous pogroms perpetrated by his Ukrainian Cossacks in 1648 decimated entire Jewish villages. Some of the children remained miraculously alive in the rubble of their burned families and houses. Since then those children and their descendants have been called Beney-Kedoshim, in its abbreviated form: Bak." ("Children of Martyrs").
(130–1) Vilna, where Jews: "… made up more than a third of the general population. … The city had always been known for its learned rabbis and its yeshivas, but in the nineteenth century there began to emerge a number of secular leaders. Some advocated assimilation. Others were Zionists … . Their antagonists were the Yiddishists. … Whether religious, Zionist, or socialist they found in Vilna a fertile ground."

(131–43, 162–6, 168, 173–92) Jonas Bak's parents: their youth, their marriage, their life and the lives of their children: "Chayim was born in the 1870s, a son of a family of wood merchants. Early in life he married Grandmother Rachel and fathered two sons and a daughter, David and much later my father and Aunt Tsilla." Samuel's memories of childhood visits in his grandparents' home.

(146–50) Samuel wakes his parents in the middle of the night: "… a collapse of the chimney's ashes had caused the bedroom stove to emit a very dangerous gas that had almost killed us. If it hadn't been for my throwing up the forbidden cake, all three of us might well have been found sleeping forever, forever. … Grandmother Shifra donated a lot of money to the local synagogue to have some poor Jews say prayers and study the holy scriptures on our behalf."

(147, 154–5, 195–203) Xenia the housekeeper, who takes Samuel every week to visit his grandparents, Chayim and Rachel Bak: "Mother had warned me that the housekeeper's explanations were to be taken with the utmost reserve. But I was only five. Perhaps even today some of the housekeeper's popular beliefs, prejudices, and certitudes remain deposited under layers of old varnish in some forgotten place in my soul."

(159–62) Grandmother Rachel and her daughter-in-law, Samuel's mother Mitzia, disagree on the appropriate length of his pants. Each of his weekly visits to his grandparent's involves Rachel lengthening his pants. His mother's response: "Her diligent hands regularly unstitched Grandmother's work and Rachel, well aware of the disrespect to her opinion, passed to an offensive mode by making my pants increasingly longer and with totally incongruous textures, colors, and prints. The two women must have seen in me a neutral ground for pursuing their ongoing battle. … Father would not react. At most he would reply 'You know my mother,' which meant nothing, or maybe everything."

(172, 287–8, 291, 305, 433–4) On Judaism: "Occasionally our Jewish God becomes a subject of conversation between my two pairs of grandparents. … usually provoked by my questions. … Every child knows that in order to retain pleasant relationships one must avoid certain subjects or raise them only when some shouting and yelling would make everyone feel better."

(207–15) Samuel's memories of his father: "He loved playing games. … And I never knew where his fun ended and the seriousness began. He used to utter the most outlandish stuff with the coolest of expressions, and he often baffled me."

(233–9) Mitzia's father's father Shmuel Yochel, married at his Bar Mitzvah to escape being taken into the Czarist army: "He lived till his early nineties … According to Mother's calculations . . . the number of his children reached twenty-five. … Shmuel was widowed three times, and his last daughter was conceived when he was seventy-two."

(239–40, 253–78) Mitzia's parents: Khone Yochel, Shmuel's son, apprenticed to Isaac Nadel in Vilna, marries Isaac and Yentl's daughter Shifra. Shifra's reaction to the proposal: "What had … made her able to cope all those years with her numbing chores had been the hope that one day she would depart. Depart from the stale reality of her parents' home, the blind father and the unloved mother. This could only have been achieved by uniting herself in marriage to someone far away. … Why didn't they search farther than the four walls of home?" Shifra's marriage to Khone, her four children Mitzia, Yetta, Rakhmiel, and Izia. Of his grandmother Shifra: "Few people have ever conveyed to me such a feeling of protection and shelter."

(240–6) Khone's sister Hanna accompanies her brother to Vilna, is apprenticed to a baker and adopted by the Polish governess of an ancient Polish family, but must renounce her family and heritage. She is baptized, becomes Janina, and is educated at a school associated with the Benedictine Convent. She marries a Polish chemical engineer, and eventually returns to her family and is accepted by her father Shmuel: "'God will always take care of you. His ways are a mystery to us, a mystery, but you are welcome in your coming and in your going, and I bless you.'"

(251–3) Shifra and Rachel, dear friends, had tried to interest their children in each other: "However by 1930 it was too late for parental matchmaking; the world had grown 'modern'. … Jonas and Mitzia … were always convinced that their decision to marry was their own."

(287–8, 292–8) "For me, in the beginning the world was created in Polish … ." Samuel attends a Yiddish kindergarten, falls in love with a little girl: "Since the object of my love was fluent in Polish but sometimes spoke to me in Yiddish, I began gradually to absorb the new language."

Pre-war anti-Semitism

(157) In 1920, Jonas, at 12 or 13, had beaten up two Christian boys, and locked them in the coal cellar: "They had dared to call him 'dirty Jew' and he had dared to teach them a lesson. … Father finally liberated them – in the presence of his own father, the boys' distraught mothers, and a local policeman …." Grandfather Chayim recalls: "'We were lucky that a small bundle of cash, intended to compensate the families but gone astray in the official's pocket, settled the affair. The policeman was very kind and understanding.'"

(288–91) Samuel, age 5, is spat upon in the street while returning from kindergarten with his mother: "'Zjid! Filthy kike!'" As a result, his parents transfer him to a Yiddish school: "Because my face had been spat on, I had to understand the why of it, to realize what it meant to be a Jew. I had to acquire our language and culture. … His nasty impulse was my 'existentialist' experience. I was made into a Jew by the act of the 'other'." 1938.

The coming of war

(224–7, 315) Fleeing the German occupation of Western Poland, acquaintances of Samuel's father from Warsaw stay with them en route to safety: "They knew Father had a way of creating dental prostheses that contained double bottoms or hollow crowns capable of hiding diamonds. By such means they might hope to carry their valuables past border controls. … In our home every bed, sofa, and empty space that could hold a mattress was offered as temporary lodging to the unlucky refugees, or rather those lucky individuals who had so far succeeded in escaping the Nazi boot." Autumn 1939 to autumn 1940.

(248–9, 279–80, 317) Vilna is within the area annexed by the Soviet Union: "A Russian general confiscated the Jewish middle-class apartment …." of grandparents Khone and Shifra, who move in with Chayim and Rachel, June 1940: "I remember the year of the Soviet occupation, between June 1940 and June 1941, as a time of relative happiness for me. How even closer to each other my two sets of grandparents grew to be, living now in the same flat. And how available in their patience for my little person they became during this interval." Samuel is 7.

(309–16) The Soviet era, 1940: "Distressing news about the increase of 'actions' against Jews in the countries controlled by the Nazis started to spread among the adults and greatly affected the general mood. There was more and more talk of emigration, but such a solution required a lot of courage and a lot of means. … few of those who still lived in the comfort of their homes and still had their worldly goods tried to move. The tribal ties that traditionally kept Jewish families together did not encourage individual departures. And the stress of uncertainty about our future only reinforced the power of such ties."

(317–19) With the Soviet annexation of Vilna, a Soviet colonel moves in with them: "He was much younger than we anticipated, better educated, and very accommodating. … Yet, for our housekeeper's fanatic nature the Soviet officer was a sworn enemy. Only her own person was the rightful representative of the true Russian soul." He stays only until the autumn.

(319–24) "... my first day in a Socialist grammar school had arrived. The school was to teach me Yiddish and Russian and introduce me to the Lithuanian language." The teacher tells the story of a little girl, lost: "'Do not worry about me, dear citizens,' said the little girl; 'Whenever I see the picture of Comrade Stalin I know where I am, and I know that I am being protected. He is a father who loves me even more than my parents do. Now I am safe' ... ." Mitzia takes Samuel out of school and teaches him at home, Autumn 1940.

(325–6) "In the streets of Vilna, at ten o'clock in the morning on Sunday, June 22, the sirens started to sound. The German forces had attacked the Soviet Union. ... Thousands of panicking and disoriented Jews, aware of what the hordes of Nazis were going to bring, were trying to follow in the steps of the Red Army's retreat and find refuge in Russia's mainland." Two of his father's friends offer to take them along: "We had five minutes to pack one small suitcase for the three of us, wear on ourselves anything else we hoped to save, and join them in their vehicle." Samuel's parents decide not to leave.

Life under German occupation

(216–19, 327) Two months after the Germans enter Vilna, Samuel's father had been taken to a slave labour camp, radios confiscated, telephones diconnected, and hunger had set in: "Vilna was hungry, and those providers who passed the various military roadblocks with their merchandise and managed to save them from confiscation expected a very lucrative barter." Xenia finds a farmer who trades his sack of potatoes for father's tuxedo. Summer 1941.

(227–9) Jonas converts their assets to gold, which he hides in the plaster casts of his dental patients. Later they are expelled from their house, and eventually hear that the last remnants of their belongings were taken to the dump: "Who knows if anyone ever checked the contents of those 'white mouths'? I hope they did not. I prefer to imagine the plaster casts reaching their final destination intact, lying in the fraternal mass graves of discards and debris with all their multiheaded eagles and gold ingots safely hidden inside."

(304–5) Betrayals: "The Lithuanian thugs were being paid ten rubles for every Jew delivered to the Germans. Busy fighting the Russians, the Germans badly needed volunteers ...."

Creation of the ghetto

(203–4, 229, 282–3) As they are forced out of their home for the ghetto, Samuel wonders of Xenia: "The looting of Jewish belongings was common. I am sure that she was joined in this by the janitor and by some of the neighbors who had been waiting patiently for their share. Compared to the loss of the lives of our dear ones, the dispossession and the dispersion of material belongings seemed to us trivial." 6, 7 September 1941.

(290, 327–31) "... a few Lithuanian policemen with guns and clubs in their hands arrived in our courtyard. ... while the older one was interrogating Mother about the number of persons present and ordering her to take whatever we were able to carry and quickly descend to the building's courtyard, the younger turned around and nonchalantly touched with his menacingly outstretched club whatever object he fancied." Samuel and his mother join the others and walk in the pouring rain to the ghetto. 6, 7 September 1941.

(331–4) Samuel and his mother spend one night in the newly formed ghetto, in an apartment: "It was now occupied by two dozen people, like us freshly ejected. ... There was sitting room only. Air was scarce and pervaded by the smell of drying shoes and wet wool." In the morning, Samuel and his mother find a way out of the ghetto through a delivery entrance.

Daily life in the ghetto

(40, 47) "Most ghetto policemen and executives of the ghetto administration provided themselves and their families and friends with better conditions … that granted the chance to live a bit longer. … Our double standards sadden me. I know that many 'kapos' … were no more vicious than today's men of power, whom society greatly admires. Doesn't the struggle for survival in extreme conditions merit a more generous understanding?"

(347) Their time in the ghetto after having escaped from the Benedictine Convent in early 1942, until the ghetto's liquidation, September 1943: "Mother became employed in the accounting offices of the Judenrat. Father was sent to work in a welding unit on the outside."

Deportation

(6, 21–2, 24–5) Deportation from the Vilna Ghetto by truck to the HKP camp; Samuel carries the "Pinkas" hidden under his coat: "… it is dear to me not so much for what I have already put into it as for the space that it still provides." The truck is loaded: "Crowded to the maximum, piled up against each other, we look like a compact accumulation of human spare parts." September 1943. (HKP stands for *Heeres Kraftfahrpark*, military vehicle repairs.)

Mass murder sites

(59–60) An art exhibit in the Vilna Ghetto, 28 March to 4 April 1943: "On the eve of the show's opening, several German trucks unloaded hundreds of people from a nearby defunct ghetto and dumped them in the raw paving-stones of the Judenrat's large courtyard. … A myriad of yellow stars sewn on their clothing helped to distinguish living matter from inanimate objects. … Later we learned that they got no further than Vilna's notorious suburb Ponar, where they were met with machine guns. … But their poor belongings, stained with blood and torn by bullets, were sent back to the ghetto for further use."

(248–51, 281) Samuel visits Aunt Yetta, Uncle Yasha, and Tamara, in the village of Ponar, early summer, 1941: "The neighbors told us that the Red Army was digging huge trenches for an underground fuel depot. … After the Red Army retreated and the Germans arrived, the woods of Ponar became a place of executions; and the deep-dug Russian holes meant for fuel became mass graves of Vilna Jews and the Jews of many neighboring towns. … My two grandfathers, Khone and Chayim … were arrested … and then shot. Several months later, on Yom Kippur 1941, my two grandmothers, Shifra and Rachel, were brought … to Ponar and shot with thousands of others."

Slave labour camps and factories

(19–20) 23 September 1943: the Vilna Ghetto is cleared of: "… most of the ghetto's nineteen thousand inhabitants … my parents and I were among the two thousand prisoners retained in two Vilna labor camps, Kailis and HKP. … The HKP labor camp, created on the eve of the ghetto's liquidation, was to hold me until March 1944."

(34–6) Arrival at the HKP camp, Samuel and his mother reunite with his father: "We are given round metal tags to be worn around the neck. Each one bears a hammered number. The number substitutes for our name and must therefore be hammered into our memory. These metal tags as well as the yellow stars on the front and back of our clothing must be visible at all times."

(47–8) Bedbugs in their straw mattresses, which are periodically "de-bugged": "The war between Jews and bedbugs is one thing and the war of Germans against Jews another. Both are constant features of the camp's life. There may be brief lulls, but these never last long."

(51–3) A father, mother, and teenage son escape from the HKP camp, but are found and returned to the camp where they are tortured and hanged: "… several prisoners whose identity tag numbers were close to those of the fugitives were selected and immediately taken to be shot. … It was obvious that anyone who dared to flee automatically condemned to death those with identity numbers close to his. Very few would have taken it on themselves to buy their freedom with other people's lives. Similarly no prisoner wanted to sacrifice his life for someone else's attempt to escape."

Witness to mass murder

(6, 73–7) 27 March 1944, the children are rounded up from the HKP camp and taken away in trucks: "The sobs of the children fade with the rattle of departing trucks, and the sound of retreating army boots leaves behind a silence of death. … A mounting sound of moaning grows in crescendo and turns to a fortissimo of wailing cries, a chorale of hundreds of bereaved parents." Samuel is hidden with two other children; later they hear that: "Several mothers who clung to their children were taken away on the first of the trucks. Others, who opposed the soldiers were gunned down."

(178) Samuel refers to a post-war account of Jewish prisoners, and the fate of Jews who are: "… taken by force to Ponar and turned into dead bodies dumped in a pile. The sheer weight of cadavers will flatten them into an anonymous similarity. The Nazis will call them 'figuren' and will force Jewish prisoners, in leg-irons, to dig them out and burn them, transforming their remains into smoke and ashes. The dead will achieve a degree of equality that does not exist in the most egalitarian of societies."

(377) After the war, Samuel renews his friendship with the poets Avrom Sutzkever and Shmerke Kaczerginski: "Shmerke used to interview various survivors, scrupulously transcribing their oral testimonies. He worked on these texts for endless hours. Sutzkever too wrote and wrote. … With the end of the war he was invited to bear witness in one of the Nuremberg trials."

Resistance, ghetto revolts, individual acts of courage and defiance

(5–7, 28) Yiddish poets of the Vilna Ghetto, Avrom Sutzkever and Schmerke Kaczerginski, give the 9-year-old Samuel the *Pinkas*, a book that contained a century of records of the Vilna Jewish community, in order for him to record the destruction of the ghetto and its community: "I was happy to add my childish drawings to its yellowing pages if for no other reason than that sheets of paper had become very scarce. Thus we became constant companions." 1942 to March 1944.

(22–4) In the ghetto, Samuel had sculpted a clay Moses, based on a postcard of Michelangelo's *Moses* that he had found. The sculpture was presented to Jacob Gens, head of the Jewish Council. As the ghetto is being liquidated, Samuel wonders: "Recently I heard a rumor that the Germans have killed Gens. What now will become of my Moses?"

(26, 29–31, 470) Samuel's teacher in the ghetto, Rokhele Sarovski: "She taught me Yiddish and Polish spelling, arithmetic, and much else. I especially loved geography because it permitted me to travel beyond the narrow boundaries of the ghetto. She refused any payment for her time and devotion." She introduces Samuel to the two poets, with whom she shares a room.

(28–9, 55–6, 58–9) Art in the ghetto: "Genuine artists tried in the bleakest of times to reassure themselves of their humanity and give value to their existence. In this way art could grant the spirit an escape that the body's imprisonment categorically forbade. … performances of theater, music, choral singing, and readings of poetry began to attract large audiences. An exhibition of paintings by the most prominent of the still surviving artists was planned. ... my drawings were to be a significant part of its display." April 1943.

(49) At the HKP slave labour camp, where the men worked to convert gasoline-fuelled engines to wood-burning, Samuel describes a noon-hour "frenzy": "With one of the Jewish laborers on guard ... the others cut, dismantled, and unscrewed certain parts ... and immediately reattached them by a very superficial welding. The work had to pass the scrutiny of a very rigorous control, and at the same time break down a few days after the truck's new assignment to an army unit. ... I'm not sure these activities influenced or modified the ultimate outcome of the war, but though modest, this contribution of the HKP men to the allied war effort was immensely courageous."

(50–1) Samuel's parents' work at the HKP camp: his father first as a welder, then as dental assistant to the camp's doctor: "He used the utensils to melt metal and make plausible imitations of gold coins. ... At times a coin that looked like gold, extracted at the right moment from one's pocket, could create a miracle. ... Whatever looked like gold could increase some people's willingness to take risks." His mother's job is with the women, cleaning and repairing the bloodied and torn uniforms, to prepare them for the next round of German soldiers, they: "... did it with malicious pleasure, hoping the uniforms would soon return with fresh holes and new bloodstains."

(54–8) An artist from the Vilna Ghetto paints signs in the HKP camp, and portraits for the Germans: "'I spend my time painting families that I can curse as much as I like. When the oil dries, I can even spit in their faces and wipe it off.'" Late autumn 1942.

(347) Samuel refers to: "... the night in which the ghetto was ordered to deliver unto the hands of his executioners the partisan Vittenberg ...." 1943. (Itsik Vitenberg was leader of the "Fareynigte Partizaner Organizatsie" the "FPO" or United Partisan Organization of the Ghetto.)

Partisan activity

(26–7) Sutzkever and Kaczerginski escape the ghetto and join the partisans in the forest: "All partisans are supposed to fight the Germans, but some fight each other. It is widely known that many Polish partisans hate Jewish partisans and try to finish off any Jews the Germans may have missed."

Specific escapes

(5–8, 11–14, 21–2, 87–90, 488–9, 492–4) The survival and rediscovery of the *Pinkas* by the curator of the National Historical Museum of Lithuania in the 1990s: "The document was an ancient, Jewish, leather-bound manuscript, and it contained modern drawings. She knew that I was their author."

(17, 84–8, 215, 220) After hiding in the camp, Samuel is to be smuggled outside: "Father's face is very tense. I know that he whispers into my ear important matters but I can hardly hear his voice. My heart is pounding. Something that sounds like a waterfall is resounding in my ears. My gaze tries to be focused on his moving lips. Will I ever see him again?" Samuel is carried in a burlap sack on his father's back to where he can escape. A woman delivers him to Aunt Janina and his mother. Late March 1944; Samuel is not yet 11.

(22, 30, 341–6) The sisters of the Benedictine Convent hiding the Baks are accused of helping the Soviet Forces; the convent is raided: "Later we learned that the sisters were evacuated with amazing brutality and sent off to a labor camp." The group of hiding Jews escapes through the attic: "Ironically we had to seek refuge in the ghetto as a place of last resort."

(60–3) As a child in an adult world, Samuel writes of wanting to be invisible, like Janusz Korczak's character Matthew: "Matthew knew how to become invisible. He was capable of observing others totally undisturbed and of escaping from the most dangerous predicaments. To paint the invisible was quite a challenge."

(78–9) Samuel's hiding place is not discovered during the round-up of the children on 27 March 1944 at the HKP camp, as his father relates: "'The Germans who came to check this corridor were of the local unit. Luckily they vaguely know me. When one of them came near the stuff piled up against the door it was clear that he was going to find you. I pulled from my coat's lining one of the gilded rubles and pushed it quickly into his hand. He closed his fingers, let it drop into his pocket, and called out to his companion that everything was all right, and suddenly both were gone.'"

In hiding, including Hidden Children

(77–83) After the children's *Aktion* in the camp, Samuel is hidden in his parents' bunk while his mother tries to find a hiding place outside the camp: "I must keep myself from falling asleep. Sleep would take away the control over immobility. Immobility is indispensable. But in my head thoughts run wild. Again an unknown fear takes hold of me. … I am so scared of being discovered by the parents of my friends who were torn away that I fear the Jews more than I fear the Germans. … The horror that can be expected from the Germans does not come as a surprise, but what about my own people, the people I am supposed to trust? I feel guilty for having escaped the fate of those other children."

(84, 87, 303–4, 402) Samuel, who had been baptized by Janina as "Zygmunt", prepares to hide as a Christian; Father's reminder as Samuel leaves the camp: "'Don't forget to show Aunt Janina that you remember the prayers.'"

(219–20) Summer 1941 at home: "… I had been cautioned about the way times were changing. I was also told that in spite of the troubling nature of events, I was to be informed of everything as if I were a young adult. It was dangerous to remain a child. I had to grow up quickly. I tried my best, but the mind of a boy of eight had its limitations."

(299–301, 304, 306) Samek Epstein, Samuel's friend, and the son of his parent's friends Mania and Lola, is hidden in the cupboard of the Epstein's maid: "… a loyal and a decent person. … She did her best to be very discreet, very secretive. But somebody in the neighborhood denounced her. They found the boy and arrested the woman. … The Lithuanian police dragged a crying Samek to the courtyard, shot him, and left him lying in a pool of blood." 1941, Samek is 8.

(348–53) Following Samuel's escape from the HKP camp, March 1944, he is reunited with his mother at Aunt Janina's, who tries to find a hiding place for mother and son. Janina finds an elderly woman, with: "… a small closet. Inside there was no opening for light or air. The cracks in the wood had to suffice. An old mattress of a child's bed covered the entire surface of the floor." Aunt Janina declines.

(357–8) Samuel and his mother are allowed to join the nine other Jews hiding among looted documents in the Benedictine Convent. He describes the dynamics between them: "One would have expected a social leveling and an ideological tolerance, but this was not the case. Perhaps the dire conditions of life, and the struggle for survival at any cost, had reinforced in them their different identities and beliefs as a way of maintaining their self-respect."

Righteous Gentiles

(63, 79, 84, 88, 242, 246–7, 303, 348–9) "Mother's converted Aunt Janina …" helps Samuel and his mother escape from the HKP camp. Samuel remembers her: "She was our most trustworthy and often our only support in the most horrendous of times. She was the axis of our plans and often their courageous executor. She was the only home port we had. Whenever our boat was in need of urgent repair or on the point of sinking, she was there!"

(225, 317) Jews fleeing East come to Vilna; Samuel reports: "The refugees tried to obtain visas distributed by the Japanese Consul in Kaunas, a man who in time became a real legend." The Japanese diplomat was Chiune Sugihara, summer 1940.

(302, 335–40) Samuel and his mother escape from the ghetto after only one night, September 1941. They appeal to Aunt Janina for help; she appeals to her Benedictine Convent and the Church of St Catherine: "The mother superior, with the authorization of her bishop, agreed to create a hiding place for a woman and child in the heart of the convent's 'clausura', the closed cloister. This privilege was extended later to Mother's sister Yetta and her husband and my father."

(353–6, 358–61) After Janina helps them escape from the HKP camp, Samuel and his mother return to the Benedictine Convent in search of refuge; there they find: "Behind a wailing wall of looted manuscripts, in a secret space made from a small slice of the corridor's last section and of the last room to which it led, several survivors of the liquidated ghetto had formed an ingenious shelter. ... Sister Maria and Father Stakauskas, a Catholic priest and former professor of history who was employed to supervise and sort the looted material, were providing the hidden Jews with food and other necessities. ... Their courage and devotion went beyond anything I have ever encountered."

(358, 489) On Sister Maria, Maria Mikulska, born in 1903, died 12 August 1994, the Benedictine nun who hid Samuel and his mother and nine other Jews: "Her optimism and her courage nourished the energies that were vital for our survival."

(488–91) Rimantas Stankevicius, a Lithuanian Christian from Vilnius, finds Samuel in Weston in 2000: "... he devoted much of his personal time to the remembrance of those righteous men and women who, despite the barbarity of the Nazi occupation, had committed themselves to saving Jews. ... he was arranging for a plaque to commemorate Sister Maria, Father Stakauskas, and a certain Vladas Zemaitis." Samuel sends a message to the commemoration.

Liberation

(41–5, 362) July 1944, Samuel and his mother emerge from their hiding place after the Soviet Army retakes Vilna: "Unexploded bombs, walls ready to crumble, isolated snipers, revenge-thirsty partisans, and the unfamiliar Red Army soldiers frighten the inhabitants and keep the streets empty. Only shadowlike figures, disheveled, creased and covered by dust, thirsty like us for the forgotten taste of freedom, solitary or in very small groups, haunt Vilna's streets."

(42, 65, 207, 215, 220) Samuel, at liberation, anticipating the reunion with his father who would have celebrated his birthday 7 July: "I am thinking of my last glimpse of Father's face. Mother and I do not yet know that only ten days ago, a few days before this birthday on which he would have become thirty-seven, Father was killed by a German machine gun." Samuel's mother hears of his death, after the city is liberated: "Father's hands had been tied behind his back." At Ponar, 1944.

(45–7) Friends from the ghetto at liberation, Nadia, with her daughter, tells Samuel's mother of the murder of her husband after liberation by Jewish partisans: "One of the partisans had identified her husband as a former ghetto policeman and had gunned him down."

(63–6, 363) After the Soviet Army liberates Vilna, Samuel and his mother return to Aunt

Janina: "When Janina saw us in her doorway, a little shriek burst forth from her throat, but then there was no further sound and her mouth remained open. Her eyes told us that she could hardly believe what she saw. She stretched out her arms. She had to hold us to convince herself that we were real."

(364–6) "We had been liberated and the Lithuanian Socialist Republic reborn ...." Mitzia finds work: "... in a state-owned food store. ... The choosy customers were mostly wives of the upper echelon. ... the general public was famished. Even the soldiers on the front were hungry, but this did not concern the privileged class. ... Where were the basic ideas of equality and justice that theoretically grounded the Communist society?"

(367–8) Documentation after Vilna's liberation by the Soviets: "... Avrom Sutzkever's published reports about the German crimes ... Two hundred of his pages would appear in Ilya Ehrenburg's 'Black Book'. My story appeared among Sutzkever's lighter chapters that were intended to soothe devasted readers with a few happy endings." Peretz Markish comes to Vilna: "Markish, speaking to Mother with satisfaction and pride, informed her that an order for my transfer to an exclusive institute of 'geniuses' was on its way."

(374–89) Summer 1944 to summer 1945, the year in "Red Vilna": "I lived among adults who, in a world tattered and transformed by catastrophe, must themselves have felt like abandoned and lost children." Mitzia and Yetta, with Samuel and Tamara escape by train to the Polish border, a trip that normally took three to five hours: "It lasted four full days, days of short advances and long periods of waiting." From there they continue on to Lodz to arrange passage to Palestine.

Displaced Persons camps

(97–8, 424–5) Samuel and his mother come to Landsberg in late 1945. They are interviewed by Nathan Markovsky, "Markusha", and brought into the camp: "After a few months Markusha became my stepfather. I believe that Mother must have chosen him from among a large number of suitors because she thought he would be good for me." Samuel was 12; with Markusha's help: "I had a room of my own, lots of space for painting, and the means to go regularly to Munich for tutoring in an art school."

(258–9, 427) "It was after the end of the war, and I was living among survivors of the Holocaust who were in need of telling over and over again their experiences of recent years. ... Pain, loss, and bewilderment were everywhere. Talking about people from our past, and in particular about those who had perished, gave us a sense of rescuing them from extinction. As if the dead were being summoned to cleanse us of the guilt of having survived."

(410–20) At the entrance into the Tempelhof DP camp in Berlin, the American soldiers try to ascertain whether those seeking refuge were indeed Jewish refugees: "There were obviously many Jewish survivors among us, but some people looked as if they belonged to other nationalities. Some even looked like Germans trying to pass for Jews." They leave Tempelhof for a perilous journey to Munich and the Landsberg DP camp.

(421, 424–8, 472) Samuel's three years in Landsberg, aged 12 to 15: "It was a place that allowed me to regain many of the pleasures of a 'normal existence'. Things that people take for granted: a decent space to live, sufficient food and clothing, some schooling, direction and care from the elders, close friendships, and the freedom from fear for one's life."

(429–31, 441) "The DP camp was supposed to be a place of brief passage, but the world did not want us and we had nowhere to go. ... Jewish leaders acted energetically. ... Ben-Gurion

... came to visit the survivor's diaspora in the DP camps of Germany. ..." Also Leonard Bernstein and Yehudi Menuhin.

Stories of individuals, including family members

(3, 14–17, 19, 105–8, 115–16, 432, 439) Samuel's mother and her "post-war Zionism", her life with Markusha in Israel, her death at the age of 60 in 1971 after being taken ill during Samuel's daughter Ilana's ninth birthday party: "The last image that she took with her must have been of little Ilana's joyous bewilderment at the magician's fabulous hocus-pocus."

(5, 8) Schmerke Kaczerginski gives Samuel the "Pinkas", survives as a partisan and retrieves the "Pinkas" from rubble at the HKP camp: "In Kaczerginski's hands, the 'Pinkas' was immediately designated for a Holocaust museum he was already trying to create in Soviet Vilna." 1944.

(10, 138–9, 143) Samuel's uncle David Bak: "... he joined the Communist Party of Poland, was put in prison, and managed to escape to Soviet Russia. There he saw his idols betray him, was arrested, accused of Trotskyism, and exiled to Siberia." He survives but chooses to remain in the Soviet Union after the war ends.

(31–3) In the ghetto, Rokhele takes Samuel to meet a young painter, a potential tutor, but they find only his painting: he had earlier been taken to the Lukiszki Prison, "... from which very few ever returned." Samuel views his painting of a boy seated at a table: "It was an art that managed to save itself from oblivion by generating images in the mind and work of another artist. I am grateful for what he passed on to me, and I regret not remembering his name. ... in my daily toiling with brushes and colors there flickers a small flame in his honor."

(36–9, 81–2) The three who share their room in the HKP camp: Salomon, Katia, and "Maman", who had come from a smaller ghetto nearby. After the children's *Aktion* and when Samuel is hidden, the three move out, fearing to be implicated: "'We would prefer not to be involved. Best luck from the three of us.'"

(62–3, 70–2, 145) The relationship between Jonas and Mitzia, Samuel's parents: "Whenever faced with her husband's not-so-secret indiscretions she would repeat a phrase that she had coined: 'It is better to be a partner in a flourishing business than the sole owner of a failing one.' Later she would cry behind a locked door, while her little son, his ear laid against it, would search his childish mind for things he might have done that were responsible for her unhappiness."

(72–3, 392–4) Friends at the HKP camp, Misha, the camp doctor whom Samuel's father assists, and his wife Slava, and their daughter: "They survived the liquidation of the camp, passed through the DP camps in Bavaria, and in 1948 settled in Israel, as we did." They hide Samuel during the children's *Aktion*, March 1944.

(99–102, 104–5, 439–40, 442–3, 447–9) Samuel's stepfather Markusha: "He never got over the tragic death of his first daughter in the ghetto of Kovno and the subseqent loss of his wife and second child. He was plagued by horrible dreams that brought him back to the terror of the camps. ... the screams. ... became the familiar sounds that invaded many nights of my adolescent years." Markusha's love of chess is passed on to Samuel: "Chessboard and figures were painted as metaphors of life's human struggle." His death in 1972 at the age of 78.

(108–13, 116–22, 363, 377–97, 400–6, 442) Mitzia's younger sister Aunt Yetta: her survival with her daughter Tamara, their escape together from Vilna, their re-uniting in Israel, and her death in Germany in 1987, staying with Tamara: "Shortly after our liberation, the resurrected

Yetta appeared one day, with five-year-old Tamara at her side, at Janina's gate. ... Later we all left for Poland."

(111–12, 391, 442–3, 451–60) Yerachmiel (Uncle Rachmila), Mitzia and Yetta's brother: "I greatly admired this Zionist pioneer, this rebel against maternal authority, insurgent fighter against the British, and founder of a heroic kibbutz in the middle of swamps infested by malaria."

(113, 119, 402–4, 410, 442) Zygmunt, who married Aunt Yetta in Lodz after the war: "He had survived the ghetto of Czestochowa, where his wife and children had perished. ... Zygmunt was not very bright, nor was he well educated, but he was a very decent man, a devoted and helpful husband, and a warm and loving father to little Tamara."

(118–19, 363, 370–3) Aunt Yetta's husband and Tamara's father, Yasha, deported from the Vilna Ghetto to a slave labour camp: "Later, as the Red Army was approaching, he was among a large group of prisoners whom the Nazis killed by putting them in boats and drowning them in the Baltic Sea." Of his Uncle Yasha: "The ghetto transformed him, revealing all that was best in him. ... People who remembered him in the final days of his life spoke of him with affection."

(143–4) Samuel's aunt Tsilla (Bak): "... she and her husband and their baby, fleeing to Kiev to escape the German occupation of Vilna, would meet their death, riddled by the bullets of a Nazi machine gun, most probably on the precipice of the mass grave at Babi Yar."

(259–61, 263, 406–7, 410) Mitzia's Uncle Arno, who had been brought with his parents to Berlin as they sought medical treatment for Isaac's eye injury, had stayed on in Berlin when his parents returned to Vilna. He had been the hope when Samuel and his mother made their way to Berlin in October 1945, they find: "... Arno Nadel and his wife were sent to Auschwitz, and no one had heard from them again."

(442) Uncle Izia, Mitzia's youngest brother: "... badly injured when battling in the ranks of the Red Army. He had escaped to Italy where he was being treated for severe head wounds, and he too planned to go to the new Jewish state."

Post-war life and career

(9, 13, 15, 17, 436) His wife Anna and their three daughters, Daniela, Ilana, and Mikhal, with whom he has lived in Israel, Paris, and Rome.

(121–2, 166–9, 436–8) Josée, Samuel's second wife, to whom the book is dedicated. They married in 1992, and moved from Lausanne to Boston.

(191) On criticism of his art: "I have had to learn to ignore those who feel that my kind of art is a joke or an offence, and who point their fingers at me. ... The sound of friendly voices speaking seriously about my work is a music I treasure."

(369–70) Samuel's art teachers in newly liberated Vilna: "... the very distinguished Mr. Makoynik. ... He spoke of the unity of time and space, and I realized that he would never teach me to paint an apple that looked like an apple." And: "... Professor Serafinovicz, with her angelic name and manner." She had found broken plaster casts from Vilna's academy of fine arts, and used them for models: "Many years later ... these abused fragments reentered my art and filled many of my canvases."

(386, 396, 406–9) With the help of the "Brichah", they are able to obtain authentic-looking documents to leave the Soviet Zone. In October 1945, Samuel, his mother, and an orphaned Jewish girl leave Lodz, and Aunt Yetta and Tamara who are to follow, for a harrowing journey to Berlin.

(390–401) Summer, autumn 1945, in Lodz, Samuel: "... found refuge in the sheltered atmosphere of Professor Richtarski's studio. ... I concentrated on portraits and still lifes. ... Our small kitchen table was often transformed into a base for a painting's model. ... 'Is it a still life, or can it be eaten?' was my little Cousin Tamara's regular question."

(432, 440, 443–54) Reluctantly giving up the opportunity to study art in Paris, the family prepares to leave Landsberg for the difficult voyage to Israel, to Uncle Rachmila and Aunt Riva.

(465–84) His educational experiences, his painting: "Bridging the gap between the inner projection of a mental vision and the final, physical result of the completed canvas is the essence of my craft and passion."

Personal reflections

(6) On writing his memoir: "The story writes itself through the one who summons the recollections, and not the other way around. It is a journey into memory that is more than an attempt to save the past from oblivion; it searches for some kind of restoration or mending."

(16) "My past had taken from me the capacity to deal with aggression." May 1967, Israel.

(66–7) "... I have been a perpetual wanderer. ... Although I have managed to hold on to individual friendships and have cultivated several languages and cultures, I am everywhere and nowhere at home. I have no geography of my own and am always afraid of losing my identity and those transportable roots that I keep neatly folded in a suitcase."

(91) "Countering the stern traditions of our ancient religion, I have made paintings that evoke the concerns of our time and invite observers to invest them with their own reflections. A representative of the people of the book, I sometimes see myself as a book, my mind an amalgam of stories and images, a mortal 'Pinkas'. As a boy I added my images to old texts. Today I am adding new texts to my old images."

(107–8) On his mother's memory of family: "Her stories had charged me with a grave responsibility. I was the last link. I had promised myself ... by writing about what was still retained in my memory, to save these dead from oblivion."

(129) "My paintings are meant to bear personal testimony to the trauma of surviving. They depict troubling images of a world shadowed by the dissipating clouds of yet another universal flood."

(171) Grandfather Khone and his discussion with Samuel as a child on viewing paintings: "'How is it that distance makes us understand what nearness does not?'"

(342) "Ten improbable miracles were the minimal rate for survival. Nine miracles, if the tenth did not happen, were not enough."

(374) "We survivors were badly equipped to deal with loss and mourning. Testimonies that gave proof of death were rare. Many of our dear ones who disappeared might still be vaguely hoped for. Denial, too, led us to avoid considering them lost. ... Even where we were certain of the fate of our loved ones, as in the case of those murdered at Ponar, the setting evoked such horror that it offered no place to commune with the dead or search for solace. As there were no funerals and no rituals that could be put in place, our mourning had to go on for years."

Places mentioned in Europe (page first mentioned)

Auschwitz Main Camp/Auschwitz I (410), Babi Yar mass murder site (Kiev) (144), Bad Reichenhall (430), Baltic Sea (119), Bavaria/Bayern (72), Berlin (57), Cologne/Köln (117), Czestochowa (119), Dachau concentration camp (95), East Prussia/Ost Preussen (260),

Feldafing Displaced Persons camp (97), Frankfurt-on-Main/Frankfurt-am-Main (421), Gare du Nord (Paris) (133), Germany/Deutschland (8), Greece/Ellas (458), Hanover/Hannover (416), Heidelberg (482), HKP ("Heereskraftfahrpark") slave labour camp (6), Italy/Italia (9), Kailis slave labour camp (20), Kassel (417), Kiev/Kyjiv (144), Königsberg/Kaliningrad (260), Kosovo (66), Kovno/Kaunas (100), Kutno (386), Landsberg am Lech (420), Landsberg Displaced Persons camp (97), Lausanne (66), Liège/Lüttich (372), Lithuania/Lietuva (10), Lodz/Litzmanstadt (119), Lukiszki/Lukiskiu prison (Vilna) (31), Marseille (440), Minsk (358), Munich/München (98), Nuremberg (483), Odessa/Odesa (199), Paris (9), Poland/Polska (62), Ponar/Paneriai (25), Prague/Praha (24), Riga (425), Rome/Roma (3), Salonika/Thessaloniki (458), Soviet Union/Union of Soviet Socialist Republics (13), Switzerland/Schweiz/Suisse/Swizzeria (120), Tempelhof Displaced Persons camp (410), Ukraine/Ukrajina (129), Venice/Venezia/Venedig (129), Vevey (167), Viliya River (44), Vilna ghetto (5), Vilna/Wilno/Vilnius (3), Warsaw ghetto (33), Warsaw/Warszawa/Warschau (62), Zakopane (78)

Places mentioned outside Europe (page first mentioned)

Baku (243), Boston (3), Caspian Sea (243), Cyprus/Kypros/Kibris (440), Egypt/Al Misr (14), Galilee (129), Haifa/Hefa (391), Israel/Yisrael (9), Jerusalem/Yerushalayim (12), Leningrad/St Petersburg (264), Manchuria (264), Middle East (10), Moscow/Moskva (10), New York City (66), Ottoman Empire (129), Palestine (129), Pittsburgh (477), Port Arthur/Dalian (264), Ramat Chen (9), Ramat Gan (10), Safed/Tzfat (129), Shanghai (224), Siberia/Sibir (132), Stalingrad/Volgograd/Tsarytsin (20), Tel Aviv (10), Tokyo (264), United States of America (19), Ural Mountains (321), Waco (Texas) (442), Washington (DC) (421), Weston (Massachusetts) (3)

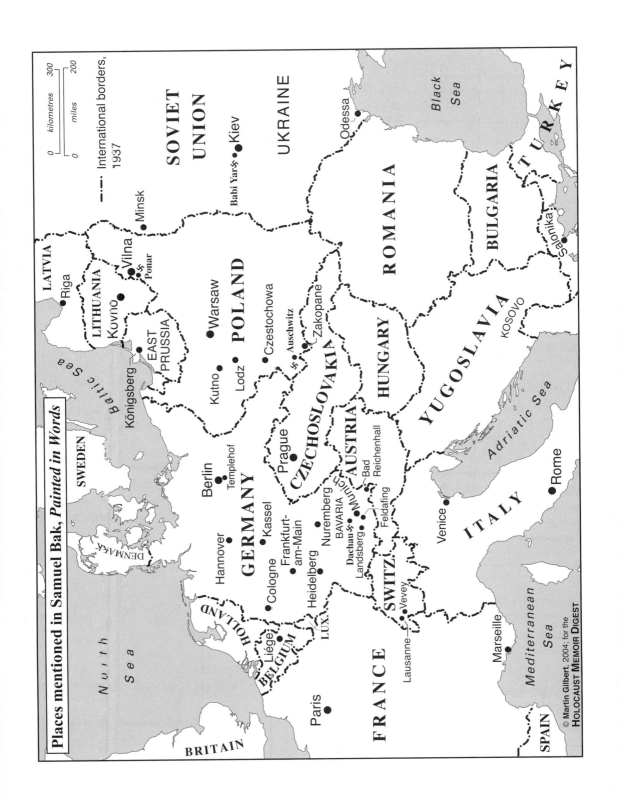

Places mentioned in Samuel Bak, *Painted in Words*

International borders, 1937

0 kilometres 300
0 miles 200

NORTH SEA

Sea

BRITAIN

Baltic Sea

SWEDEN

DENMARK

LATVIA
Riga

LITHUANIA
Kovno
Vilna
Ponar

Minsk

SOVIET UNION

EAST PRUSSIA
Königsberg

Babi Yar ☆ ● Kiev

UKRAINE

HOLLAND

BELGIUM
Liége
LUX.

Paris

FRANCE

GERMANY
Berlin
Templehof
Hannover
Kassel
Cologne
Frankfurt-am-Main
Heidelberg
Nuremberg
BAVARIA
Munich
Dachau ☆
Landsberg
Bad Reichenhall
Feldafing

Warsaw
Kutno
Lodz
Czestochowa
Auschwitz ☆
Zakopane

POLAND

Prague
CZECHOSLOVAKIA

AUSTRIA

HUNGARY

ROMANIA

Odessa

Black Sea

SWITZ.
Lausanne
Vevey

ITALY
Venice
Rome

YUGOSLAVIA
KOSOVO

Adriatic Sea

BULGARIA

Salonika

TURKEY

Marseille

SPAIN

Mediterranean Sea

© Martin Gilbert, 2004; for the
HOLOCAUST MEMOIR DIGEST

Study Guide

INTRODUCTION

This Study Guide is intended to elaborate on aspects of the *Digest*.

The term "Holocaust", which has entered into common usage in the past few decades, comes from classical Greek and means "consumed by fire: a burnt offering". In Hebrew, which is both the language of prayer among Jews and the language of the State of Israel, the Holocaust is called "Shoah" (catastrophe), and in Yiddish, the traditional language of East European Jews, it is "Hurban" (destruction).

Since 1945, the Holocaust has come to refer to the planned, systematic murder of Jews who were living in European lands occupied or dominated by Germany during the Second World War. The war began with the German invasion of Poland on 1 September 1939. What had started as the random killing of Jews became, with the German invasion of the Soviet Union in June 1941, the mass murder of Jews on a daily basis. The surrender of Germany on 8 May 1945 brought the war in Europe to an end; six million Jewish men, women, and children had been killed.

From the first days of their liberation in 1945, many survivors felt the need to record their eyewitness accounts, to memorialize their destroyed families, to remember their pre-war way of life. The first such memoirs, written soon after the war, introduced the Holocaust to the public consciousness. In recent years, the passage of time and a growing interest in their experiences during that traumatic time have been the impetus for many other survivors to record their memories for posterity.

The will to live, to maintain hope, to survive, and to rebuild – this gives the Holocaust its universality. Jews are known as the People of the Book, that book being the Bible, the narrative of their origins, laws, and early history. The need to write and record, to document, and to remember are an integral part of Jewish tradition. This makes the Holocaust a window onto both the best and the worst of human behaviour. The Holocaust was not the only genocide of the twentieth century; it was almost certainly the most documented one.

Each survivor's experiences are unique; each memoir contains aspects of the Holocaust that add to our knowledge of that terrible time. The *Holocaust Memoir Digest*, by reviewing the published memoirs of Jews who survived the Holocaust, provides a guide and reference for the teaching not only of the Holocaust, but also of recent history, human relations, the pattern of genocide, and the psychology of good and evil.

TOPICS

The entry for each memoir in the *Holocaust Memoir Digest* consists of the following six parts:

1. The **author, title**, and **publishing details**.
2. A one-sentence **focus** that sets the geographic area and time.
3. A list of **features** that are not part of the memoir itself but added to it.
4. The **contents** of the memoir, divided into twenty-six categories.
5. A list of **places** mentioned in the memoir, both in Europe and beyond.
6. A **map** or **maps** showing each place in Europe mentioned in that memoir.

The first two of the twenty-six categories are **Pre-war Jewish home and community life** and **Pre-war anti-Semitism**. These describe what life was like throughout Europe for Jews, some of whose ancestors had lived in these countries for many hundreds of years. In **Pre-war Jewish home and community life**, survivors write about the culture, education, traditions, community structure, and the life Jews led as they struggled to grapple with changing twentieth-century values. Should they maintain family and religious traditions, or seek assimilation? Should they work toward a better economic situation where they lived, or would they find better opportunities elsewhere? Should they seek to fulfil their Zionist aspirations, or was carving out a life in the "desert" of Palestine too difficult?

One of the main factors that determined how pre-war European Jewish families faced these questions is that many of them lived amidst an all-pervasive **Pre-war anti-Semitism**, the second category of the *Digest*. They lived in a Christian world that was in many ways foreign to them or had alienated them.

The segregation and humiliation of Jews, legalized under the Nuremberg Laws of 1935, had begun in Germany when Hitler came to power in 1933. Hitler separated the Jews from the general population by making them into scapegoats – by taking advantage of latent anti-Semitism and blaming Jews for Germany's ills. He then removed Jews from their positions in government, the law, universities, schools, and hospitals. German colleagues took over their positions; those who had worked under them moved up the ladder. Jewish businesses were confiscated, or "sold" for a fraction of their worth to local people who were loyal to the Nazi Party.

By the time Jews were separated physically from the larger German community, those of Hitler's compatriots who had accepted his plan, and benefited from this exclusion of the Jews, were not particularly interested in helping the Jews when persecution intensified. This segregation and humiliation extended to Austria in March 1938, when it became part of the German Reich, and to the Sudetenland region of Czechoslovakia in October 1938.

The coming of war and **Life under German occupation** categories describe how the beginning of the war in September 1939, the sudden violent imposition of Nazi rule, and the constant struggle for survival affected the memoir writer. In each country that Germany conquered between September 1939 and June 1941 – Poland in September 1939, Denmark and Norway in April 1940, Holland, Belgium, France, and Luxembourg in May 1940, Yugoslavia and Greece in April 1941 – anti-Jewish legislation was put in place, often upheld by the local collaborationist regime. Jewish businesses and possessions were confiscated.

In Poland, from the first days of the German conquest, Jews were rounded up and beaten, and several thousand were murdered. Later the Jews were forcibly removed from their homes and crowded into ghettos.

Ghettos were established in Poland in many towns in which Jews were confined amid considerable hardship and privation. Some ghettos existed for only a short time. Others lasted up to four years. This is described in the two categories **Creation of the ghetto** and **Daily life in the ghetto**. Having lost their property and livelihood, the only further value Jews represented to the Nazi occupier was in their labour. Thus the struggle by Jews for survival in the ghettos centred on trying to find food and obtain valid work permits, both of which were tightly controlled and restricted.

Those Jews deemed by the Nazis no longer "essential" were rounded up and removed from the ghettos. The category **Deportation** describes the physical movement of Jews from their home towns or ghettos, in most cases to their deaths. Usually deportations took place by train, and were undertaken with deliberate deception, and promises that were recognized as false only when it was too late. The destination of the deportation trains was a tightly guarded secret. Only a few deportees returned.

Starting in June 1941, when Germany invaded the Soviet Union, four "commandos" of specially trained SS killing squads, the *Einsatzgruppen*, rounded up Jews in hundreds of towns and villages, and took them by force to nearby ditches, ravines, and forests, where they were shot. The largest of these **Mass murder sites** were located near cities that had large Jewish populations. These sites include Babi Yar outside Kiev, Rumbuli outside Riga, Ponar outside Vilnius, and the Ninth Fort outside Kaunas, at each of which tens of thousands of Jews were killed. Also included in this *Digest* category are smaller sites where thousands of Jews were murdered by shooting.

Transit camps: Drancy in France, Malines in Belgium, Westerbork in Holland, and Fossoli in Italy were among the principal transit camps to which Jews were taken for short periods of time and then deported to an "unknown destination in the East" – in most cases, to their deaths. Other transit camps were to be found throughout Europe.

December 1941 saw the first systematic gassing of Jews. This took place in German-occupied Poland, near the village of Chelmno (in German "Kulmhof"), which became the first death camp. Belzec (pronounced Belzhets), Sobibor, and Treblinka were also **Death camps** in German-occupied Poland to which, with Chelmno, as many as two million Jews were deported and killed. A fifth death camp, Maly Trostenets, was situated near Minsk in German-occupied Byelorussia.

The only Jews who survived for more than a few days in the death camps were a small group of slave labourers forced to dispose of the bodies, usually in mass graves where the bodies were then burned. These labourers were also used to sort the clothing and belongings of the victims: material that was later redistributed among the SS, the German armed forces, and the German people. Almost none of the slave labourers in the death camps survived.

Many German factory owners took advantage of the plentiful labour supply and built factories and labour camps close to the ghettos and camps, as described in the category **Slave labour camps and factories**. Those Jews who were able to work had a better chance of survival, despite the harsh conditions in those camps which ensured a high turnover of labourers. Many memoir writers survived as slave labourers.

The deception practised by the SS in their killing operations depended on secrecy and the complete control of information. Northwest of Prague, the SS established a ghetto in the former Czechoslovak garrison town of **Theresienstadt (Terezin** in Czech). It was here that the Red Cross was shown what was "happening" to the Jews during a massive deception operation, complete with Jewish children at play. Much of the art, poetry, and music created by the Jews during the Holocaust came from those who were interned in Theresienstadt. Most of those who did not succumb to the privations in Theresienstadt were deported to Auschwitz and Maly Trostenets and killed.

While mass murder by shooting continued in the East throughout the last six months of 1941 and for all of 1942, experimental means were being investigated in German-occupied Poland to make killing more "efficient". What had begun at Chelmno with exhaust fumes was "perfected" at **Auschwitz-Birkenau**, where Zyklon B gas pellets were thrown into sealed "shower" rooms. The bodies were then burned in crematoria. This method of killing began in the summer of 1942. By the autumn of 1944, five crematoria were operating.

Although "Auschwitz" has come to refer to the whole facility, it consisted of three large camps in close proximity. The original and Main Camp, with its single crematorium, was known as Auschwitz I. Birkenau, where four of the five crematoria were located, was known as Auschwitz II. Auschwitz also contained several satellite slave labour camps in the vicinity, the largest of which was attached to the Buna synthetic rubber and oil factory at the nearby town of Monowitz, and was known as Buna-Monowitz, or Auschwitz III. Descriptions of Buna-Monowitz and the other slave labour camps in the Auschwitz region are to be found in the *Digest* in the category of **Slave labour camps and factories**.

In January 1945, as Soviet forces approached the Auschwitz region, the SS evacuated the camp and the surrounding slave labour camps and moved the surviving Jews westward, initially on foot. Those who were sent westward by rail were put in open railway wagons in mid-winter. Amid terrible brutality by their guards, many of the deportees were forced to "march" with little food, water, or shelter, until April. The toll from these **Death marches** was high.

When the Nazi Party came to power in Germany in 1933, it immediately established concentration camps for political prisoners. These camps were run by the SS. Dachau, outside Munich, and Sachsenhausen, north of Berlin, date from this period. These concentration camps, located on German soil, were used for German political prisoners, opponents of the Nazi regime, writers, artists, teachers, religious leaders, pastors, priests, homosexuals, common criminals, and, later, prisoners of war, particularly Russians. Towards the end of the war, tens of thousands of Jews on death marches were brought to these **Concentration camps** in Germany, among them Dachau, Bergen–Belsen, Buchenwald, Mauthausen, and their many sub-camps.

Also included in the *Digest* category of **Concentration camps** is Majdanek, although this camp had many different aspects. Located in Poland near the city of Lublin, Majdanek initially served as a concentration camp for Russian prisoners of war, who were held there in horrific conditions, and for Polish political prisoners. For the thousands of Jews who were taken to Majdanek and were later sent to Auschwitz, it was a transit camp. In addition, thousands of Jews from as close as Lublin and as far as Holland and Greece were brought to Majdanek and killed. After the defeat of the Warsaw Ghetto Revolt and the destruction of the Warsaw Ghetto, and later the revolt in Bialystok, many thousands of survivors of those revolts were taken to Majdanek and murdered during the notorious "Harvest Festival" in November 1943.

One of the main reasons that survivors have written their memoirs of the Holocaust is to bear witness, to describe what they lived through, what they saw, and what the people whom they knew had witnessed. The category **Witness to mass murder** makes it possible to begin to understand the scale of what happened.

As well as recording the details of the places to which Jews were taken, survivors also sought to chronicle the events and to write about the people who inspired them to continue, the people who helped them, and the ways in which they were able to evade death. The category **Resistance, ghetto revolts, individual acts of courage and defiance** includes acts of physical resistance, armed revolts, and also acts of "spiritual resistance": dignity in the face of inhumanity, the will to rise above the circumstances, the determination to live through the time of torment, the will to live.

Again and again, Jews fled to forests and outlying areas where they could fight the Nazi occupier. The category **Partisan activity** refers to armed resistance against the German Army and German occupation, either by Jews, or by non-Jewish resistance fighters. Unfortunately, Jews who were able to escape to the forests and fight the Germans as partisans also had to fear some Polish and Russian partisan groups who did not consider the Jews to be allies. One of the tragedies of the Holocaust is that some of those who were fighting the Nazi occupier were also fighting the Jews.

The category of **Specific escapes** refers to those few Jews who were able to escape from the deportation trains, or from those who would betray them, or from other situations of grave danger, or to find a brief respite from the constant terror.

In order to survive, many Jews went into hiding, as described in the category **In hiding, including Hidden Children**. This could involve a physical hiding place: a cellar, an attic, a cupboard, a cavity in a wall, under the floor, or in a barn. For those who did not have "typically Jewish" features and were able to pass as Christians, it also involved a psychological hiding. In such cases, along with the false identity papers, a whole new persona and demeanour had to emerge. In the struggle to find safety, families were split up; children were often hidden separately from their parents. Of those children who survived, many lost their families; nearly all lost their childhood.

Many Jews were fortunate to receive kindness and help from non-Jews. Many of these **Righteous Gentiles,** as they have become known, risked, and some even lost, their lives for helping Jews. Showing great humanity, they shared food, shelter, and risk. It is to their credit that thousands of Jews survived.

The category **Liberation** denotes the time when Soviet, American, British, Canadian, and other Allied troops liberated the camps and the areas in which many Jews had been in hiding. For the Jews, liberation meant an end to their physical suffering, and the beginning of their quest to try to find family members, and to try to find a country that would give them safe haven. Many eventually made their way to Palestine (later Israel); many went to Britain, the United States, Canada, Australia, South Africa, and Argentina.

The category **Displaced Persons camps** describes the refugee camps where survivors lived after they had been liberated. These camps were also used as a base for those who travelled to find relatives. Most survivors began to rebuild their lives while in DP camps; some spent several years there while waiting to find a country that would take them.

The category **Stories of individuals, including family members** identifies the lives and fate of individuals mentioned by the memoir writer, as well as the fate of family members if known. Each survivor identifies extended family, neighbours, friends, colleagues, and many of those individuals with whom he or she came into contact.

The category **Post-war life and career** focuses not only on the achievements of the survivors after liberation, but on their search to explore their past. The final category **Personal reflections** provides an understanding of how the survivors view the world, and gives the reader the opportunity to learn – through the survivors' own words – their philosophy, their psychology, their connection to religion, and what is important to them.

Because the borders of many countries in Europe have changed so much in the twentieth century, the names of **Places** also changed. For example, the capital of Slovakia is today Bratislava. When it was part of the Austro-Hungarian Empire, the Germans called it Pressburg, and the Hungarians knew it as Posony. The capital of Lithuania is today Vilnius. It was a part of Poland between the two world wars when Poles called it Wilno; to the Jews it was Vilna.

Many towns in the East had a Yiddish as well as a local name. Thus Brest-Litovsk was Brisk, and Wlodzimierz Wolynski (Vladimir Volynski) was Ludmir. The *Digest* shows these various spellings of towns and cities. Also, by locating each place on **Maps**, specially prepared by the *Digest* for each memoir, we can follow the memoir writer's travels, experiences, and torments.

The following is a series of questions within each category, with a key indicating which memoirs address these particular issues in that category.

Pre-war Jewish home and community life

How was a Jewish religious life observed?
Strange and Unexpected Love, Fanya Gottesfeld Heller
From Thessaloniki to Auschwitz and Back, Erika Kounio Amariglio
The Cantor's Voice, Solomon Gisser

In what ways was assimilation attempted?
When Memory Comes, Saul Friedländer
Painted in Words, Samuel Bak

What were the discussions among members of the author's family about following Zionist dreams and moving to Palestine?
When Memory Comes, Saul Friedländer

What cultural aspects created a sense of community?
Strange and Unexpected Love, Fanya Gottesfeld Heller
From Thessaloniki to Auschwitz and Back, Erika Kounio Amariglio
Painted in Words, Samuel Bak

Pre-war anti-Semitism

How did the annexation of Austria and parts of Czechoslovakia affect Jews living in those areas?
When Memory Comes, Saul Friedländer
Maus: A Survivor's Tale, Part I, Art Spiegelman
From Thessaloniki to Auschwitz and Back, Erika Kounio Amariglio

What options to flee were open to Jews who found themselves in annexed areas?
When Memory Comes, Saul Friedländer
From Thessaloniki to Auschwitz and Back, Erika Kounio Amariglio

What was the prominence of local anti-Semitic gangs?
Maus: A Survivor's Tale, Part I, Art Spiegelman
Strange and Unexpected Love, Fanya Gottesfeld Heller
Painted in Words, Samuel Bak

The coming of war

What was it like to experience the bombing raids?
The Cantor's Voice, Solomon Gisser

What was it like for Jewish soldiers in the Polish Army?
Maus: A Survivor's Tale, Part I, Art Spiegelman

What was the situation for Jewish refugees?
When Memory Comes, Saul Friedländer
Painted in Words, Samuel Bak

What were the first encounters with the Germans like?
All But My Life, Gerda Weissmann Klein

How did Soviet occupation affect Jewish life?
Strange and Unexpected Love, Fanya Gottesfeld Heller
Painted in Words, Samuel Bak

Life under German occupation

How did life change for Jews under occupation?
All But My Life, Gerda Weissmann Klein
Maus: A Survivor's Tale, Part I, Art Spiegelman
Strange and Unexpected Love, Fanya Gottesfeld Heller
From Thessaloniki to Auschwitz and Back, Erika Kounio Amariglio
The Cantor's Voice, Solomon Gisser
Painted in Words, Samuel Bak

What was the economic impact of German occupation?
All But My Life, Gerda Weissmann Klein
Maus: A Survivor's Tale, Part I, Art Spiegelman
Strange and Unexpected Love, Fanya Gottesfeld Heller
From Thessaloniki to Auschwitz and Back, Erika Kounio Amariglio
Painted in Words, Samuel Bak

How did the seeming politeness of the Germans gain confidence and dispel rumours?
From Thessaloniki to Auschwitz and Back, Erika Kounio Amariglio

How was the German chain of command established?
Strange and Unexpected Love, Fanya Gottesfeld Heller

How did the Germans use local sentiment to further their goals?
Strange and Unexpected Love, Fanya Gottesfeld Heller
Painted in Words, Samuel Bak

Creation of the ghetto

How were the smaller ghettos established?
All But My Life, Gerda Weissmann Klein
Maus: A Survivor's Tale, Part I, Art Spiegelman
Strange and Unexpected Love, Fanya Gottesfeld Heller
From Thessaloniki to Auschwitz and Back, Erika Kounio Amariglio

How were the larger ghettos formed?
The Cantor's Voice, Solomon Gisser
Painted in Words, Samuel Bak

Daily life in the ghetto

What was life like in the smaller ghettos?
All But My Life, Gerda Weissmann Klein
Maus: A Survivor's Tale, Part I, Art Spiegelman
Strange and Unexpected Love, Fanya Gottesfeld Heller

What was the day-to-day existence like in the larger ghettos?
The Cantor's Voice, Solomon Gisser
Painted in Words, Samuel Bak

Deportations

What were conditions like on the deportation trains?
From Thessaloniki to Auschwitz and Back, Erika Kounio Amariglio

Which deportations came to Auschwitz?
Maus: A Survivor's Tale, Part I, Art Spiegelman
From Thessaloniki to Auschwitz and Back, Erika Kounio Amariglio

How were deportations used to move Jews to slave labour camps?
All But My Life, Gerda Weissmann Klein
The Cantor's Voice, Solomon Gisser
Painted in Words, Samuel Bak

Were there eyewitnesses to the deportation trains?
All But My Life, Gerda Weissmann Klein

What was known of the destination of the deportation trains?
When Memory Comes, Saul Friedländer
Maus: A Survivor's Tale, Part I, Art Spiegelman
From Thessaloniki to Auschwitz and Back, Erika Kounio Amariglio

Mass murder sites

How and where did the killings take place?
Strange and Unexpected Love, Fanya Gottesfeld Heller
Painted in Words, Samuel Bak

How did the Nazis deal with enemy forces?
Maus: A Survivor's Tale, Part I, Art Spiegelman

Transit camps

What were conditions like in transit camps?
From Thessaloniki to Auschwitz and Back, Erika Kounio Amariglio

Death camps

What was known about Belzec and when?
Strange and Unexpected Love, Fanya Gottesfeld Heller

Slave labour camps and factories

What were conditions like in the slave labour camps?
All But My Life, Gerda Weissmann Klein
From Thessaloniki to Auschwitz and Back, Erika Kounio Amariglio
The Cantor's Voice, Solomon Gisser
Painted in Words, Samuel Bak

How were workers enslaved and then moved to different factories and camps?
All But My Life, Gerda Weissmann Klein
From Thessaloniki to Auschwitz and Back, Erika Kounio Amariglio
The Cantor's Voice, Solomon Gisser
Painted in Words, Samuel Bak

Theresienstadt/Terezin

No memoirs in this volume.

Auschwitz-Birkenau

What was the routine upon entry into Auschwitz?
Maus: A Survivor's Tale, Part II, Art Spiegelman
From Thessaloniki to Auschwitz and Back, Erika Kounio Amariglio
The Cantor's Voice, Solomon Gisser

What were conditions like in Auschwitz–Birkenau?
Maus: A Survivor's Tale, Part II, Art Spiegelman
From Thessaloniki to Auschwitz and Back, Erika Kounio Amariglio

How could the mind help or hinder survival?
Maus: A Survivor's Tale, Part II, Art Spiegelman
From Thessaloniki to Auschwitz and Back, Erika Kounio Amariglio

How could relationships help or hinder survival?
Maus: A Survivor's Tale, Part II, Art Spiegelman
From Thessaloniki to Auschwitz and Back, Erika Kounio Amariglio
The Cantor's Voice, Solomon Gisser

How did the author convey a sense of the number of people being killed there?
All But My Life, Gerda Weissmann Klein
Maus: A Survivor's Tale, Part II, Art Spiegelman
From Thessaloniki to Auschwitz and Back, Erika Kounio Amariglio

What was a "mussulman" and who became one?
From Thessaloniki to Auschwitz and Back, Erika Kounio Amariglio

Death marches

What was the evacuation of Auschwitz like?
Maus: A Survivor's Tale, Part II, Art Spiegelman
From Thessaloniki to Auschwitz and Back, Erika Kounio Amariglio
The Cantor's Voice, Solomon Gisser

What were the conditions on the marches?
All But My Life, Gerda Weissmann Klein
Maus: A Survivor's Tale, Part II, Art Spiegelman
From Thessaloniki to Auschwitz and Back, Erika Kounio Amariglio
The Cantor's Voice, Solomon Gisser

What period of time elapsed and what distances were covered by those on death marches?
All But My Life, Gerda Weissmann Klein
From Thessaloniki to Auschwitz and Back, Erika Kounio Amariglio

Concentration camps

What were conditions like in these camps during the war?
From Thessaloniki to Auschwitz and Back, Erika Kounio Amariglio

What were conditions like for those who came in from death marches?
Maus: A Survivor's Tale, Part II, Art Spiegelman
The Cantor's Voice, Solomon Gisser

Witness to mass murder

What were the early reports of mass murder?
All But My Life, Gerda Weissmann Klein
Maus: A Survivor's Tale, Part I, Art Spiegelman
Strange and Unexpected Love, Fanya Gottesfeld Heller
From Thessaloniki to Auschwitz and Back, Erika Kounio Amariglio

Which survivors saw mass murder at Auschwitz?
Maus: A Survivor's Tale, Part II, Art Spiegelman
From Thessaloniki to Auschwitz and Back, Erika Kounio Amariglio

What eyewitness accounts of mass murder were there in cities, slave labour camps, and other areas?
All But My Life, Gerda Weissmann Klein
Strange and Unexpected Love, Fanya Gottesfeld Heller
From Thessaloniki to Auschwitz and Back, Erika Kounio Amariglio
Painted in Words, Samuel Bak

How was mass murder carried out on death marches?
All But My Life, Gerda Weissmann Klein

Resistance, ghetto revolts, individual acts of courage and defiance

What do we know about organized resistance at Auschwitz, and the crematorium blown up at Birkenau?
Maus: A Survivor's Tale, Part II, Art Spiegelman
From Thessaloniki to Auschwitz and Back, Erika Kounio Amariglio

What could individuals do to resist?
All But My Life, Gerda Weissmann Klein
When Memory Comes, Saul Friedländer
Strange and Unexpected Love, Fanya Gottesfeld Heller
From Thessaloniki to Auschwitz and Back, Erika Kounio Amariglio
The Cantor's Voice, Solomon Gisser
Painted in Words, Samuel Bak

In what ways could Jewish Councils resist?
Strange and Unexpected Love, Fanya Gottesfeld Heller
Painted in Words, Samuel Bak

What secret messages were transmitted through the mail?
Strange and Unexpected Love, Fanya Gottesfeld Heller
From Thessaloniki to Auschwitz and Back, Erika Kounio Amariglio

What acts of a religious, educational, cultural, or artistic nature took place, and how can they be considered resistance?
All But My Life, Gerda Weissmann Klein
When Memory Comes, Saul Friedländer
Strange and Unexpected Love, Fanya Gottesfeld Heller
From Thessaloniki to Auschwitz and Back, Erika Kounio Amariglio
The Cantor's Voice, Solomon Gisser
Painted in Words, Samuel Bak

What was the penalty for resistance?
All But My Life, Gerda Weissmann Klein
Maus: A Survivor's Tale, Part II, Art Spiegelman
From Thessaloniki to Auschwitz and Back, Erika Kounio Amariglio
Painted in Words, Samuel Bak

Partisan activity

What were the betrayals, the hazards of Jews forming or joining partisan units?
Strange and Unexpected Love, Fanya Gottesfeld Heller
Painted in Words, Samuel Bak

Specific escapes

What specific escapes from deportation trains were known?
When Memory Comes, Saul Friedländer

What were some examples of day-to-day escapes?
All But My Life, Gerda Weissmann Klein
Maus: A Survivor's Tale, Part I, Art Spiegelman
Maus: A Survivor's Tale, Part II, Art Spiegelman
Strange and Unexpected Love, Fanya Gottesfeld Heller
From Thessaloniki to Auschwitz and Back, Erika Kounio Amariglio
The Cantor's Voice, Solomon Gisser
Painted in Words, Samuel Bak

What were some examples of psychological escape?
Strange and Unexpected Love, Fanya Gottesfeld Heller
From Thessaloniki to Auschwitz and Back, Erika Kounio Amariglio
Painted in Words, Samuel Bak

In hiding, including Hidden Children

What was involved in the hiding of children?
When Memory Comes, Saul Friedländer
Maus: A Survivor's Tale, Part I, Art Spiegelman
Painted in Words, Samuel Bak

What was involved in taking on a new identity in order to survive?
When Memory Comes, Saul Friedländer
From Thessaloniki to Auschwitz and Back, Erika Kounio Amariglio
Painted in Words, Samuel Bak

What was involved in finding a physical hiding place?
When Memory Comes, Saul Friedländer
Maus: A Survivor's Tale, Part I, Art Spiegelman
Maus: A Survivor's Tale, Part II, Art Spiegelman
Strange and Unexpected Love, Fanya Gottesfeld Heller
Painted in Words, Samuel Bak

What were conditions like for those in hiding?
When Memory Comes, Saul Friedländer
Maus: A Survivor's Tale, Part I, Art Spiegelman
Strange and Unexpected Love, Fanya Gottesfeld Heller
Painted in Words, Samuel Bak

What were the risks involved in hiding Jews?
Maus: A Survivor's Tale, Part I, Art Spiegelman
Strange and Unexpected Love, Fanya Gottesfeld Heller
Painted in Words, Samuel Bak

Righteous Gentiles

What kinds of offers were made by non-Jews to help their Jewish friends?
When Memory Comes, Saul Friedländer
Strange and Unexpected Love, Fanya Gottesfeld Heller

From Thessaloniki to Auschwitz and Back, Erika Kounio Amariglio
Painted in Words, Samuel Bak

Who were to be the beneficiaries of non-Jews who supplied real assistance?
All But My Life, Gerda Weissmann Klein
When Memory Comes, Saul Friedländer
Maus: A Survivor's Tale, Part II, Art Spiegelman
Strange and Unexpected Love, Fanya Gottesfeld Heller
From Thessaloniki to Auschwitz and Back, Erika Kounio Amariglio
The Cantor's Voice, Solomon Gisser
Painted in Words, Samuel Bak

How could even kindness be seen as an act of righteousness?
All But My Life, Gerda Weissmann Klein
Maus: A Survivor's Tale, Part II, Art Spiegelman
Strange and Unexpected Love, Fanya Gottesfeld Heller
From Thessaloniki to Auschwitz and Back, Erika Kounio Amariglio
The Cantor's Voice, Solomon Gisser

What were the risks to non-Jews who helped?
Strange and Unexpected Love, Fanya Gottesfeld Heller

In what ways have the Righteous been recognized?
Painted in Words, Samuel Bak

Liberation

What evidence did survivors have that Germany might lose the war?
All But My Life, Gerda Weissmann Klein
When Memory Comes, Saul Friedländer
Strange and Unexpected Love, Fanya Gottesfeld Heller
From Thessaloniki to Auschwitz and Back, Erika Kounio Amariglio
Painted in Words, Samuel Bak

How did liberation from the Germans not end the threat of death?
All But My Life, Gerda Weissmann Klein
Maus: A Survivor's Tale, Part II, Art Spiegelman
Strange and Unexpected Love, Fanya Gottesfeld Heller
From Thessaloniki to Auschwitz and Back, Erika Kounio Amariglio
Painted in Words, Samuel Bak

What was the situation involved in returning home?
All But My Life, Gerda Weissmann Klein
Maus: A Survivor's Tale, Part I, Art Spiegelman
Maus: A Survivor's Tale, Part II, Art Spiegelman
From Thessaloniki to Auschwitz and Back, Erika Kounio Amariglio
Painted in Words, Samuel Bak

Displaced Persons camps

Who was able to benefit from the DP camps?
Maus: A Survivor's Tale, Part II, Art Spiegelman
Strange and Unexpected Love, Fanya Gottesfeld Heller
From Thessaloniki to Auschwitz and Back, Erika Kounio Amariglio
Painted in Words, Samuel Bak

Who was able to be of assistance in the DP camps?
Strange and Unexpected Love, Fanya Gottesfeld Heller
From Thessaloniki to Auschwitz and Back, Erika Kounio Amariglio
The Cantor's Voice, Solomon Gisser
Painted in Words, Samuel Bak

Stories of individuals, including family members

What was the fate of parents, siblings, and extended family?
What was the fate of friends, and those met along the way?
These categories are addressed in every memoir.

Gerda Klein writes of one friend: "I cannot help but want to tell her story, for I might be the only one left in the world who knows it." In which cases might this be true?

Post-war life and career

How did marriage and children help survivors reaffirm their commitment to life?
All But My Life, Gerda Weissmann Klein
Maus: A Survivor's Tale, Part II, Art Spiegelman
Strange and Unexpected Love, Fanya Gottesfeld Heller
From Thessaloniki to Auschwitz and Back, Erika Kounio Amariglio
The Cantor's Voice, Solomon Gisser
Painted in Words, Samuel Bak

Which survivors were able to return home only after an absence of many years?
When Memory Comes, Saul Friedländer
Strange and Unexpected Love, Fanya Gottesfeld Heller

How have their experiences in the Holocaust inspired survivors to write and teach about the Holocaust?
All But My Life, Gerda Weissmann Klein
When Memory Comes, Saul Friedländer
Strange and Unexpected Love, Fanya Gottesfeld Heller
From Thessaloniki to Auschwitz and Back, Erika Kounio Amariglio
Painted in Words, Samuel Bak

Personal reflections

Compare Gerda Klein's sense of "belonging" to America and Samuel Bak's sense "I am everywhere and nowhere at home", which Saul Friedländer echoes.

Compare Saul Friedländer's father with Fanya Heller's father, the importance of religion, their mechanisms for coping.

Compare Gerda Klein's sense that she "discharged a burden" with Samuel Bak's sense of writing to "save the dead from oblivion". In what ways is it important to remember these lives?

Compare Saul Friedländer's and Solomon Gisser's view of religion.

How did the sense of hope that Vladek Spiegelman expresses contrast with that of Erika Amariglio's community, whose sense of hope was used against them?

How can survival be "a privilege and a burden" to Gerda Klein, Vladek Spiegelman, and Fanya Heller?

Erika Amariglio, with her first-hand knowledge of the documentation of Auschwitz, has no patience for those who might question the facts of the Holocaust. Vladek Spiegelman wants his son to be prepared "just in case". Can knowledge of the events be sufficient to prevent another catastrophe from occurring?

GENERAL QUESTIONS

How did the following elements help the Germans to carry out their genocide?

Segregation
Restrictions
Confiscations
Control of information
Ruthlessness in dealing with those opposed to Nazism

What part did economics play in the Holocaust and in the German war effort, in terms of confiscated assets, and slave labour?

What is meant by "hunger", as experienced by the Jews?
What is meant by "fear"?
What is meant by "hope"?

In what ways can "courage" and "defiance" comprise real resistance?

Why were some non-Jews willing to help, and for what reasons did they help?

To what extent has the reality of Auschwitz alerted us to the potential for evil in the world?

What is meant by "crimes against humanity" and why is it important to know what happened during the Holocaust?

GLOSSARY OF TERMS USED BY THE MEMOIR WRITERS

Compiled by Sir Martin Gilbert

Aktion / Aktsia (German: "action"): a raid on the ghetto, the round-up and arrest of Jews, often accompanied by mass slaughter.

Aliyah (Hebrew: "going up"): *Aliyah la-Torah*: going up to the *bimah* (reader's desk) in synagogue to read from the *Torah*. *Aliyah le-Regel*: going up to Jerusalem for the pilgrim festivals. A third meaning was immigration to Ottoman and British Mandate Palestine, and (since 1948) to Israel. In the 1930s, as Britain imposed severe restrictions on Jewish immigration, illegal immigration was known as *Aliyah Bet* (*Aliyah B*).

Altalena: a ship hired by the *Irgun* in southern France to bring immigrants and arms, for its own use, into Israel shortly after the foundation of the State. The Prime Minister, David Ben Gurion, ordered the *Irgun* to hand over the ship to the Israeli army and to give up its arms. When they refused to do so, he instructed the army to open fire. Forty of those on board were killed, and the ship was sunk just off Tel Aviv. The story of the *Altalena* is told in a museum in Tel Aviv.

Amcha (Hebrew: "a Jew", "the Jewish people"): "one of us", used as a form of code word between Jews to ascertain whether the person spoken to was Jewish.

American Jewish Joint Distribution Committee (*the Joint*): an organization set up in 1914 to help Jewish refugees in the Russian–Polish borderlands during the First World War; active to this day in Jewish welfare work worldwide.

Anschluss (German: "unification"): the union of Germany and Austria, forbidden by the Versailles Treaty of 1920, but secured by Hitler in March 1938.

Appel (German: "roll call"): in the slave labour and concentration camps, inmates were lined up and counted, usually both before they went out to work and after their return. It was often a time of torment and danger.

Armia Krajowa (Polish: "Home Army"): Polish underground movement loyal to the Polish government in London.

Armia Ludowa (Polish: "People's Army"): Polish underground movement loyal to Moscow, and predominantly Communist.

Aryan side (*Warsaw*): the non-Jewish sections of Warsaw after the creation of the Warsaw Ghetto, which was surrounded by a high brick wall.

Aussiedlung (German: "resettlement"): a euphemism for deportation, usually to a death camp.

Bet Am (Hebrew: "House of the People"): the name often given to a Jewish community house or centre.

Banderowtzi / Banderovtsi: members of a clandestine and violently anti-Jewish paramilitary force, the Ukrainian Insurgent Army (Ukrainska Povstanska Armyia), organized at the end of 1942, and named after the Ukrainian nationalist leader Stefan Bandera.

Bar-Mitzvah (Hebrew: "son of the covenant"): a Jewish boy's coming of age, on his thirteenth birthday, when he is able to assume religious obligations as an adult.

Block (also *bloc*): a barrack in a concentration camp usually designated with a number or a letter.

Blood Libel: an accusation levelled against the Jews, especially during the Middle Ages, that they murdered Christian children in order to use their blood in the baking of unleavened bread (*matza*) at Passover. The Blood Libel, which persisted throughout the nineteenth century, was revived by the Nazis in their campaign of hatred against the Jews.

Boche (French: "a German", plural: *les Boches*): slang word for Germans.

Bread and Salt: the traditional East European offering to a newcomer or a stranger, as a sign of friendship.

Bricha (Hebrew: "flight"): the organization set up by Jews from Palestine in September 1944, to smuggle Jewish survivors out of Europe, in defiance of the British Mandate restrictions. It was first active in Vilna and Rovno after the liberation of those two towns, and later was centred on the Displaced Persons camps in southern Germany. The main route led through Austria to Italy, and then by sea to Palestine. Those brought by the *Bricha* who were intercepted by the British were sent to internment camps in Cyprus.

Bund (Yiddish: "union"): the Jewish Social Revolutionary party, founded in Russia in 1898 as an association of Jewish workers worldwide, committed to world revolution and social equality.

Bunker: a hiding place, often in a cellar, or dug underneath a building.

Camps: places where Jews and other opponents of Nazism were confined, under strict guard. See also *Concentration camps*, *Death camps* and *Slave labour camps*.

Canada (*Kanada*): a large hutted area at Auschwitz-Birkenau set aside for the sorting of the belongings of Jews deported to the camp from all over Europe. A vast storehouse of clothing and personal possessions.

Centos (Polish acronym): pre-war Polish Jewish welfare organization for orphans.

Concentration camps: camps where the Nazis incarcerated their opponents behind barbed wire and high walls; places of extreme brutality by the guards, who were often common criminals; places to which Jews were deported. Each Concentration camp had a crematorium to burn the bodies of those who died or had been murdered there. Jews were murdered in gas chambers in the Death camps (see below), and at Auschwitz and Majdanek.

Crematorium/crematoria (*crematory*): places in concentration camps where the corpses of those who had died, or been murdered, were burned. Auschwitz had five, each one attached to a gas chamber where the murders took place.

Death camps: concentration camps in which almost all those deported there were murdered within a few hours, usually by gas.

Displaced Persons camp (*DP camp*): post-war camps in which survivors of the Holocaust were gathered, and awaited rehabilitation.

Dowry: the property, movable and immovable, brought into a marriage by the bride. Thus the Biblical Rebecca took maidservants with her, on her way to marry Isaac. By Talmudic times, it was customary for the bride to be endowed by her father. Among ultra-Orthodox Jews, the amount set aside by the bride's parents is often used to enable their new son-in-law to continue his Talmudic studies. Throughout the ages, "dowering the bride" (*Hakhnasat kallah*) was a communal responsibility, considered especially meritorious, and one of the highest precepts of Judaism.

Dulag (German: abbreviation for *Durchgangslager*): transit camps in the SS concentration camp system.

East (as in "to the East", "somewhere in the East"): the "unknown destination" of almost all the deportation trains from mid-1942 to mid-1944. As a result of the escape of four Jews from Auschwitz in April and May 1944, the main "unknown destination" was revealed as Auschwitz-Birkenau, a death factory. Another long-kept secret destination "in the East" was the death camp at Maly Trostenets, near Minsk.

Einsatzgruppen "Operational Squads" (singular *Einsatzgruppe*): mobile killing squads that operated behind the front line in German-occupied eastern Poland and western Russia from the first days of the German invasion of the Soviet Union in June 1941. Four squads were in action, A, B, C and D, each located in a different region in the wake of the advancing German Army, and massacring Jews in every town and village throughout the conquered region, listing their killings with methodical detail. As many as a million Jews were murdered by the squads, often with the help of local collaborators: in ravines, abandoned quarries, anti-tank ditches, and pits dug especially for the killings.

Eretz Yisrael (Hebrew: "the Land of Israel"): A phrase used frequently in the Bible. It was used between 1922 and 1948, before the establishment of the State, by Jews to describe the British Mandate of Palestine.

Family Camp (at Auschwitz-Birkenau): also known as the "Czech Family Camp", a substantial section of Birkenau in which some 10,000 Jews from the Theresienstadt Ghetto, most of them Czech Jews, were kept together as families and not subjected to the full rigours of the camp. They were even allowed to receive Red Cross parcels, and to send postcards. This device enabled the SS to maintain that Auschwitz was a camp of "protective custody", not extermination. After several months, almost all those in the Czech Family Camp were taken to the gas chambers and murdered. Gypsies at Auschwitz were also kept in a "family camp".

(*FPO*) *Fareynigte Partizaner Organizatsie* (Yiddish: United Partisan Organization, Vilna Ghetto): a clandestine Jewish partisan organization set up in the Vilna Ghetto at the beginning of 1942. On 1 September 1943, the first clashes took place between the FPO and the German occupation authorities. On 23 and 24 September, during the liquidation of the Ghetto, and round-ups for deportation to local slave labour camps and to Estonia, a few hundred members of the FPO managed to escape to the forests and formed two fighting units. On 13 July 1944 the survivors of these units entered Vilna as liberators alongside the Soviet Red Army.

Folkschul (Yiddish: a Jewish "people's school"): usually a non-religious school.

Gestapo (*Geheime Staatspolizei*, of which *Gestapo* is an acronym): the much-feared German Secret State Police.

(*HKP*) *Heeres Kraftfahrpark* (German: "Army Motor Vehicle Depot"): workshops in Vilna, where several thousand Vilna Ghetto Jews worked and lived in a special labour camp attached to the workshops. The man in charge, Major Karl Plagge, was later recognized as a Righteous Gentile for his efforts to help the Jews while they were working for him, and to warn them of danger.

Haftorah (Hebrew: "conclusion"): the section of the prophetical books of the Bible that are recited in synagogue after the Reading of the Law (*Torah*) at morning services on the Sabbath and festivals, during the afternoon on fast days, and at both services during the fast of the Ninth of Av (*Tisha b' Av*). In Sephardi and Eastern communities, a minor may be given the privilege of reading the *Haftorah*.

Haganah (Hebrew: "defence"): a Jewish self-defence organization established in Palestine in 1921. In 1938 it set up a clandestine organization (*Aliyah Bet*) to bring Jews to Palestine despite the British restrictions. In 1948 the *Haganah* became the principal component of the Israel Defence Forces.

Hanukkah (Hebrew: "dedication"): the Jewish festival commemorating the victory of the Maccabees (between 165 and 163 BCE) over the Hellenistic Syrians, who had tried to eradicate the Jewish religion. The main observance of *Hanukkah* is the kindling of the festival lamp, the *Hanukiyah*, each night of the eight-day holiday.

High Holy Days: the solemn festivals of the Jewish New Year, *Rosh Hashana* and the Day of Atonement, *Yom Kippur*.

Hitler Youth (*German: Hitlerjugend, HJ*): the National Socialist youth movement, established as the Adolf Hitler Boys Storm Troops in 1922, renamed Hitler Youth in 1926. By 1935 it comprised 60 per cent of German youth between the ages of ten and eighteen. The Nazi ideology that the movement took was permeated with hatred of Jews. Many Hitler Youth members were later active in the Final Solution – the plan to wipe out all of Europe's Jews.

Hlinka Guard: Slovak militia named after the Slovak nationalist Andrej Hlinka (who died in 1938). When it was established in 1938 it acted against Jews, Czechs, socialists, and all opposition to Slovak independence. From 1941 its members were trained in SS camps in Germany. In 1942 it participated in the deportation of Slovak Jews to the death camps in German-occupied Poland. Its members wore black uniforms.

International Brigade: military formation made up largely of volunteers from all over the world who went to Spain between 1936 and 1939 to fight on the Republican side against the Franco nationalists. Several thousand Jews, including many from North America, joined the Brigade in the hope of playing an active part against fascism.

Internment camps: camps, mostly in German-dominated Western Europe, in which Jews were held before being sent to transit camps – and then to death camps.

Irgun (Hebrew: *Irgun Zvai Leumi*, National Military Organization): an anti-British minority organization, established in the mid-1930s in Mandate Palestine. Denounced by mainstream Jewish political figures, it carried out a series of attacks against British targets, and violent reprisal actions against Arabs In 1949 it became a political party, Herut, which later evolved into Likud, and was represented in Israel's Parliament. Its leader, Menachem Begin, became prime minister of Israel in 1977.

Jewish Brigade: Jewish soldiers in the British Army, who in 1944 were given their own military formation and Star of David insignia within the British forces. After fighting against the Germans in Italy, many of them were active after the war in helping Jews to escape from Central and Eastern Europe and to make their way from Austria to Italy – and in due course to Palestine.

Jewish Co-ordinating Committee: a relief organization in the Warsaw Ghetto. After the ghetto uprising it focused its efforts on helping those who had survived, including providing them with false papers. It also tried to help Jews in the Czestochowa Ghetto after it had been destroyed.

Jewish Council (German: *Judenrat*): Jewish administrations established in the ghettos at German insistence. They were responsible for all aspects of Jewish internal life in the ghetto, including health and education. Some collaborated with the Germans, or were forced to do so; most resisted German demands, even taking a lead in helping Jewish resistance. Jewish Council members, including those who had collaborated, suffered the fate of all Jews in the ghettos. The head of the Jewish Council in Warsaw, Adam Czerniakow, committed suicide rather than hand over to the Germans the daily quota of Jews they had demanded for deportation to Treblinka.

Jewish Fighting Organization (JFO): see Glossary entry for *ZOB*.

"*Jewish Uncle*": a Christian who committed himself to helping Jews, despite the hostility of his Christian neighbours to this course of action.

Joint: see the Glossary entry for *American Jewish Joint Distribution Committee*.

Kabala (also *Kabbalah*): a mystical Jewish system developed in the eleventh and twelfth centuries, which seeks to find an inner meaning to the scriptural writings.

Kapo: a supervisor of concentration camp or slave labour camp inmates, himself a prisoner. Often a common criminal. The word is believed to derive from the Italian word "*capo*" – "chief". Some kapos were cruel in the extreme; others could act fairly.

Kol Nidrei (Hebrew: "All Vows "): the opening prayer of the Day of Atonement. The phrase, based on the first two words of that prayer – which is mostly in Aramaic – has come to mean the whole evening service in synagogue at the opening of the Day of Atonement.

Kristallnacht (German: "Night of Broken Glass"): the night of 9/10 November 1938, when hundreds of synagogues throughout Germany and Austria were destroyed, and many Jewish businesses and homes ransacked. Ninety-two Jews were also murdered that night, and tens of thousands of Jewish men sent to concentration camps.

Lagerführer (German: camp chief). If the head was a woman, then *Lagerführerin*.

Levi: the surname of members of the Biblical tribe who descended from the third son of the patriarch Jacob. Aaron, the High Priest, belonged to the tribe of Levi. The Levites were chosen to carry the Sanctuary during the Israelites' 40 years in the wilderness, and later to serve in the Temple. In synagogue, they are called up for an *aliyah* after the *Cohens* (Priests) to the Reading of the Law (*Torah*).

Maftir (Hebrew: "one who concludes"): the honour reserved for the last worshipper summoned for an *aliyah* to the Reading of the Law (*Torah*). It comprises the final verses of the portion being read that Sabbath or Festival from the Torah scroll. On the Sabbaths before Passover and the Day of Atonement, *Maftir* is usually given to a rabbi or a learned and pious layman.

Marshall Plan: United States aid package, introduced in 1947, to rebuild the war-shattered economies of Europe. The Soviet Union rejected the plan and made all its Eastern European Communist satellites do likewise. Named after its founder, General George C. Marshall, Chief of Staff of the United States Army, 1939–45, and Secretary of State, 1947–49. In recognition of the success of his plan, Marshall was awarded the Nobel Peace Prize.

Masada: King Herod's palace and fortress overlooking the Dead Sea. In the final stages of the Jewish revolt against Rome (which lasted from 132 to 135CE) the surviving rebels held out against a Roman siege until the wall was breached. The Jews committed collective suicide to avoid capture.

Matza (Hebrew: plural *matzot*): unleavened bread, a thin, dry biscuit-type bread eaten by Jews during the eight days of Passover, in memory of the exodus from Egypt, when there was no time to bake leavened bread.

Megilla (Hebrew: "scroll"): usually refers to the Scroll of the biblical Book of Esther, which is read in synagogue on the festival of *Purim*.

Melina (Yiddish: a hiding place) a word mostly used in Poland and Lithuania, often in a cellar, or behind a cupboard.

Molotov Cocktail: a crude explosive device, usually a bottle filled with gasoline and ignited through a rag stuffed into the neck of the bottle. First used by the Finns in their defence against the Russians in the Russo-Finnish War (1939-40), and named by them derisively after the Soviet Foreign Minister at that time, Vyacheslav Molotov.

Mussulman/muselmänner: an emaciated concentration camp prisoner who had given up the will to live, and was near death.

Nazi–Soviet Non-Aggression Pact (also known as the *Molotov–Ribbentrop Pact*): the agreement between Hitler and Stalin, concluded in August 1939, whereby Nazi Germany and the Soviet Union agreed publicly to cease their public animosity, and agreed secretly to partition Poland. A week later, German forces invaded Poland from the west. Soviet forces then moved in to occupy the eastern half of Poland. Molotov and Ribbentrop were the respective Soviet and German Foreign Ministers who negotiated the pact.

Nebich (Yiddish: "poor thing"): an unfortunate person.

Nyilas: Hungarian fascists who rampaged through Budapest in late 1944, murdering many thousands of Jews. Thousands more Jews were protected from the Nyilas gangs by the Swedish diplomat Raoul Wallenberg and his fellow diplomats in the city.

Oberkapo: a senior supervisor in a concentration camp (see *Kapo*).

Palestine Mandate: the governance of Palestine, between the Mediterranean Sea and the River Jordan, granted to Britain by the League of Nations in 1922 as a Mandate. Britain relinquished the Mandate in 1948, when David Ben-Gurion declared a Jewish State (Israel). The West Bank and Gaza Strip areas of the Mandate were occupied in 1948 by Jordan and Egypt respectively, until occupied by Israel in 1967.

Papal Nuncio: the senior representative of the Pope and the Vatican in foreign capitals. The Papal Nuncio in Budapest – Angelo Rotta – was particularly active in trying to protect Jews.

Politische Abteilung (PA) "Political Department": at Auschwitz, run by the Gestapo, to record admissions to and transfers from the camp.

Purim (Hebrew: "lots"): Jewish festival commemorating the deliverance of Persian Jewry from their intended destruction by the Grand Vizier, Haman. It was one of the king's wives, Esther, a Jew, who secured the salvation of the Jewish community. The festival is celebrated with the reading of the history of that time, from the *Megillat Esther*, "The Book of Esther". It is a time of parties and entertainment, in which children participate with enthusiasm.

Quisling: the surname of the head of the wartime Norwegian collaborationist regime in Norway, Vidkun Quisling. The word became synonymous with treachery.

Reichsautobahn Lager (German): slave labour camp run by the German road-building administration, for the construction of the autobahn network. Jews were among those who worked in the camps.

Reichsicherheitshauptampt (*RSHA*) "Reich Security Main Office": formed in Berlin on 22 September 1939, the central office to coordinate the fight against "enemies of the regime". It was organized by the SS in conjunction with the German police and governmental bureaucracy, and made up of seven departments (Amter). It was one of the fourteen divisions of Amt (Department) IV - known as IV B 4, and headed by Adolf Eichmann - that was responsible for the "Jewish Question".

reparations: money paid by the German government, and by some German companies, in recognition of the personal suffering and material losses suffered by Jews during the Holocaust. The German government initiated this process in 1952, under the Luxembourg Agreement with the State of Israel.

resettlement: a deliberate and deceptive German euphemism for deportation, usually to a death camp. The German word was *aussiedlung*.

Rosh Hashana: the Jewish New Year, marking the start of the High Holy Days.

SS (*Schutz Staffeln,* of which SS is an abbreviation): "Defence Squad", created in Munich in the 1920s to protect Nazi Party speakers from attacks by their opponents; from 1933, responsible for administering the concentration camps and slave labour camps, and with carrying out the racist policies of the Nazi regime. Following the German invasion of the Soviet Union in June 1941, SS mobile killing squads – *Einsatzgruppen* – murdered at least a million Jews. The SS was headed by Heinrich Himmler.

Sad Eyes: the eyes of a Jewish person who was trying to find safety by pretending to be a Christian; a reference to the way a Jew in hiding or in disguise could be recognized by a non-Jew. These "sad eyes" could be the cause of exposure and betrayal.

Selection/Selektsia: the act of dividing Jews into two groups: those who were to be taken away and murdered, and those who were to return to the ghetto or concentration camp barracks – to work, and await yet another selection. Selections often took place during mass roll calls.

Shabbat (Hebrew), *Shabbos* (Yiddish): the Jewish Sabbath, beginning on Friday night at sundown. The Jewish day of rest.

Shanda (Yiddish: a shame, a scandal): to make *a shanda fur die goyim* is to do something embarrassing to Jews in a place where non-Jews can observe it.

Shtetl (Yiddish: a small town or village): in Eastern Europe, where Jews lived in self-contained and self-sustaining communities, far from the cities, often extremely poor, and largely cut off from the nearby non-Jewish towns, or the non-Jewish parts of the town.

Siberia: Eastern region of the Soviet Union, from the Ural mountains to the Pacific Ocean; the location of many Soviet labour camps and labour camp zones of the utmost severity.

Slave labour camps: SS-run camps, often attached to factories and factory zones, in which large numbers of Jews – and other captive peoples – worked amid extreme severity, and in which many died because of the harsh conditions and brutality of the guards.

smous: a derogatory term for Jews (in Belgium).

Sonderbehandlung (SB) "Special Treatment": a Nazi euphemism for execution.

Sonderkommando: groups of Jewish prisoners forced by the Germans to work in and around the gas chambers disposing of the corpses. In almost every case the group selected were murdered within a few months, and replaced by others who were also murdered.

szmalcownicy: the Polish word for blackmailers, extortioners.

Tarbut (Hebrew: "culture"): A pre-war Jewish educational and cultural system established throughout Eastern Europe. Particularly active in Poland, where, by 1935, there were 183 elementary and nine secondary *Tarbut* schools, seventy-two kindergartens, four teachers' seminaries, four evening schools, and an agricultural school. In all *Tarbut* schools, Hebrew was the principal language of instruction. Both biblical and modern Hebrew literature were taught. The education was Zionist oriented, and many pupils went as pioneers to Palestine.

Todt Organization: a German organization, originally headed by a Nazi Party engineer, Fritz Todt (who died accidentally in 1942). The Todt Organization, which employed Jewish and non-Jewish slave labour, was responsible for the construction of projects of strategic importance, including the Siegfried Line defence in western Germany, railway facilities for the German army on the Eastern Front, and the "West Wall" fortifications to protect against an Allied landing in northern France.

Torah: the Five Books of Moses (the Pentateuch).

Transit camps: camps to which Jews were taken, and then held until they were deported to a death camp.

Uberleben (Yiddish, German: "to live through"): the hope of Jews during the Holocaust – to live through the time of torment, to survive.

Umschlagplatz (German: "collection place"): a railway siding from which Jews were deported. In Warsaw, they were brought there on a regular basis from all over the ghetto and held until deported by train to Treblinka.

UNESCO (*United Nations Educational, Scientific and Cultural Organization*): established in 1946 to further "a universal respect for human rights, justice and the rule of law, without distinction of race, sex, language or religion", in accordance with the United Nations Charter. Dedicated to the free flow of information, and the preservation of freedom of expression.

UNRRA (*United Nations Relief and Rehabilitation Administration*): set up in the aftermath of the Second World War to help refugees and Displaced Persons. Among its tasks was the distribution of food.

Ustachi: a fascist force in the wartime independent State of Croatia, responsible for the mass murder of Serbs and Jews. The concentration camps under its control were much feared.

Vichy: a town in central France, which, following the German defeat of France in June 1940, became the capital of the "Vichy" government, headed by Marshal Pétain, and subservient to Germany. Vichy's police were active in the round-up of Jews for deportation. The word "Vichy" became synonymous with collaboration.

Volksdeutsche (also known as "ethnic Germans"): German minorities living outside the German Reich, including the Sudeten Germans in Czechoslovakia and the Volga Germans in the Soviet Union. Some groups had lived many hundreds of miles from Germany for several centuries. Many became strong supporters of Nazism after the German Army occupied the regions in which they lived, and benefited considerably from the German occupation.

Yom Kippur: the Day of Atonement, the holiest 24 hours in the Jewish religious calendar, a time of prayer and fasting, and seeking forgiveness from God.

Wehrmacht: the German armed forces. In 1939 they consisted of 2,700,000 men, and in 1943 of more than 13 million. Separate from the armed forces of the SS (*Waffen SS*).

Yeshiva (plural *yeshivot*): an institution of learning in which Jews pursue the study of the Torah. The word comes from the Hebrew verb *yashav*, "to sit". The system of study is based on the keen debate of biblical and rabbinical sources. Many famous *yeshivot* were destroyed during the Holocaust. Some were able to renew their existence after the war, mostly in the United States and Israel.

ZOB (Polish *Zydowska Organizacja Bojowa*, "Jewish Fighting Organization"): established in Warsaw on 28 July 1942, when the mass deportations to Treblinka were taking place. Determined to offer armed resistance against the German occupation forces, it organized two ghetto uprisings in Warsaw, the first in January 1943 and the second – the Warsaw Ghetto Revolt – in April 1943. In August 1944, many of its members who had survived the crushing of the ghetto revolt participated in the Polish Uprising in Warsaw.

Zachor (Hebrew: "to remember"): a basic Jewish precept.

Zohar: the classical work of the *Kabala* containing a record of the divine mysteries said to have been granted to a second-century Jewish teacher, Rabbi Simeon ben Yohai, and his mystic circle. The word means "illumination" or "brightness".

Zloty: the Polish currency.

Zytos (Polish, acronym): a Jewish relief agency in the Warsaw Ghetto.

SS POSITIONS AND RANKS MENTIONED IN THE MEMOIRS

Reichsführer: the head of the SS (Heinrich Himmler)
Oberstgruppenführer: Colonel-General
Obergruppenführer: General
Gruppenführer: Lieutenant-General
Brigadeführer: Major-General
Oberführer: Brigadier
Standartenführer: Colonel
Obersturmbannführer: Lieutenant-Colonel
Sturmbannführer: Major
Haupsturmführer: Captain
Obersturmführer: Lieutenant (UK), First Lieutenant (USA)
Untersturmführer: Second Lieutenant
Oberscharführer: Sergeant-Major
Scharführer: Sergeant
Unterscharführer: Lance-Sergeant
Sturmmann/Rottenführer: Corporal
Obergrenadier: Lance-Corporal
Grenadier/Panzergrenadier: Private

REFERENCE WORKS CONSULTED

Danuta Czech, *Auschwitz Chronicle 1939–1945*, I.B. Tauris, London and New York, 1990.

Ilya Ehrenburg, Vasily Grossman, *The Complete Black Book of Russian Jewry*, translated and edited by David Patterson, Transaction Publishers, New Jersey, 2002.

Martin Gilbert, *Atlas of the Holocaust*, 3rd edition (with gazetteer), Routledge, London and New York, 2002.

Martin Gilbert, *The Holocaust: A History of the Jews of Europe During the Second World War*, Henry Holt, New York, 1985.

David J. Hogan, David Aretha, editors, *The Holocaust Chronicle*, publisher Louis Weber, Publications International, Lincolnwood, Illinois, 2000.

Rachel Kostanian-Danzig, *Spiritual Resistance in the Vilna Ghetto*, The Vilna Gaon Jewish State Museum, Vilnius, 2002.

Michael Matsas, *The Illusion of Safety: The Story of the Greek Jews During the Second World War*, Pella Publishing Company, New York, 1997.

Czeslaw Pilichowski, *Obozy hitlerowskie na ziemiach polskich 1939–1945: Informator encyklopedyczny*, Glowna Komisja Badania Zbrodni Hitlerowskich w Polsce, Warsaw, 1979.

Professor Cecil Roth, Dr Geoffrey Wigoder, editors, *Encyclopaedia Judaica*, Keter Publishing House, Jerusalem, 1996.

INDEX

Compiled by the editor

Study Guide Maps

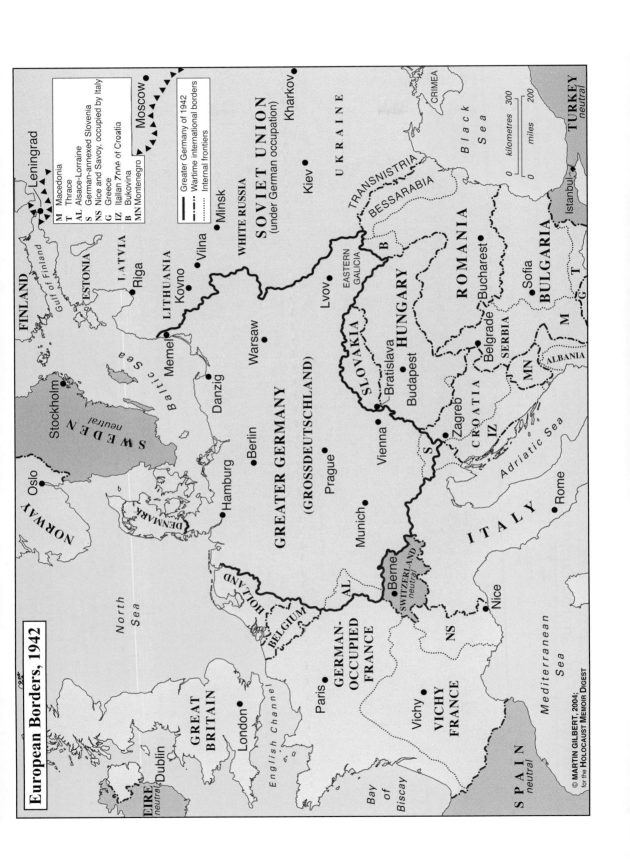

European Borders, 1942

M Macedonia
T Thrace
AL Alsace-Lorraine
S German-annexed Slovenia
NS Nice and Savoy, occupied by Italy
G Greece
IZ Italian Zone of Croatia
B Bukovina
MN Montenegro

Greater Germany of 1942
Wartime international borders
Internal frontiers

NORWAY

Oslo

SWEDEN
neutral

Stockholm

FINLAND

Leningrad

Gulf of Finland

ESTONIA

LATVIA

Riga

LITHUANIA

Memel

Kovno

Vilna

Minsk

WHITE RUSSIA

SOVIET UNION
(under German occupation)

Moscow

Kharkov

Kiev

UKRAINE

North
Sea

DENMARK

Baltic Sea

Hamburg

Berlin

Danzig

Warsaw

GREATER GERMANY

(GROSSDEUTSCHLAND)

Prague

Munich

Vienna

Lvov

EASTERN
GALICIA

SLOVAKIA

Bratislava

Budapest

HUNGARY

B

TRANSNISTRIA

BESSARABIA

ROMANIA

Bucharest

GREAT
BRITAIN

London

English Channel

EIRE
neutral

Dublin

Bay
of
Biscay

Paris

GERMAN-
OCCUPIED
FRANCE

HOLLAND

BELGIUM

AL

Berne

SWITZERLAND
neutral

S

Zagreb

CROATIA

IZ

Belgrade

SERBIA

MN

ALBANIA

M

Sofia

BULGARIA

T

G

Black
Sea

CRIMEA

TURKEY
neutral

Istanbul

Vichy

VICHY
FRANCE

NS

Nice

ITALY

Rome

Adriatic Sea

Mediterranean
Sea

SPAIN
neutral

0   kilometres   300
0   miles   200

© MARTIN GILBERT, 2004;
for the HOLOCAUST MEMOIR DIGEST

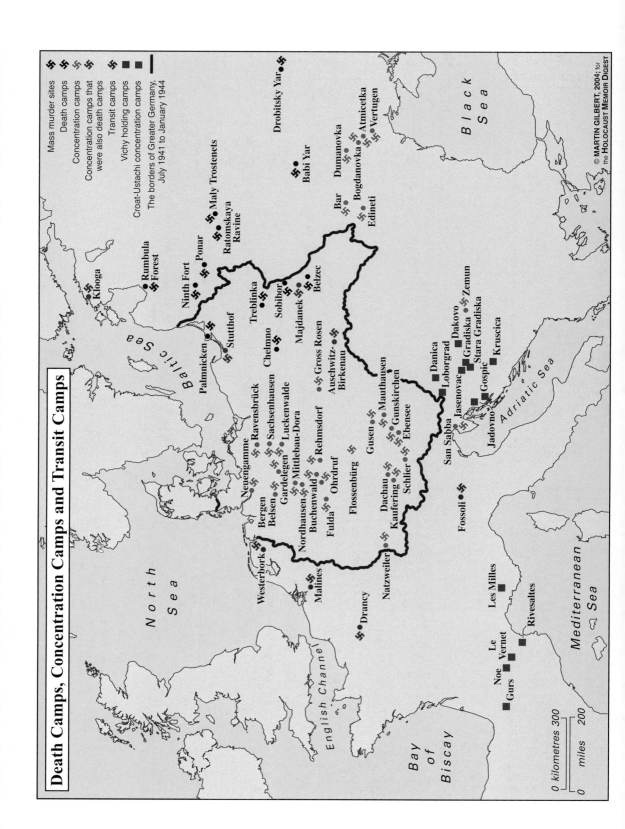

Death Camps, Concentration Camps and Transit Camps

Mass murder sites
Death camps
Concentration camps
Concentration camps that were also death camps
Transit camps
Vichy holding camps
Croat-Ustachi concentration camps
The borders of Greater Germany, July 1941 to January 1944

Klooga

Rumbula Forest

Ninth Fort
Ponar
Ratomskaya Ravine
Maly Trostenets

Palmnicken
Stutthof
Treblinka
Chelmno
Sobibor
Majdanek
Belzec
Gross Rosen
Auschwitz-Birkenau

Bar
Dumanovka
Bogdanovka
Atmicetka
Vertugen
Edineti

Babi Yar

Drobitsky Yar

Neuengamme
Westerbork
Bergen Belsen
Ravensbrück
Sachsenhausen
Luckenwalde
Gardelegen
Mittlebau-Dora
Nordhausen
Buchenwald
Rehmsdorf
Fulda
Ohrdruf
Flossenbürg
Gusen
Mauthausen
Gunskirchen
Ebensee
Schlier
Dachau
Kaufering
Natzweiler

Malines
Drancy

San Sabba

Danica
Loborgrad
Dakovo
Zemun
Gradiska
Stara Gradiska
Gospic
Kruscica
Jasenovac
Jadovno

Fossoli

Les Milles
Rivesaltes
Le Vernet
Noe
Gurs

North Sea

Baltic Sea

Black Sea

Adriatic Sea

Mediterranean Sea

English Channel

Bay of Biscay

0 kilometres 300
0 miles 200

© MARTIN GILBERT, 2004; for the HOLOCAUST MEMOIR DIGEST

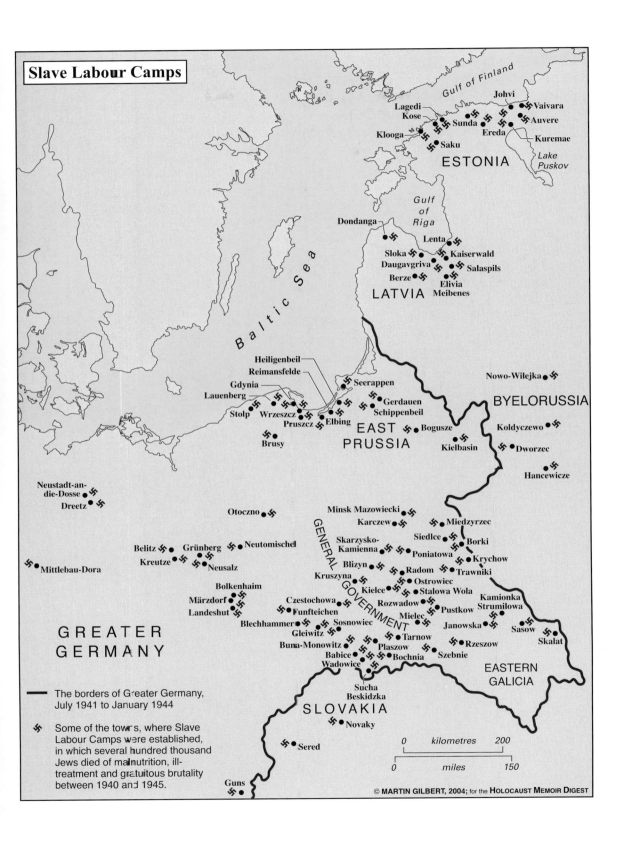

Slave Labour Camps

Gulf of Finland

Johvi
Lagedi ᛋᛋ Vaivara
Kose ᛋᛋ Sunda ᛋᛋ Auvere
Klooga ᛋᛋ Ereda
Kuremae
ᛋᛋ Saku
Lake Puskov

ESTONIA

Gulf of Riga

Dondanga ᛋᛋ
ᛋᛋ Lenta ᛋᛋ
Sloka ᛋᛋ ᛋᛋ Kaiserwald
Daugavgriva ᛋᛋ ᛋᛋ Salaspils
Berze ᛋᛋ Elivia
Meibenes

LATVIA

Baltic Sea

Nowo-Wilejka ᛋᛋ

Heiligenbeil —
Reimansfelde — ᛋᛋ Seerappen
Gdynia — ᛋᛋ Gerdauen **BYELORUSSIA**
Lauenberg — ᛋᛋ ᛋᛋ Schippenbeil
Stolp ᛋᛋ Wrzeszcz ᛋᛋ Koldyczewo ᛋᛋ
Pruszcz ᛋᛋ Elbing **EAST** ᛋᛋ Bogusze ᛋᛋ Dworzec
Brusy ᛋᛋ **PRUSSIA** Kielbasin
Hancewicze ᛋᛋ

Neustadt-an-die-Dosse ᛋᛋ
Dreetz ᛋᛋ
Otoczno ᛋᛋ
Minsk Mazowiecki ᛋᛋ
Karczew ᛋᛋ ᛋᛋ Miedzyrzec
GENERAL Siedlce ᛋᛋ ᛋᛋ Borki
Belitz ᛋᛋ Grünberg ᛋᛋ Neutomischel Skarzysko- ᛋᛋ Poniatowa
Kreutze ᛋᛋ Kamienna ᛋᛋ Krychow
ᛋᛋ Neusalz Blizyn ᛋᛋ Radom ᛋᛋ Trawniki
ᛋᛋ Mittlebau-Dora Kruszyna ᛋᛋ ᛋᛋ Ostrowiec
Bolkenheim ᛋᛋ Kielce ᛋᛋ ᛋᛋ Stalowa Wola Kamionka
Märzdorf ᛋᛋ Rozwadow ᛋᛋ Strumilowa
Landeshut ᛋᛋ Czestochowa ᛋᛋ Mielec ᛋᛋ Pustkow
Funfteichen ᛋᛋ Janowska ᛋᛋ Sasow
Blechhammer ᛋᛋ Sosnowiec Skalat ᛋᛋ
Gleiwitz ᛋᛋ Tarnow ᛋᛋ Rzeszow
GREATER Buna-Monowitz ᛋᛋ Plaszow ᛋᛋ
GERMANY Babice ᛋᛋ Bochnia Szebnie ᛋᛋ
Wadowice ᛋᛋ **EASTERN**
GOVERNMENT **GALICIA**

Sucha
Beskidzka
SLOVAKIA ᛋᛋ Novaky

ᛋᛋ Sered

| 0 | kilometres | 200 |
| 0 | miles | 150 |

Guns ᛋᛋ

— The borders of Greater Germany, July 1941 to January 1944

ᛋᛋ Some of the towns, where Slave Labour Camps were established, in which several hundred thousand Jews died of malnutrition, ill-treatment and gratuitous brutality between 1940 and 1945.

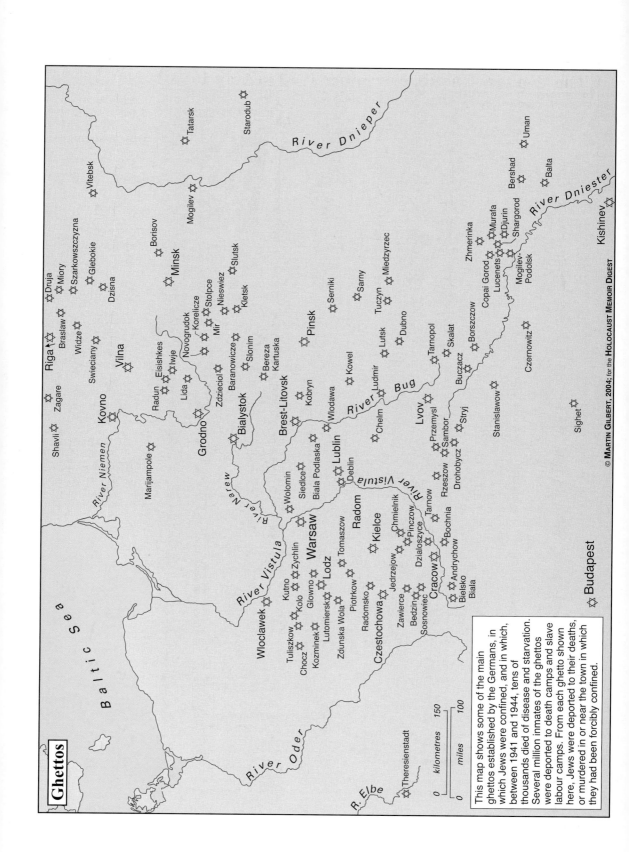

Ghettos

Baltic Sea

River Oder

R. Elbe

Theresienstadt

0 kilometres 150
0 miles 100

River Vistula

Wloclawek

Tuliszkow
Chocz
Kozminek
Lutomiersk
Zdunska Wola
Radomsko
Czestochowa
Zawierce
Bedzin
Sosnowiec
Biala
Bielsko

Kutno
Kolo
Glowno
Lodz
Piotrkow

Zychlin

Wolomin
Siedlce
Biala Podlaska

River Narew

River Niemen

Shavli

Zagare

Marijampole

Kovno

Radun Eisishkes
Lida
Zdzieciol

Vilna

Swieciany

Druja
Braslaw
Widze

Miory
Szarkowszczyzna
Glebokie
Dzisna

Borisov

Minsk

Mogilev

Vitebsk

Starodub

Tatarsk

River Dnieper

Novogrudok
Korelicze
Mir
Nieswiez
Kletsk
Slonim

Stolpce
Slutsk

Baranowicze

Bereza
Kartuska

Serniki

Pinsk

Sarny

Grodno

Bialystok

Brest-Litovsk

Kobryn
Wlodawa

Lublin
Deblin

Radom

Tomaszow

Kielce

Chmielnik
Jedrzejow
Pinczow
Dzialoszyce
Tarnow
Bochnia
Andrychow

Cracow

Warsaw

River Vistula

Chelm

Kowel

Ludmir

River Bug

Lutsk
Dubno

Tuczyn

Miedzyrzec

Przemysl
Rzeszow
Sambor
Drohobycz

Lvov

Tarnopol

Skalat

Buczacz

Stryj

Stanislawow

Borszczow

Czernowitz

Sighet

Zhmerinka

Copai Gorod
Lucenets
Murafa
Djurin

Mogilev-
Podolsk

Shargorod

Bershad

Balta

Uman

River Dniester

Kishinev

Budapest

Riga

© MARTIN GILBERT, 2004; for the HOLOCAUST MEMOIR DIGEST

This map shows some of the main ghettos established by the Germans, in which Jews were confined, and in which, between 1941 and 1944, tens of thousands died of disease and starvation. Several million inmates of the ghettos were deported to death camps and slave labour camps. From each ghetto shown here, Jews were deported to their deaths, or murdered in or near the town in which they had been forcibly confined.

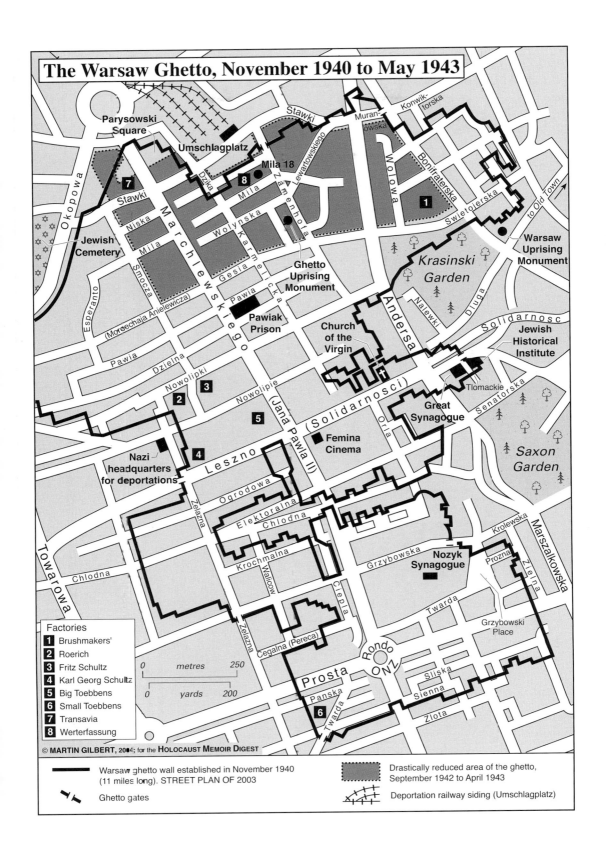

The Warsaw Ghetto, November 1940 to May 1943

Parysowski Square

Umschlagplatz

Mila 18

Stawki

Muran-owska

Konwik-torska

Wolowa

Bonifraterska

Swietojerska

to Old Town

7

8

1

Okopowa

Stawki

Niska

Mila

Smocza

Marchlewskiego

Jewish Cemetery

Wolynska

Karmelicka

Gesia

Zamenhofa

Lewartowskiego

Dzika

Warsaw Uprising Monument

Krasinski Garden

Nalewki

Dluga

Ghetto Uprising Monument

Esperanto

(Mordechaja Anielewicza)

Pawia

Pawia

Dzielna

Nowolipki

Pawiak Prison

Pawia

Church of the Virgin

Andersa

Solidarnosc

Jewish Historical Institute

Tlomackie

3

2

5

Nowolipie

Jana Pawla II)

(Solidarnosci)

Orla

Great Synagogue

Senatorska

Saxon Garden

Femina Cinema

Nazi headquarters for deportations

4

Leszno

Ogrodowa

Elektoralna

Chlodna

Krochmalna

Walicow

Zelazna

Ciepla

Grzybowska

Nozyk Synagogue

Twarda

Krolewska

Prozna

Zielna

Marszalkowska

Towarowa

Chlodna

Zelazna

Cegalna (Pereca)

Rondo ONZ

Grzybowski Place

Prosta

Panska

Twarda

Sliska

Sienna

Zlota

6

Factories
1 Brushmakers'
2 Roerich
3 Fritz Schultz
4 Karl Georg Schultz
5 Big Toebbens
6 Small Toebbens
7 Transavia
8 Werterfassung

0 metres 250

0 yards 200

© **MARTIN GILBERT, 2004**; for the HOLOCAUST MEMOIR DIGEST

— Warsaw ghetto wall established in November 1940 (11 miles long). STREET PLAN OF 2003

Ghetto gates

Drastically reduced area of the ghetto, September 1942 to April 1943

Deportation railway siding (Umschlagplatz)

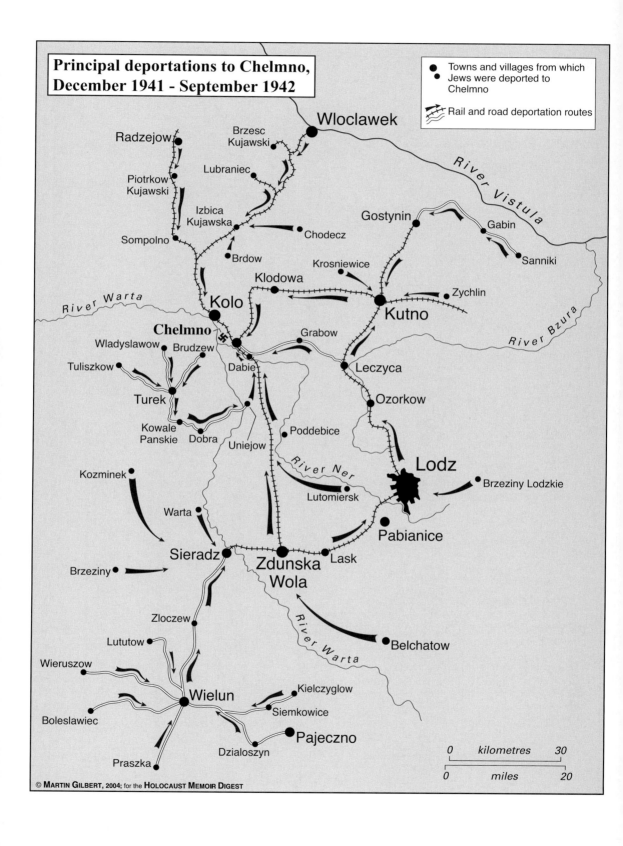

Principal deportations to Chelmno, December 1941 - September 1942

Towns and villages from which Jews were deported to Chelmno

Rail and road deportation routes

Wloclawek

Radzejow

Brzesc Kujawski

Lubraniec

Piotrkow Kujawski

Izbica Kujawska

Sompolno

Chodecz

Brdow

Gostynin

Gabin

Sanniki

River Vistula

Krosniewice

Klodowa

River Warta

Kolo

Kutno

Zychlin

River Bzura

Chelmno

Grabow

Wladyslawow

Brudzew

Dabie

Leczyca

River Ner

Tuliszkow

Turek

Ozorkow

Kowale Panskie

Dobra

Uniejow

Poddebice

Lodz

Kozminek

Lutomiersk

Brzeziny Lodzkie

Warta

Pabianice

Sieradz

Lask

Brzeziny

Zdunska Wola

Zloczew

Belchatow

River Warta

Lututow

Wieruszow

Wielun

Kielczyglow

Siemkowice

Boleslawiec

Pajeczno

Praszka

Dzialoszyn

0 kilometres 30

0 miles 20

© Martin Gilbert, 2004; for the Holocaust Memoir Digest

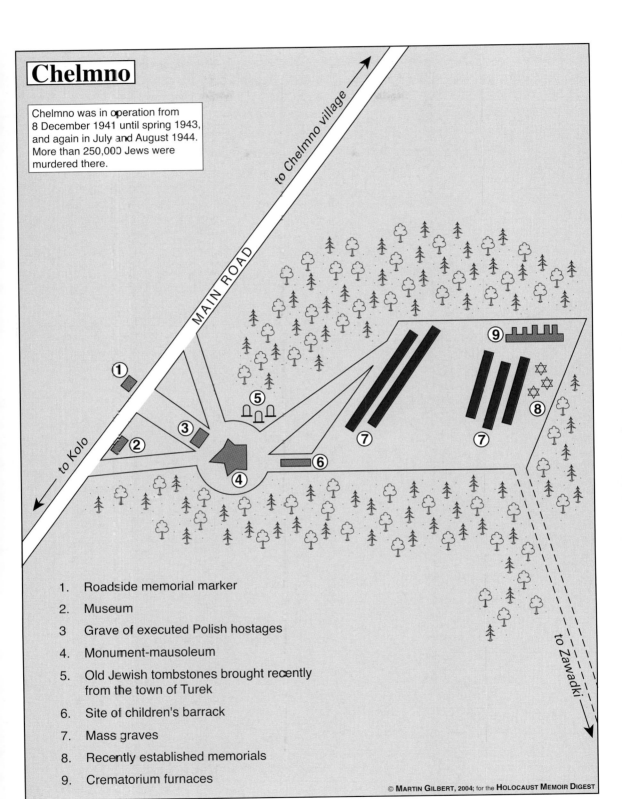

Chelmno

Chelmno was in operation from
8 December 1941 until spring 1943,
and again in July and August 1944.
More than 250,000 Jews were
murdered there.

to Chelmno village →

MAIN ROAD

to Kolo

to Zawadki

1. Roadside memorial marker

2. Museum

3 Grave of executed Polish hostages

4. Monument-mausoleum

5. Old Jewish tombstones brought recently
   from the town of Turek

6. Site of children's barrack

7. Mass graves

8. Recently established memorials

9. Crematorium furnaces

© MARTIN GILBERT, 2004; for the HOLOCAUST MEMOIR DIGEST

Principal deportations to Belzec, 1942

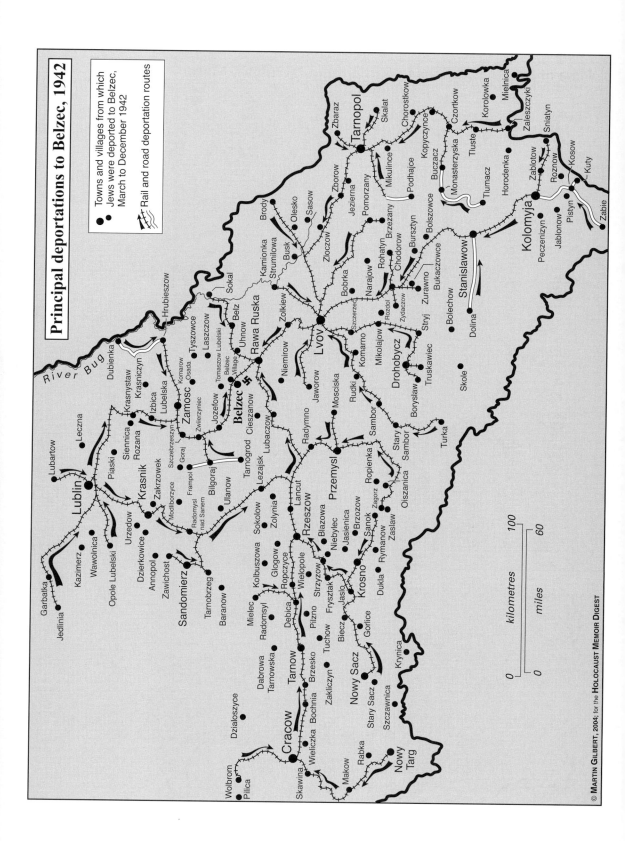

- Towns and villages from which Jews were deported to Belzec, March to December 1942
- Rail and road deportation routes

© Martin Gilbert, 2004; for the Holocaust Memoir Digest

Some of the deportations to Belzec from Germany, March - April 1942

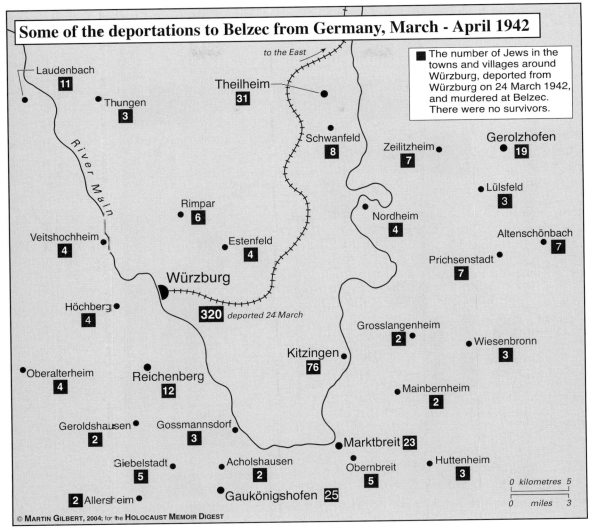

The number of Jews in the towns and villages around Würzburg, deported from Würzburg on 24 March 1942, and murdered at Belzec. There were no survivors.

to the East

Laudenbach **11**

Thungen **3**

Theilheim **31**

Schwanfeld **8**

Zeilitzheim **7**

Gerolzhofen **19**

Lülsfeld **3**

Rimpar **6**

Nordheim **4**

Altenschönbach **7**

Veitshochheim **4**

Estenfeld **4**

River Main

Würzburg

320 *deported 24 March*

Prichsenstadt **7**

Höchberg **4**

Grosslangenheim **2**

Wiesenbronn **3**

Kitzingen **76**

Oberalterheim **4**

Reichenberg **12**

Mainbernheim **2**

Geroldshausen **2**

Gossmannsdorf **3**

Marktbreit **23**

Giebelstadt **5**

Acholshausen **2**

Obernbreit **5**

Huttenheim **3**

2 Allersheim

Gaukönigshofen **25**

0 kilometres 5
0 miles 3

© MARTIN GILBERT, 2004; for the HOLOCAUST MEMOIR DIGEST

Some of the towns in Germany from which Jews were deported to Belzec in March and April 1942

Rail deportation routes from Germany to Belzec, March and April 1942

Dortmund

Julich

GREATER

Piaski

Izbica / Lubelska

Belzec

Bad Kissingen

Bamberg

Würzburg

see map above

Nuremburg

GERMANY

SLOVAKIA

Augsburg

Lindau

SWITZERLAND
neutral

0 kilometres 150
0 miles 0

© MARTIN GILBERT, 2004; for the HOLOCAUST MEMOIR DIGEST

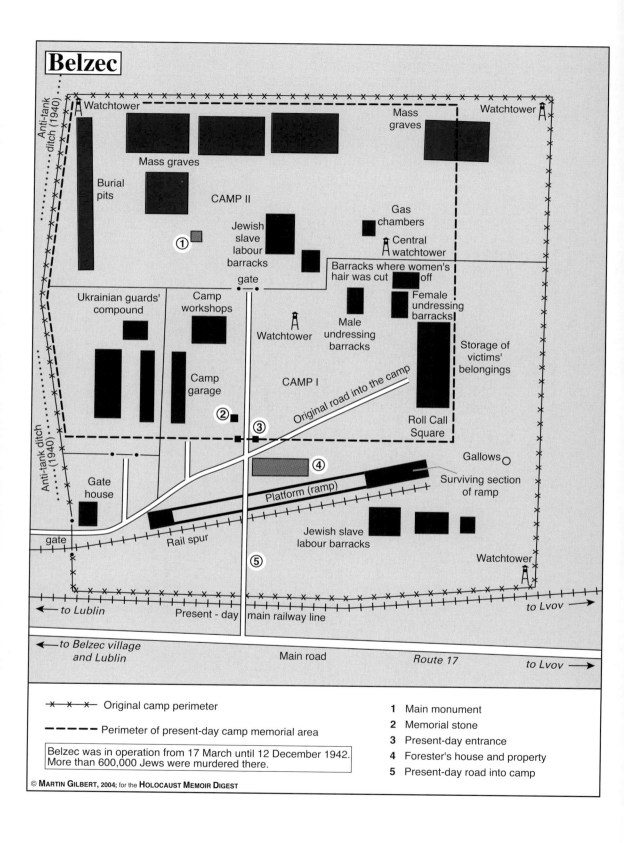

Belzec

Anti-tank ditch (1940)

Watchtower

Mass graves

Watchtower

Burial pits

Mass graves

CAMP II

Gas chambers

① Main monument

Jewish slave labour barracks

Central watchtower

gate

Barracks where women's hair was cut off

Female undressing barracks

Ukrainian guards' compound

Camp workshops

Watchtower

Male undressing barracks

Storage of victims' belongings

Camp garage

CAMP I

Original road into the camp

② Memorial stone

③ Present-day entrance

Roll Call Square

Gallows

Anti-tank ditch (1940)

④ Forester's house and property

Surviving section of ramp

Gate house

Platform (ramp)

gate

Rail spur

Jewish slave labour barracks

Watchtower

⑤ Present-day road into camp

← to Lublin

Present - day main railway line

to Lvov →

← to Belzec village and Lublin

Main road

Route 17

to Lvov →

—×—×—×— Original camp perimeter

— — — — Perimeter of present-day camp memorial area

Belzec was in operation from 17 March until 12 December 1942. More than 600,000 Jews were murdered there.

1 Main monument
2 Memorial stone
3 Present-day entrance
4 Forester's house and property
5 Present-day road into camp

© MARTIN GILBERT, 2004; for the HOLOCAUST MEMOIR DIGEST

Principal deportations to Sobibor, 1942-1943

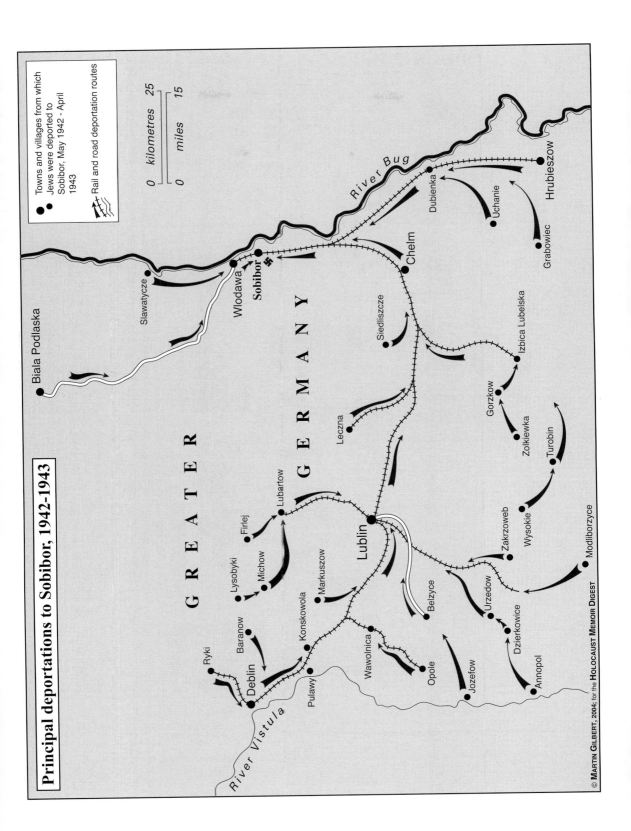

Towns and villages from which Jews were deported to Sobibor, May 1942 - April 1943

Rail and road deportation routes

| 0 | kilometres | 25 |
| 0 | miles | 15 |

GREATER GERMANY

River Bug

River Vistula

Biala Podlaska

Slawatycze

Wlodawa

Sobibor

Chelm

Dubienka

Uchanie

Hrubieszow

Grabowiec

Siedliszcze

Izbica Lubelska

Gorzkow

Zolkiewka

Turobin

Leczna

Lubartow

Firlej

Lysobyki

Michow

Markuszow

Lublin

Wysokie

Zakrzoweb

Modliborzyce

Konskowola

Belzyce

Urzedow

Baranow

Ryki

Deblin

Pulawy

Wawolnica

Opole

Jozefow

Dzierkowice

Annopol

© Martin Gilbert, 2004; for the **Holocaust Memoir Digest**

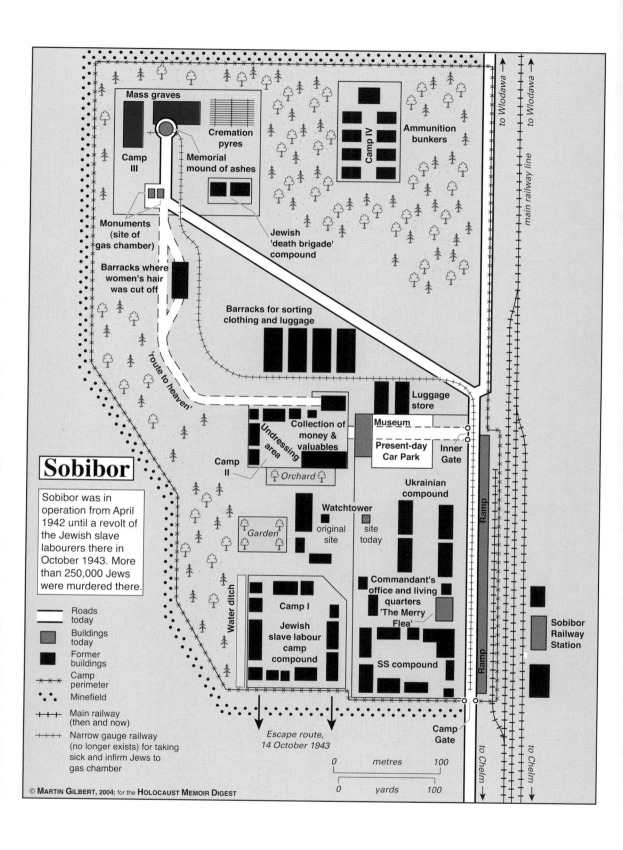

Mass graves

Cremation pyres

Camp III

Memorial mound of ashes

Camp IV

Ammunition bunkers

Monuments (site of gas chamber)

Jewish 'death brigade' compound

Barracks where women's hair was cut off

'route to heaven'

Barracks for sorting clothing and luggage

Luggage store

Museum

Present-day Car Park

Inner Gate

Collection of money & valuables

Undressing area

Camp II

Orchard

Ukrainian compound

Watchtower

original site

site today

Garden

Commandant's office and living quarters 'The Merry Flea'

Ramp

Sobibor Railway Station

Water ditch

Camp I

Jewish slave labour camp compound

SS compound

Ramp

Sobibor

Sobibor was in operation from April 1942 until a revolt of the Jewish slave labourers there in October 1943. More than 250,000 Jews were murdered there.

Roads today

Buildings today

Former buildings

××× Camp perimeter

•••• Minefield

+++ Main railway (then and now)

+++ Narrow gauge railway (no longer exists) for taking sick and infirm Jews to gas chamber

Camp Gate

Escape route, 14 October 1943

0   metres   100

0   yards   100

to Wlodawa

to Wlodawa

main railway line

to Chelm

to Chelm

© MARTIN GILBERT, 2004; for the HOLOCAUST MEMOIR DIGEST

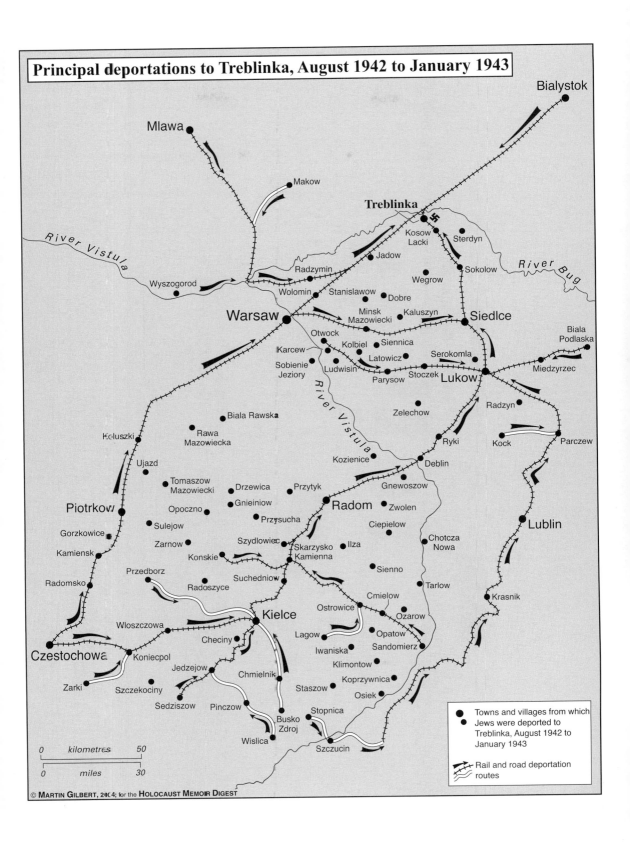

Principal deportations to Treblinka, August 1942 to January 1943

Bialystok

Mlawa

Makow

River Vistula

Treblinka

Wyszogorod

Kosow Lacki

Sterdyn

Radzymin

Jadow

Wegrow

Sokolow

River Bug

Wolomin

Stanislawow

Dobre

Warsaw

Minsk Mazowiecki

Kaluszyn

Siedlce

Otwock

Biala Podlaska

Karcew

Kolbiel

Siennica

Sobienie Jeziory

Ludwisin

Latowicz

Serokomla

Miedzyrzec

Parysow

Stoczek

Lukow

River Vistula

Zelechow

Radzyn

Biala Rawska

Ryki

Kock

Parczew

Koluszki

Rawa Mazowiecka

Kozienice

Deblin

Ujazd

Tomaszow Mazowiecki

Drzewica

Przytyk

Gnewoszow

Piotrkow

Opoczno

Gnieiniow

Radom

Zwolen

Lublin

Gorzkowice

Sulejow

Przysucha

Ciepielow

Kamiensk

Zarnow

Szydlowiec

Ilza

Chotcza Nowa

Radomsko

Konskie

Skarzysko Kamienna

Sienno

Przedborz

Suchedniow

Tarlow

Radoszyce

Cmielow

Krasnik

Wloszczowa

Kielce

Ostrowice

Ozarow

Checiny

Lagow

Opatow

Czestochowa

Koniecpol

Iwaniska

Sandomierz

Zarki

Jedzejow

Chmielnik

Klimontow

Szczekociny

Staszow

Koprzywnica

Sedziszow

Pinczow

Osiek

Busko Zdroj

Stopnica

Wislica

Szczucin

0 kilometres 50

0 miles 30

● Towns and villages from which
• Jews were deported to Treblinka, August 1942 to January 1943

Rail and road deportation routes

© Martin Gilbert, 2004; for the Holocaust Memoir Digest

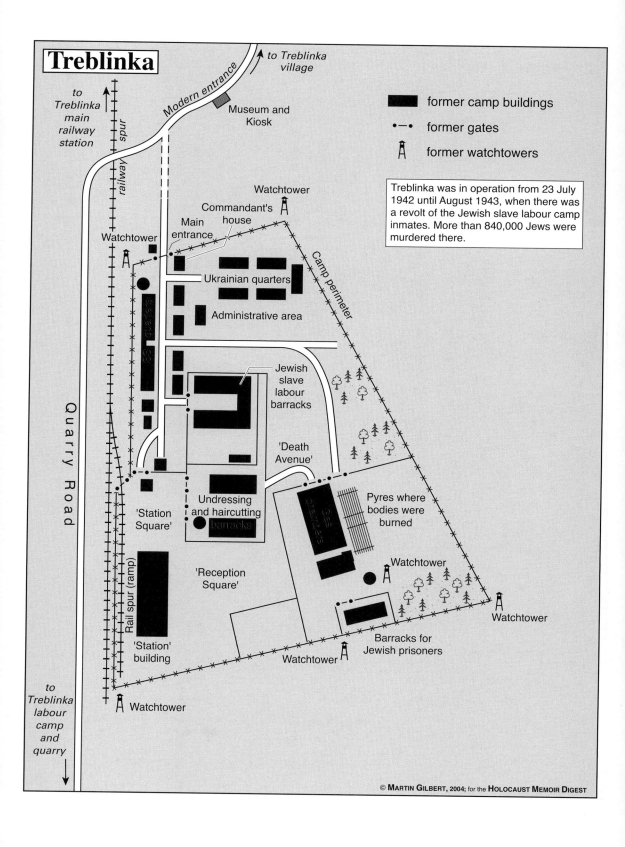

Treblinka

to Treblinka village

Modern entrance

Museum and Kiosk

to Treblinka main railway station

railway spur

◼ former camp buildings

●—● former gates

former watchtowers

Treblinka was in operation from 23 July 1942 until August 1943, when there was a revolt of the Jewish slave labour camp inmates. More than 840,000 Jews were murdered there.

Watchtower

Commandant's house

Main entrance

Watchtower

Ukrainian quarters

Camp perimeter

Administrative area

SS quarters

Jewish slave labour barracks

'Death Avenue'

Pyres where bodies were burned

Gas chambers

Quarry Road

'Station Square'

Undressing and haircutting barracks

'Reception Square'

Watchtower

Rail spur (ramp)

'Station' building

Barracks for Jewish prisoners

Watchtower

Watchtower

to Treblinka labour camp and quarry

Watchtower

© MARTIN GILBERT, 2004; for the HOLOCAUST MEMOIR DIGEST

Deportations across Europe to Sobibor and Treblinka, 1943

North
Sea

Baltic Sea

● Towns and villages from which
Jews were deported across
Europe to Treblinka and
Sobibor, March - July 1943

Rail and river deportation routes

Westerbork

to Sobibor

Treblinka

HOLLAND

Berlin

Siedlce

Sobibor

Vught

GREATER
GERMANY

Kielce Radom

to Treblinka

Teschen

River Danube

Vienna

SWITZERLAND
neutral

Zagreb

to Treblinka

Belgrade

Iron
Gates

River Danub

Lom

Black Sea

Adriatic Sea

Nis   Pirot

Pristina

Kriva
Palanka

Sofia

THRACE

Kumanova

Nea Orestia
Didimoticon

Skopje

Stip

Zilahovo
Drama
Paranestion
Xanthi
Komotini

Veles

MACE-
DONIA

Souflion

Seres

Kavalla

Sarzashaban

Gevgelija

Bitola

Thassos

Dedeagatch
Samothrace

Aegean Sea

Between 3 and 22 March 1943 more than 9,000
Jews were deported from Macedonia and Thrace
to Treblinka. Almost all were murdered within a
few hours of reaching the camp. Twenty trains
were used for these deportations. The deportations
from Thrace included a long section by barge from
the Bulgarian town of Lom to Vienna.

Most Dutch Jews were deported to Auschwitz,
but between 2 March and 20 July 1943 more than
34,000 were deported to Sobibor. All but twenty
of them were murdered there - most of them
within a few hours of reaching the camp.

0   kilometres   300

0   miles   200

© MARTIN GILBERT, 2004; for the HOLOCAUST MEMOIR DIGEST

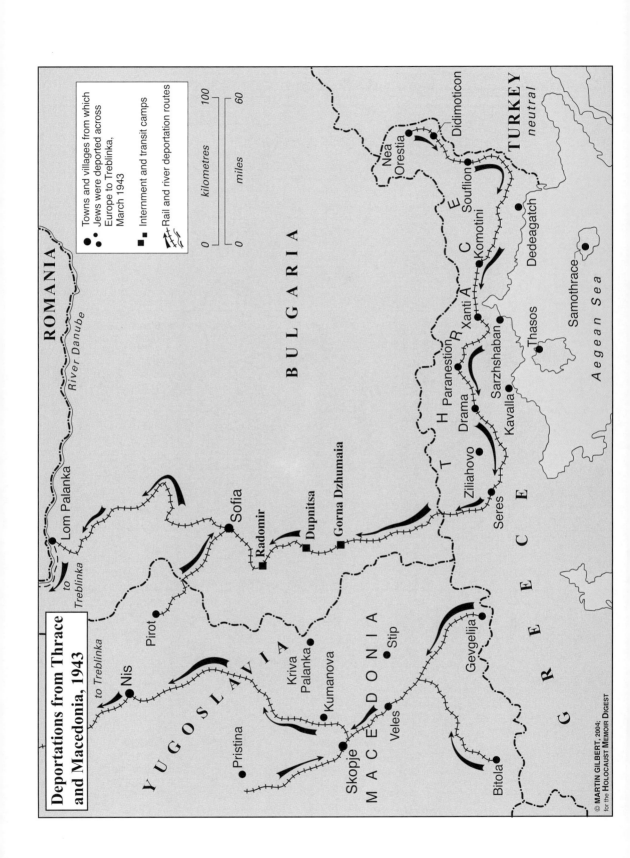

Deportations from Thrace and Macedonia, 1943

● Towns and villages from which Jews were deported across Europe to Treblinka, March 1943

■ Internment and transit camps

⌇⌇⌇ Rail and river deportation routes

kilometres 0 ——————— 100

miles 0 ——————— 60

ROMANIA

River Danube

to Treblinka
Lom Palanka

YUGOSLAVIA

to Treblinka
Nis

Pirot

Pristina

Kumanova

Kriva Palanka

Stip

MACEDONIA

Skopje

Veles

Bitola

Gevgelija

Sofia

Radomir

Dupnitsa

Gorna Dzhumaia

BULGARIA

GREECE

THRACE

Paranestion

Xanti

Drama

Ziliahovo

Seres

Sarzhshaban

Kavalla

Komotini

Souflion

Nea Orestia

Didimoticon

TURKEY
neutral

Dedeagatch

Thasos

Samothrace

Aegean Sea

© MARTIN GILBERT, 2004;
for the HOLOCAUST MEMOIR DIGEST

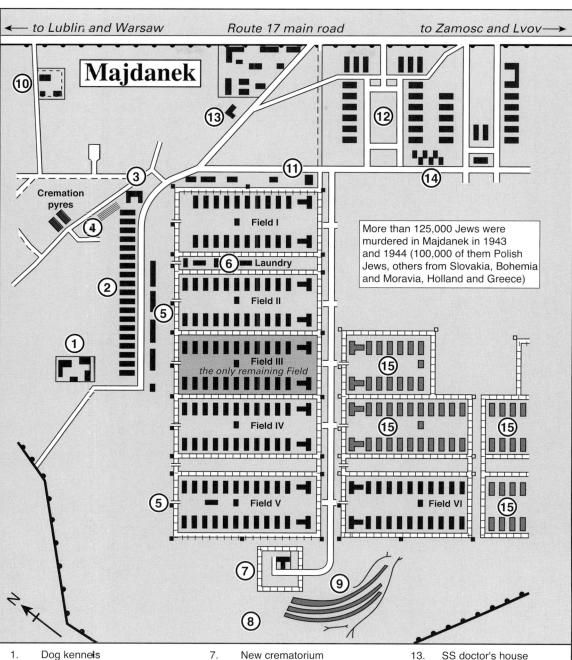

← to Lublin and Warsaw   Route 17 main road   to Zamosc and Lvov →

Majdanek

More than 125,000 Jews were murdered in Majdanek in 1943 and 1944 (100,000 of them Polish Jews, others from Slovakia, Bohemia and Moravia, Holland and Greece)

Cremation pyres

Field I

Laundry

Field II

Field III
the only remaining Field

Field IV

Field V

Field VI

1.	Dog kennels	7.	New crematorium	13.	SS doctor's house
2.	Stores	8.	Areas of mass executions	14.	Present administration building
3.	Baths and gas chambers	9.	Mass execution pits	15.	Planned extension, early to mid 1944
4.	Selection yard	10.	Commandant's house	I - VI	Barracks ("Fields")
5.	Guardhouse	11.	SS Womens' quarters	▪	Watchtowers
6.	Old crematorium	12.	SS quarters and commandant's offices		Camp perimeter

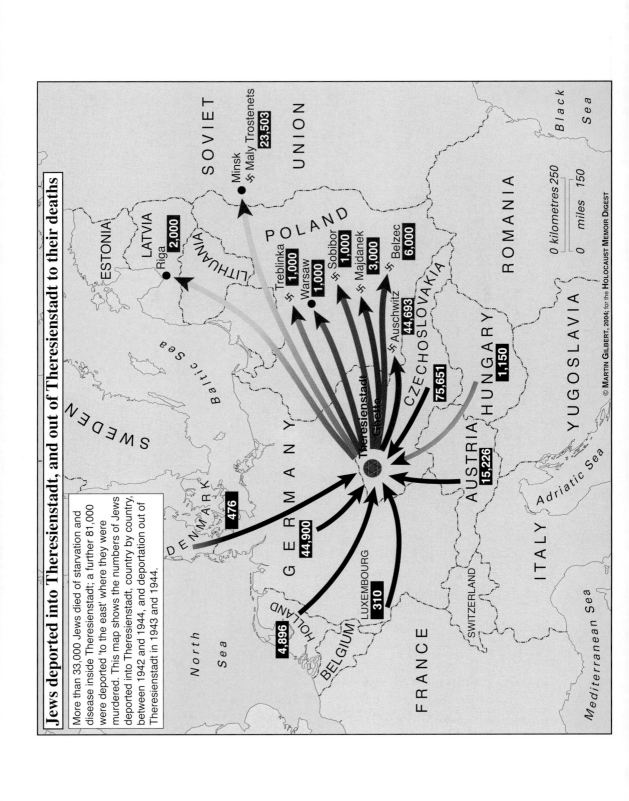

Jews deported into Theresienstadt, and out of Theresienstadt to their deaths

More than 33,000 Jews died of starvation and disease inside Theresienstadt; a further 81,000 were deported 'to the east' where they were murdered. This map shows the numbers of Jews deported into Theresienstadt, country by country, between 1942 and 1944, and deportation out of Theresienstadt in 1943 and 1944.

SOVIET UNION

Minsk
✠ Maly Trostenets **23,503**

ESTONIA

LATVIA
Riga **2,000**

LITHUANIA

POLAND

Treblinka **1,000**
Warsaw **1,000**
Sobibor **1,000**
Majdanek **3,000**
Belzec **6,000**
✠ Auschwitz **44,693**

Baltic Sea

SWEDEN

DENMARK **476**

GERMANY **44,900**

HOLLAND **4,896**

BELGIUM

LUXEMBOURG **310**

FRANCE

SWITZERLAND

CZECHOSLOVAKIA

Theresienstadt Ghetto

75,651

AUSTRIA **15,226**

HUNGARY **1,150**

ROMANIA

YUGOSLAVIA

ITALY

Adriatic Sea

Mediterranean Sea

North Sea

Black Sea

0 kilometres 250
0 miles 150

© MARTIN GILBERT, 2004; for the HOLOCAUST MEMOIR DIGEST

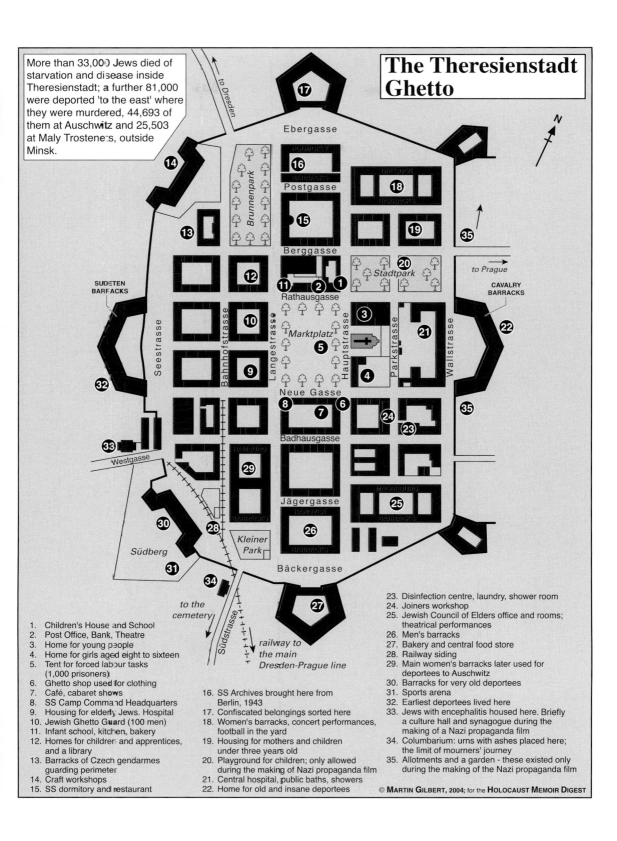

The Theresienstadt Ghetto

More than 33,000 Jews died of starvation and disease inside Theresienstadt; a further 81,000 were deported 'to the east' where they were murdered, 44,693 of them at Auschwitz and 25,503 at Maly Trostenec, outside Minsk.

to Dresden

Ebergasse

PODMOKLY BARRACKS

Postgasse

DRESDEN BARRACKS

Brunnenpark

Berggasse

Stadtpark

to Prague

Rathausgasse

SUDETEN BARRACKS

CAVALRY BARRACKS

Seestrasse

Bahnhofstrasse

Langestrasse

Marktplatz

Hauptstrasse

Parkstrasse

Wallstrasse

Neue Gasse

Badhausgasse

Westgasse

HAMBURG BARRACKS

Jägergasse

HANOVER

MAGDEBURG BARRACKS

Kleiner Park

Südberg

Bäckergasse

to the cemetery

Südstrasse

railway to the main Dresden-Prague line

1. Children's House and School
2. Post Office, Bank, Theatre
3. Home for young people
4. Home for girls aged eight to sixteen
5. Tent for forced labour tasks (1,000 prisoners)
6. Ghetto shop used for clothing
7. Café, cabaret shows
8. SS Camp Command Headquarters
9. Housing for elderly Jews. Hospital
10. Jewish Ghetto Guard (100 men)
11. Infant school, kitchen, bakery
12. Homes for children and apprentices, and a library
13. Barracks of Czech gendarmes guarding perimeter
14. Craft workshops
15. SS dormitory and restaurant

16. SS Archives brought here from Berlin, 1943
17. Confiscated belongings sorted here
18. Women's barracks, concert performances, football in the yard
19. Housing for mothers and children under three years old
20. Playground for children; only allowed during the making of Nazi propaganda film
21. Central hospital, public baths, showers
22. Home for old and insane deportees

23. Disinfection centre, laundry, shower room
24. Joiners workshop
25. Jewish Council of Elders office and rooms; theatrical performances
26. Men's barracks
27. Bakery and central food store
28. Railway siding
29. Main women's barracks later used for deportees to Auschwitz
30. Barracks for very old deportees
31. Sports arena
32. Earliest deportees lived here
33. Jews with encephalitis housed here. Briefly a culture hall and synagogue during the making of a Nazi propaganda film
34. Columbarium: urns with ashes placed here; the limit of mourners' journey
35. Allotments and a garden - these existed only during the making of the Nazi propaganda film

© MARTIN GILBERT, 2004; for the HOLOCAUST MEMOIR DIGEST

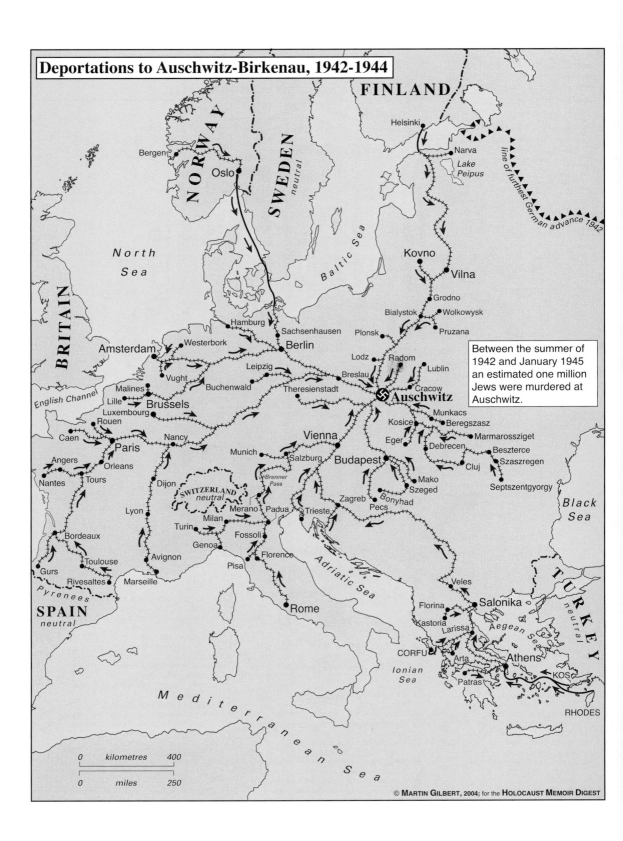

Deportations to Auschwitz-Birkenau, 1942-1944

FINLAND

NORWAY

SWEDEN *neutral*

BRITAIN

North Sea

Baltic Sea

line of furthest German advance 1942

Helsinki

Narva

Lake Peipus

Bergen

Oslo

Kovno

Vilna

Grodno

Bialystok   Wolkowysk

Pruzana

Hamburg

Sachsenhausen

Plonsk

Amsterdam   Westerbork

Leipzig

Berlin

Lodz   Radom

Lublin

Breslau

Vught

Theresienstadt

Cracow

✡ **Auschwitz**

English Channel

Malines

Buchenwald

Munkacs

Lille

Brussels

Kosice   Beregszasz

Luxembourg

Eger

Marmarossziget

Rouen

Nancy

Vienna

Debrecen   Beszterce

Caen

Munich

Salzburg

Budapest   Cluj   Szaszregen

Angers   Orleans

Paris

Septszentgyorgy

Nantes   Tours

Dijon

SWITZERLAND neutral

Brenner Pass

Mako

Szeged

Lyon

Merano   Padua

Zagreb   Pecs   Bonyhad

Black Sea

Bordeaux

Turin   Milan

Fossoli

Trieste

Avignon   Genoa

Florence

Adriatic Sea

Veles

Toulouse

Pisa

Florina

Salonika

Gurs

Rivesaltes   Marseille

Kastoria   Larissa

Pyrenees

Rome

CORFU

Arta

Athens   KOS

SPAIN *neutral*

Aegean Sea

TURKEY *neutral*

Ionian Sea

Patras

RHODES

Mediterranean Sea

Between the summer of 1942 and January 1945 an estimated one million Jews were murdered at Auschwitz.

| 0 | kilometres | 400 |
| 0 | miles | 250 |

© Martin Gilbert, 2004; for the Holocaust Memoir Digest

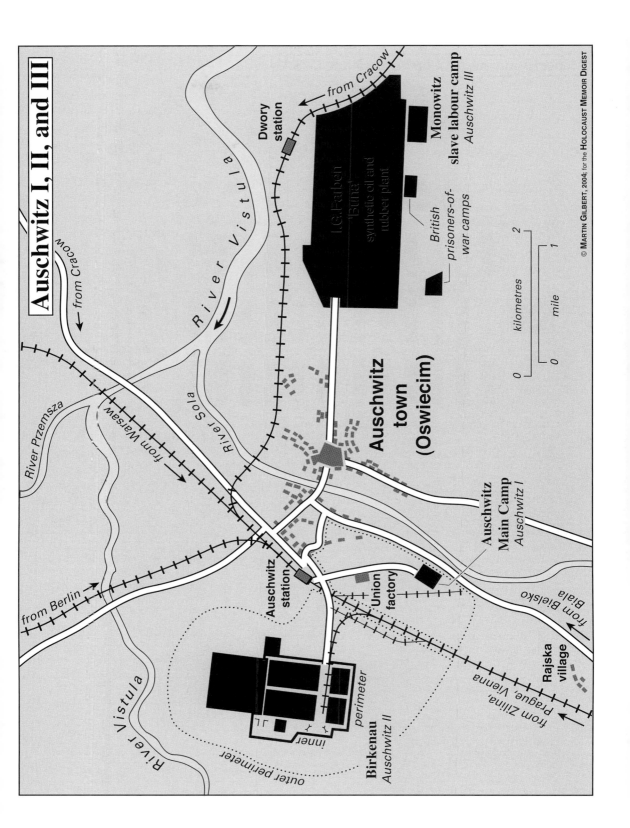

Auschwitz I, II, and III

from Cracow

from Cracow

River Vistula

River Vistula

River Sola

River Przemsza

from Warsaw

from Berlin

Dwory station

I.G.Farben 'Buna' synthetic oil and rubber plant

British prisoners-of-war camps

Monowitz slave labour camp
Auschwitz III

0   kilometres   1   2

0   mile   1

Auschwitz town (Oswiecim)

Auschwitz Main Camp
Auschwitz I

Auschwitz station

Union factory

inner perimeter

outer perimeter

Birkenau
Auschwitz II

from Bielsko Biala

Rajska village

from Zilina, Prague, Vienna

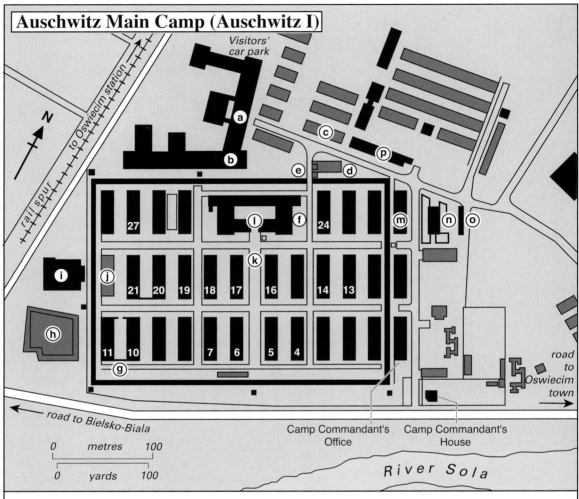

Auschwitz Main Camp (Auschwitz I)

N

Visitors' car park

to Oswiecim station

rail spur

a

b

c

p

e

d

27

l

f

24

m

n

o

i

j

k

21 20 19 18 17 16 14 13

h

11 10 7 6 5 4

g

road to Bielsko-Biala

| 0 | metres | 100 |
| 0 | yards | 100 |

Camp Commandant's Office

Camp Commandant's House

road to Oswiecim town

River Sola

a. Entrance
b. Reception building for new prisoners
c. Stores, warehouse, workshops
d. SS Guardroom
e. Entrance gate inscribed 'Arbeit macht frei' (work makes you free)
f. Place where camp orchestra played
g. Wall of Death, where prisoners were executed by shooting
h. Gravel pit, site of executions
i. Warehouse for belongings taken from deportees. The poison gas canisters were also stored here

j. Laundry
k. Assembly Square (Appelplatz)
l. Camp kitchen
m. SS hospital
n. Gas chamber and Crematorium (Crematorium I)
o. Political section (Camp Gestapo)
p. SS garages, stables and stores

Block 4: Extermination exhibition
Block 5: Exhibition of material evidence of crimes
Block 6: Exhibition of everday life of prisoners
Block 7: Exhibition of living and sanitary conditions
Block 10: Exhibition of sterilization experiments

Block 11: Death block exhibition
Block 13: Denmark and Germany exhibitions
Block 14: National exhibition, formerly Soviet exhibition
Block 16: Czechoslovak exhibition
Block 17: Yugoslavia and Austria exhibition
Block 18: Hungarian and Bulgarian exhibitions
Block 19: Prisoners' hospital
Block 20: Prisoners' hospital
Block 21: Prisoners' hospital
Block 24: Museum archive
Block 27: Exhibition, 'Suffering and struggle of Jews'

■ Brick perimeter wall   ■ Watchtowers

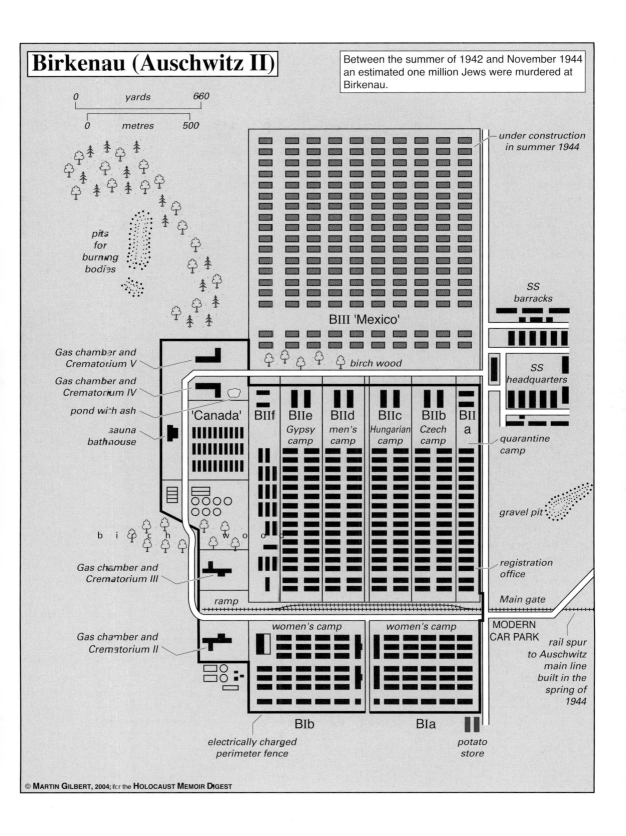

Birkenau (Auschwitz II)

Between the summer of 1942 and November 1944 an estimated one million Jews were murdered at Birkenau.

0   yards   660

0   metres   500

pits for burning bodies

under construction in summer 1944

BIII 'Mexico'

SS barracks

birch wood

SS headquarters

Gas chamber and Crematorium V

Gas chamber and Crematorium IV

pond with ash

sauna bathhouse

'Canada'

BIIf

BIIe — Gypsy camp

BIId — men's camp

BIIc — Hungarian camp

BIIb — Czech camp

BIIa

quarantine camp

gravel pit

b i r c h   w o o d

Gas chamber and Crematorium III

registration office

ramp

Main gate

Gas chamber and Crematorium II

women's camp

women's camp

MODERN CAR PARK

rail spur to Auschwitz main line built in the spring of 1944

BIb

BIa

electrically charged perimeter fence

potato store

© Martin Gilbert, 2004; for the Holocaust Memoir Digest

Escape route of Rudolf Vrba and Alfred Wetzler, 7-25 April 1944

EAST UPPER SILESIA

POLAND

Oswiecim

Birkenau

Buna-Monowitz

Auschwitz

River Vistula

River Sola

Pisarowice

Porabka

River Vistula

Bielsko-Biala

fired on by a German patrol

Zywiec

Forest

Milowka

Zwardon

Rajcza

Skalite

Sol

Cadca

Beskid Mountains

SLOVAKIA

Zilina

Southward route of the two escapees
Railway from Poland to Slovakia
International borders, 1937
SS-run camps

0   kilometres   15
0   miles   10

© **MARTIN GILBERT, 2004;** for the HOLOCAUST MEMOIR DIGEST

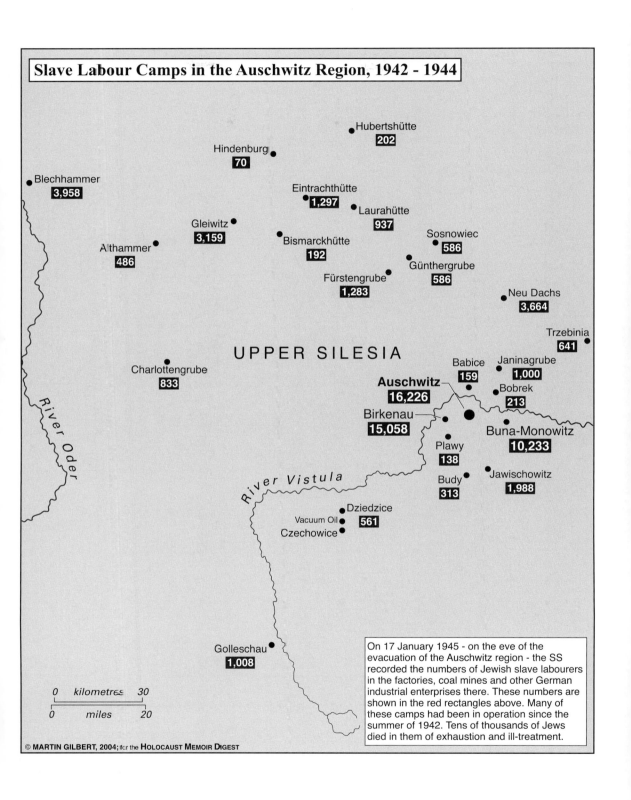

Slave Labour Camps in the Auschwitz Region, 1942 - 1944

Hubertshütte
202

Hindenburg
70

Blechhammer
3,958

Eintrachthütte
1,297

Laurahütte
937

Gleiwitz
3,159

Bismarckhütte
192

Sosnowiec
586

Althammer
486

Günthergrube
586

Fürstengrube
1,283

Neu Dachs
3,664

UPPER SILESIA

Trzebinia
641

Charlottengrube
833

Babice
159

Janinagrube
1,000

Auschwitz
16,226

Bobrek
213

Birkenau
15,058

Buna-Monowitz
10,233

Plawy
138

Budy
313

Jawischowitz
1,988

River Oder

River Vistula

Dziedzice
561

Vacuum Oil
Czechowice

Golleschau
1,008

On 17 January 1945 - on the eve of the
evacuation of the Auschwitz region - the SS
recorded the numbers of Jewish slave labourers
in the factories, coal mines and other German
industrial enterprises there. These numbers are
shown in the red rectangles above. Many of
these camps had been in operation since the
summer of 1942. Tens of thousands of Jews
died in them of exhaustion and ill-treatment.

0   kilometres   30

0   miles   20

© MARTIN GILBERT, 2004; for the HOLOCAUST MEMOIR DIGEST

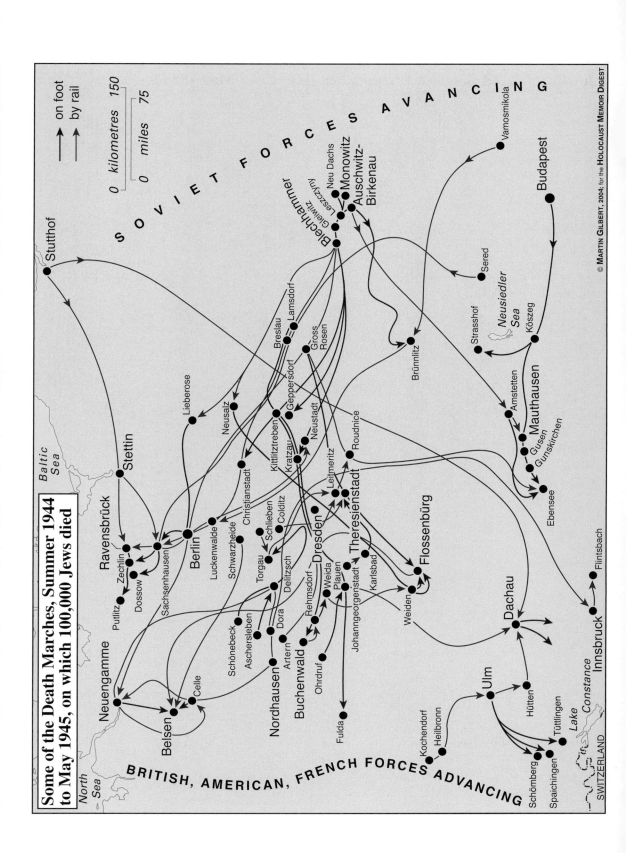

Some of the Death Marches, Summer 1944 to May 1945, on which 100,000 Jews died

SOVIET FORCES AVANCING

BRITISH, AMERICAN, FRENCH FORCES ADVANCING

© MARTIN GILBERT, 2004; for the HOLOCAUST MEMOIR DIGEST

on foot
by rail

kilometres 0 75 150
miles 0

North Sea
Baltic Sea
Neusiedler Sea
Lake Constance
SWITZERLAND

Stutthof
Neu Dachs
Monowitz
Auschwitz-Birkenau
Leszczyny
Gleiwitz
Blechhammer
Vamosmikola
Budapest
Sered
Strasshof
Köszeg
Brünnlitz
Amstetten
Mauthausen
Gusen
Gunskirchen
Ebensee
Lamsdorf
Breslau
Gross Rosen
Geppersdorf
Neustadt
Roudnice
Lieberose
Neusalz
Kittlitztreben
Kratzau
Leitmeritz
Stettin
Christianstadt
Theresienstadt
Flossenbürg
Ravensbrück
Zechlin
Putlitz
Dossow
Sachsenhausen
Berlin
Luckenwalde
Schwarzheide
Colditz
Schlieben
Torgau
Delitzsch
Dresden
Rehmsdorf
Weida
Plauen
Johanngeorgenstadt
Karlsbad
Weiden
Dachau
Flintsbach
Neuengamme
Belsen
Celle
Schönebeck
Aschersleben
Dora
Artern
Nordhausen
Buchenwald
Ohrdruf
Fulda
Ulm
Hütten
Tuttlingen
Kochendorf
Heilbronn
Schömberg
Spaichingen
Innsbruck

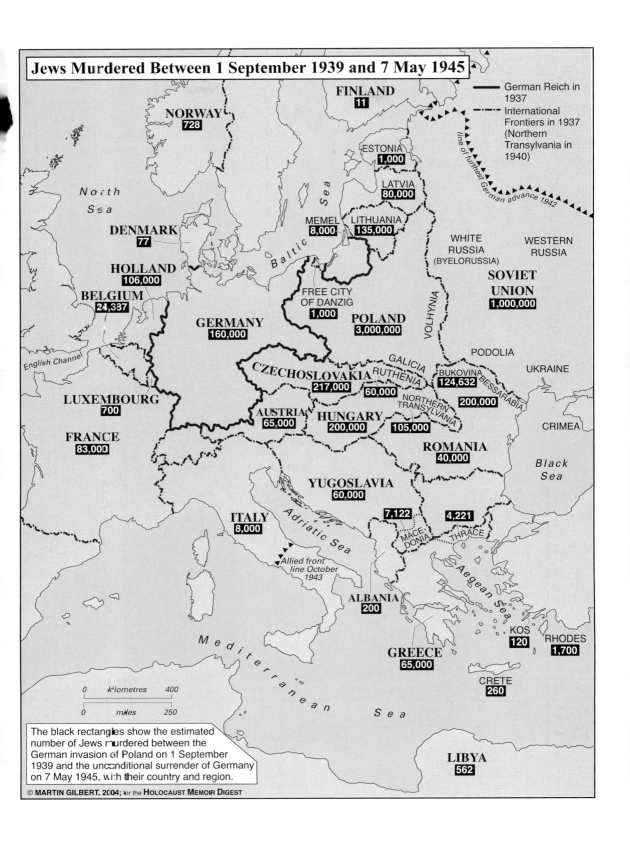

Jews Murdered Between 1 September 1939 and 7 May 1945

—— German Reich in 1937

—·—·— International Frontiers in 1937 (Northern Transylvania in 1940)

▲▲▲ line of furthest German advance 1942

FINLAND `11`

NORWAY `728`

ESTONIA `1,000`

LATVIA `80,000`

DENMARK `77`

MEMEL `8,000`

LITHUANIA `135,000`

WHITE RUSSIA (BYELORUSSIA)

WESTERN RUSSIA

HOLLAND `106,000`

BELGIUM `24,387`

FREE CITY OF DANZIG `1,000`

VOLHYNIA

SOVIET UNION `1,000,000`

North Sea

Baltic Sea

English Channel

GERMANY `160,000`

POLAND `3,000,000`

PODOLIA

UKRAINE

CZECHOSLOVAKIA `217,000`

GALICIA

RUTHENIA `60,000`

BUKOVINA `124,632`

BESSARABIA `200,000`

LUXEMBOURG `700`

AUSTRIA `65,000`

HUNGARY `200,000`

NORTHERN TRANSYLVANIA `105,000`

CRIMEA

FRANCE `83,000`

ROMANIA `40,000`

Black Sea

YUGOSLAVIA `60,000`

ITALY `8,000`

Adriatic Sea

`7,122`

MACEDONIA

`4,221`

THRACE

Allied front line October 1943

Aegean Sea

ALBANIA `200`

KOS `120`

RHODES `1,700`

GREECE `65,000`

CRETE `260`

Mediterranean Sea

| 0 | kilometres | 400 |
| 0 | miles | 250 |

LIBYA `562`

The black rectangles show the estimated number of Jews murdered between the German invasion of Poland on 1 September 1939 and the unconditional surrender of Germany on 7 May 1945, with their country and region.

Non-Jews Recognised For Having Saved Jews From Death, 1939 - 1945

North Sea

NORWAY 24

SWEDEN 10

ESTONIA 2

RUSSIA 93

DENMARK 17

Baltic Sea

LATVIA 93

LITHUANIA 513
• Kaunas

GREAT BRITAIN 13

HOLLAND 4,513

BELARUS 512

Berlin •

GERMANY 376

POLAND 5,733

Kharkov →

1,357

BELGIUM 1

CZECH REPUBLIC 104

UKRAINE 1,881

LUXEMBOURG

Vienna •

SLOVAKIA 428

FRANCE 2,262

38

SWITZ.

AUSTRIA 84

• Budapest

HUNGARY 617

MOLDOVA 53

Bordeaux •

SLOVENIA 6

ROMANIA 48

Marseille •

CROATIA 93

BOSNIA 34

SERBIA 116

SPAIN 3

ITALY 325

Adriatic Sea

YUGOSLAVIA

BULGARIA 16

Black Sea

MACEDONIA 10

61

GREECE

ALBANIA 253

TURKEY 1

Mediterranean Sea

Aegean Sea

0 kilometres 300

0 miles 200

Rhodes

–·–·– International borders, 1937

·········· Post-1991 divisions of the Soviet Union

© **MARTIN GILBERT**, 2004; for the **HOLOCAUST MEMOIR DIGEST**

The total number of non-Jews who saved Jewish lives during the Holocaust, and have been honoured by the State of Israel and the Yad Vashem Holocaust memorial in Jerusalem since 1953 reached 19,706 on 1 January 2003 (as shown on this map). They are given the title 'Righteous Among the Nations'. They are also known as 'Righteous Gentiles'. This map shows the awards given country by country, during that fifty-year period.

Also shown on the map are the cities where Jewish lives were saved by individuals who have been recognized by Yad

Vashem as Righteous: ten Armenians (including one in Budapest and one in Vienna), two Chinese (one in Kharkov, the other in Vienna), a Brazilian diplomat (in Berlin), a Portuguese diplomat (in Bordeaux), a Japanese diplomat (in Kaunas), and a United States citizen, Varian Fry, who, from Marseille, enabled many hundreds of Jews to leave Europe. The one Turkish citizen indicated on the map was also a diplomat, the Turkish Consul on the island of Rhodes.

At their own request, the Norwegian and Danish resistance movements received their honours collectively.

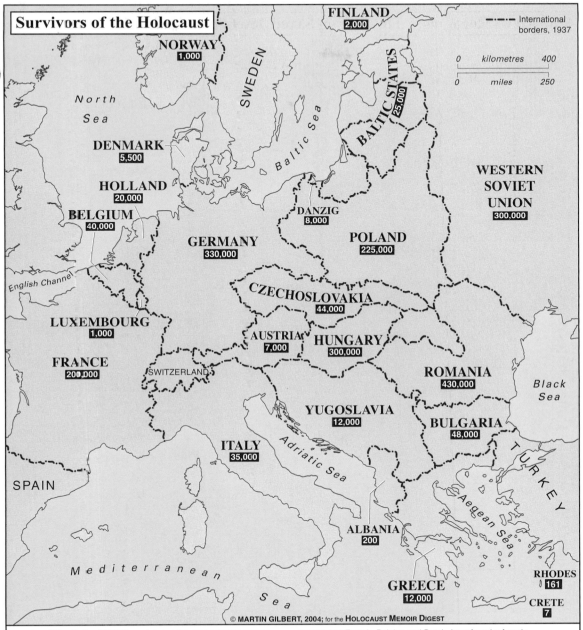

Survivors of the Holocaust

–·–·– International borders, 1937

0   kilometres   400
0   miles   250

FINLAND
2,000

NORWAY
1,000

SWEDEN

North Sea

Baltic Sea

BALTIC STATES
25,000

DENMARK
5,500

WESTERN
SOVIET
UNION
300,000

HOLLAND
20,000

DANZIG
8,000

BELGIUM
40,000

GERMANY
330,000

POLAND
225,000

English Channel

CZECHOSLOVAKIA
44,000

LUXEMBOURG
1,000

AUSTRIA
7,000

HUNGARY
300,000

FRANCE
200,000

SWITZERLAND

ROMANIA
430,000

Black Sea

YUGOSLAVIA
12,000

BULGARIA
48,000

TURKEY

ITALY
35,000

Adriatic Sea

SPAIN

Aegean Sea

Mediterranean Sea

ALBANIA
200

RHODES
161

GREECE
12,000

CRETE
7

© MARTIN GILBERT, 2004; for the HOLOCAUST MEMOIR DIGEST

In addition to the 100,000 survivors of the concentration camps, more than a million and a half European Jews survived Hitler's efforts to destroy them. The numbers are shown on this map, country by country.

Some Jews were fortunate, as in Germany, to escape from Europe before the outbreak of war, or, as in Italy, to be liberated by the Allies before the plans for their destruction could be completed. Others, as in Romania, were saved when their Government, previously anti-Jewish, changed its policy in anticipation of an Allied victory. All 48,000 Jews of Bulgaria were saved by the collective protest of the Bulgarian church, parliament and people.

The majority of the Polish Jews shown here survived because they found refuge at the beginning of the war in Soviet Central Asia. More than 20,000 French, Belgian and Dutch Jews found refuge in Switzerland, Spain and Portugal. Almost all Denmark's 7,000 Jews were smuggled to safety in Sweden. Many Greek Jews found refuge in Turkey.

Some Jews everywhere, particularly in France, Belgium, Holland and Italy, survived because the Germans took longer to deport them than the course of the war allowed: the Allied landings on continental Europe in June 1944 coming while the deportations were still in progress.

As many as 100,000 Jews escaped death because they were hidden by non-Jews who risked their own lives to save Jews.

German-Dominated Europe, 1942; and the United States of America: A Geographic Comparison

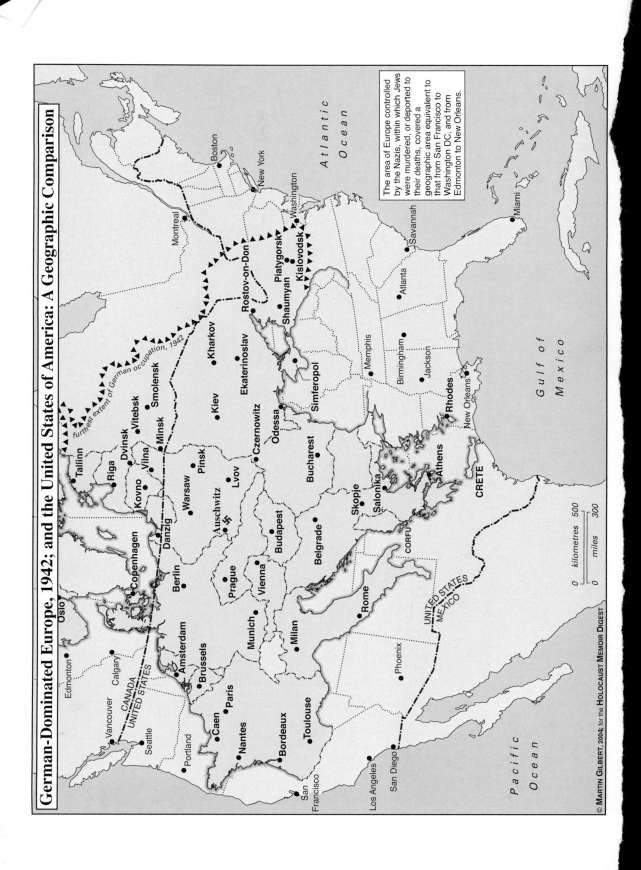

The area of Europe controlled by the Nazis, within which Jews were murdered, or deported to their deaths, covered a geographic area equivalent to that from San Francisco to Washington DC, and from Edmonton to New Orleans.

furthest extent of German occupation, 1942

Boston
New York
Montreal
Washington
Savannah
Atlanta
Memphis
Birmingham
Jackson
New Orleans
Miami
Phoenix
San Diego
Los Angeles
San Francisco
Portland
Seattle
Vancouver
Calgary
Edmonton

Tallinn
Riga
Dvinsk
Vitebsk
Smolensk
Kharkov
Rostov-on-Don
Platygorsk
Shaumyan
Kislovodsk
Kovno
Vilna
Minsk
Danzig
Pinsk
Warsaw
Lvov
Kiev
Ekaterinoslav
Czernowitz
Odessa
Simferopol
Auschwitz
Copenhagen
Oslo
Berlin
Amsterdam
Brussels
Prague
Vienna
Budapest
Belgrade
Bucharest
Skopje
Salonika
Athens
Rhodes
CRETE
CORFU
Munich
Milan
Rome
Caen
Paris
Nantes
Bordeaux
Toulouse

UNITED STATES
MEXICO
CANADA
UNITED STATES

Atlantic Ocean
Gulf of Mexico
Pacific Ocean

0   kilometres   500
0   miles   300

© MARTIN GILBERT, 2004: for the HOLOCAUST MEMOIR DIGEST